PRIDE

ON THE MOUNT

PRIDE

ON THE MOUNT

More Than a Game

 JOHN GILLOOLY

The Lyons Press
Guilford, Connecticut
An imprint of The Globe Pequot Press

The Lyons Press is an imprint of The Globe Pequot Press

10 9 8 7 6 5 4 3 2 1

Printed in the United States of America

Photographs courtesy of the Mount Saint Charles Academy.

Designed by Mimi LaPoint

ISBN 1-59228-769-7

Library of Congress Cataloging-in-Publication Data is available on file.

For Sandy, Melissa, and John-Ryan

ACKNOWLEDGMENTS

Several people played a role in telling the story of *Pride on the Mount*. It started on that summer day in 1997 when Bill and Dave Belisle agreed to let me go where no one outside the Mount Saint Charles hockey family had ever been. I always will be grateful to them for allowing me to tell a special story. Throughout the season the players on the 1997–98 Mount hockey team didn't know why I was in the locker room, but they treated me as if I belonged there. Like their sons, the parents of the Mount players made me feel like I was a member of their hockey family and they willingly talked about what it meant to be a Mount hockey parent—both good and bad. Brother Robert Croteau, Mount Saint Charles president; Richard Lawrence, Mount athletic director; and Brother Robert Lavoie, school business director (and hockey team bus driver) were always available to answer questions about Mount Saint Charles. Whenever I needed to talk to a former Mountie, alumni director Gail Bryson always had the phone number.

Several of my colleagues at the *Providence Journal* helped make the project possible. Former *Journal* sports editor Dave Bloss is the person who first encouraged me to undertake the project and Arthur Martone, the current *Journal* sports editor, is a constant source of guidance and encouragement. *Journal* sports columnist Bill Reynolds guided me through the challenge of writing a book while also working as a full-time staff writer for a daily newspaper. I would never have been able to spend the time at Adelard Arena that I did during the 1997–98 season without the help of fellow *Journal* sportswriters Bud Barker, Bob Leddy, Bob Dick, Dick Lee, and Carolyn Thornton. I will never forget the guidance former *Journal* sportswriters Ed Duckworth and the late Bill Parrillo long ago gave a young college kid who also wanted to be a sportswriter.

I'm grateful to Lyons Press editor Ann Treistman for understanding that *Pride on the Mount* was more than just a story of a high school sports team winning a lot of games and to Lisa Purcell, whose talented editorial hand is all over this book.

Finally, without the continual support of my wife, Sandy, my daughter, Melissa, and my son, John-Ryan, this book never would have become a reality.

PRIDE

ON THE MOUNT

PROLOGUE

When I talked to Sean McHugh in the fall of 1997 he was twenty-seven years old, married, and running a business, but he still vividly remembered the night when he was a sixteen-year-old member of the Mount Saint Charles hockey team.

"We had lost a game on the road. The coach didn't say a word on the bus ride home. It was close to midnight by the time we got back to the rink, but when the bus pulled into the parking lot Coach Belisle told everyone to put their uniforms back on and get on the ice.

"He shut off all the lights, except the scoreboard lights. He put the score of the game on the scoreboard so that was the only thing we could see in the rink. Then he ran the clock down just like in a game and we skated sprints in the dark for an hour. No pucks, no plays, just skating up and down the ice in the dark with a bucket on each side of the rink."

"What were the buckets for?" I asked.

"The puke," McHugh replied.

For the opportunity to skate in the dark at midnight and puke out his guts Sean McHugh drove nearly one hundred miles every school day for four straight years.

And why would any kid do that?

"Because I wanted to play for the best high school hockey team in the country," he told me that fall.

There is no definitive measure that officially determines the "best" high school hockey team in the country each year. There's no national championship game as there is in college. There's not even a national media poll for high school hockey as there is for high school football and basketball. But for almost three decades when anyone from Maine to Minnesota has talked about the best high school hockey teams in the country it's a good bet Mount Saint Charles Academy of Woonsocket, Rhode Island, has been part of the conversation.

Since 1976, the Mount Saint Charles hockey teams have been coached by a man named Normand "Bill" Belisle. Belisle was already forty-three years old when he was hired on as the Mount Saint Charles coach, yet by the end of the 2003–04 season he had coached Mount teams to 755 victories. That's more victories than any American high school hockey coach has ever recorded.

In 1978, Belisle's third year as coach, Mount Saint Charles won the Rhode Island high school hockey championship. It was the start of what would become a twenty-seven-year string of consecutive state championships—the longest of any American high school sports team, boys or girls. There were years when Mount Saint Charles unquestionably was the most talented team in Rhode Island, and in those years it steamrolled to the title. There also were years when it was the underdog, but somehow it has always emerged as champion.

Of course there are people who will say winning a Rhode Island state title is no big deal. After all, Rhode Island is the smallest state in the nation. You only have to be better than twenty-seven other teams to be its best. But, as the saying goes, "Good things come in small packages." When it comes to hockey, Rhode Island may be small, but it's definitely good.

Rhode Islanders take their hockey very seriously. In a state of only one thousand square miles there are sixteen indoor hockey rinks. That's an average of one hockey rink for every sixty-two square miles. The only state that might have more hockey rinks per square mile is Minnesota—and even that's doubtful.

But Mount Saint Charles hockey over the past three decades is more than simply a tale of high school state championships in the smallest state in the country. It is the story of how a small commuter school in an old, struggling New England mill city emerged as an influence in the fastest-growing professional sport in America. Mount Saint Charles isn't a residential prep school where players come from all over the country to play for some high school sports powerhouse. Every Mount Saint Charles player during Belisle's thirty years as coach has traveled from his home to school every morning. Yet, since the National Hockey League began its entry draft in 1969, only four American-born players have been the first-pick selections, and two of them played at Mount Saint Charles. During the 2003–04 season, six of Bill Belisle's former players played in the NHL.

It could be argued that in terms of win-loss percentage and percentage of players going on to play at the highest professional level, Mount Saint Charles hockey is the most successful high school sports team in America.

Since his first day as coach, Belisle covered his team with a blanket of secrecy. Practices were closed to outsiders—no parents, no fans, no college coaches, just Mount Saint Charles players and coaches. The word was Belisle closed his practices because his coaching style was more suited to a Marine Corps boot camp than a high school hockey rink. Rumors spread that he skated his players until they puked, that he skated them in their underwear, and that he made them go back and skate even after they won a game because he didn't think they gave 100 percent. There were plenty of rumors, but no one other than Mount Saint Charles hockey players knew for sure—and they weren't talking. For years, Belisle taped a warning sign over the inside of the door of the Mount Saint Charles dressing room, a final reminder to players as they left the inner sanctum of Mount hockey.

WHAT HAPPENS HERE, STAYS HERE.
WHAT'S SAID HERE, STAYS HERE.

For more than two decades, Mount Saint Charles players lived by that creed.

It's a little ironic that a game fostered by hard-nosed Canadian farmers has become a favorite of middle-class America. But while the American middle class has changed dramatically over the past quarter of a century, Mount Saint Charles hockey hasn't. For thirty years, Belisle has challenged his players to reach a level of intensity they never before experienced. He has made them check their middle-class comfortableness at the door of Adelard Arena so that they can pursue an abstract goal Belisle calls "Mount Pride."

Mount Saint Charles hockey isn't for every teenage hockey player. Through the years there have been plenty of players who thought they wanted to be part of it, but when they arrived at Mount they discovered that they didn't have the talent or couldn't live with the sacrifices needed to be part of the program. But for those who survived, it's a unique experience. Most came to Mount Saint Charles with a dream that their hockey talent would take them to some nirvana that they couldn't reach without hockey. Some have gone on to play in Madison Square Garden, the Molson Center, the Fleet Center, and every other NHL arena. Others have played at major colleges throughout the country. But for many, the greatest moments of their athletic careers came while they were wearing a Mount Saint Charles uniform.

When they decided to play for Bill Belisle they bought into more than just being a member of a hockey team. They bought into a philosophy that affected the rest of their lives, although most didn't realize it while it was happening. For Belisle has never preached philosophies, he only preaches hockey. He didn't institute a Spartan coaching style back in 1976 because it would develop vital life skills. He did it to win hockey games. But like the drill sergeant who instills in his recruits the lifelong qualities of discipline and self-esteem because it helps win wars, Belisle's coaching style leaves an indelible mark on both the playing styles and the psyches of his players.

"He prepares you for all that life has to ask of you," said Keith Carney, a former Mount Saint Charles star and current member of the NHL's Anaheim Mighty Ducks. "In life you need to give 100 percent and be focused. He's always trying to get your best effort. Sometimes we didn't understand why we were doing things, but we did it because he told us to do it. It gave you a feeling of accomplishment. You could say, 'I played for Bill Belisle.'"

As a member of the Rhode Island sports media I had watched and written about Mount Saint Charles hockey since Belisle became coach. More than once I was in the press box when it looked as if Mount's string of state championships was finished. One year they were only nineteen seconds away from losing the title. But somehow, some way, Belisle's players always delivered under pressure.

By the late 1990s, I started thinking of it as more than just a hockey story. Throughout the decade I had seen one veteran high school coach after another leaving the coaching ranks long before normal retirement age because they felt that teenage athletes were changing dramatically. They would talk about how it was getting tougher and tougher to get teenagers to make the same commitment to a team that kids made ten or fifteen years earlier. "Too many other things going on in their lives these days" is the way one veteran coach summarized the situation. Yet at Mount Saint Charles there had been a continuation of commitment for more than two decades.

I wanted to know how a coach, who by then was approaching seventy, could still be preaching the same values of dedication and hard work that he did in the late 1970s to teenagers of the new millennium—and get them to buy into it. I knew part of the answer would be unique to Mount Saint Charles. That it couldn't happen anyplace other than Adelard Arena, the home of the Mount Saint Charles hockey team. But I felt there must be some things happening at Mount that could be applicable to most of the six million high school athletes and two hundred thousand high school teams in America. After all, the Mount Saint Charles hockey players were American teenagers who, other than the two hours each day they spent playing hockey, lived in a world of the Internet and twenty-four-hour cable television.

After more than two decades of writing stories about Mount Saint Charles hockey, I figured I had come to know Bill Belisle as well as anyone outside the Mount hockey family. So in the summer of 1997 I approached him and his son Dave, who had been his father's assistant coach for eighteen years, about spending a season with their team. I asked them to let me go where no other non-Mount hockey family member had ever gone. I wanted to be able to attend any practice I wished from start to finish. I wanted to walk into the Mount locker room at will, ride the team bus to games, and be in the locker room before, after, and in between periods.

I was asking them to allow me to break the golden rule written above the dressing room door. What happened there and what was said there would no longer stay there.

I wanted to find out how something as abstract as Mount Pride had spanned more than one generation of teenage hockey players.

I'm not really sure why they agreed, but they did, and they lived up to the agreement we made that summer day. I stipulated that nothing that happened that year could be off the record. If there were warts on the face of Mount Saint Charles hockey they wouldn't be covered with literary cosmetics. Bill Belisle had no problem with that. I discovered that there is a brutal honesty about the man, whether he's talking about a kid's hockey talents or his own life.

I spent the 1997–98 season as a member of the Mount Saint Charles hockey team without skates. For a variety of reasons the 1997–98 season has gone down as one of the most interesting seasons in the history of Mount Saint Charles hockey. I have used that season and the lives of the players on that team as the thread to weave through the story of what Mount Pride is all about.

Partly because of my natural tendency to procrastinate, but also because I wanted my story to have a defined ending, I didn't write this book immediately after the 1997–98 season. I assumed that within a few years the state championship string would end. After all, the close calls were starting to mount up. How many times could a Mount Saint Charles team defy sports logic, not to mention the laws of probability? The end of the string would have given me a defined ending to the story of one of the most successful high school sports programs in American history.

To be honest I thought it would happen in 1999 because thirteen members of the 1997–98 team had graduated, leaving only one senior on the 1998–99 team. But despite being on the verge of losing, again Mount came back and captured their twenty-second consecutive title. They won again the following year in a two-game state title series in which the two teams were separated by a goal or less for eighty-nine of the ninety minutes of playing time. When the 2000–01 team made it twenty-four in a row by overcoming a three-game, 140-save performance by the opposing goaltender, I knew it was time for me to finish my story. A few of the seniors on the 2001 team had been freshmen members of the 1997–98 team. They were the last group of Mount players with whom I had a direct relationship. From that point on, once again, like everyone else who has never worn a Mount Saint Charles uniform, I was an outsider.

The streak finally ended in 2004, but it didn't really change the story. The story of Mount Saint Charles hockey is a blend of history and sports dreams. More important than the victories and the titles, it is a story of how through a quarter of a century of dramatic social and technological changes a few hundred American teenagers discovered the meaning of pride through a game played on ice. It's a story that shows that there are still a few basic values that haven't changed. If they have survived what many people feel was the most turbulent quarter-century in the history of American sports, there's hope that they will be around for a long time to come.

CHAPTER 1

ount Saint Charles Academy sits high on a hill overlooking the city of Woonsocket, Rhode Island. From the school windows Mount Saint Charles teachers and administrators can see well beyond the Woonsocket city limits. Maybe that's why they have been able to adapt their school to a changing world while the city around them has struggled making the transition from a textile capital of the early 1900s to a functional city in a new century. Woonsocket, which is located on the Rhode Island–Massachusetts state line about fifteen miles north of Providence, is an American history lesson trying to be a modern city. It's not doing very well. Drive up and down the hilly streets of its residential sections; drive over the bridges that span the Blackstone, the river that runs through the middle of the city; or walk along the sidewalks of its downtown business section and you can still see what a New England mill city of the nineteenth and early twentieth century looked like. Not much of Woonsocket's architecture has changed since the turn of the twentieth century. Seventy-five to 80 percent of the city's 44,000 residents still live in the same two-and-a-half and three-decker wooden tenements that were built to house the huge influx of Canadian immigrants who came from the farmlands around Quebec to work in the city's textile and rubber mills prior to the 1930s. Many of the churches built to give the workers places to practice their Roman Catholic religion still welcome worshipers. And although some of the mill buildings that made the city a thriving textile capital at the turn of the century have given way to the wrecking ball, many still stand along the banks of the Blackstone where they were built to harness the water power of the river. But the buildings are no longer functional mills.

According to Woonsocket historian Anita Rafael, in the mid-1800s there were twenty textile mills in Woonsocket. During a post–Civil War economic boom, European businessmen, offered tax incentives by the city, found Woonsocket an especially inviting place to build new mills. But Woonsocket's twentieth-century economy was severely jolted by the general collapse of the New England cotton industry that occurred when Northern manufacturers shifted investment capital to the cheap-labor South. During the great depression of the 1930s half of the city's textile workers permanently lost their jobs. Some of the city's industries held onto a share of their earlier gains, but even more mills closed after World War II. For nearly a half century now, Woonsocket has seemed to be a city on life support. For decades, people with the money or those who knew how to help the city were moving out of rather than into Woonsocket.

So what do you do with big, old, inefficient mills? What do you do when many of the three-decker tenements that once housed two and three generations of French-Canadian families have become a haven of inexpensive housing for a new wave of Asian and Hispanic immigrants trying to gain a financial foothold in America? For more than three decades, Woonsocket city officials have been struggling to find the answers—without much success.

The city has made some recent comebacks spurred on by both government grants and private industry, but there's still a long way to go. In 1997, Woonsocket residents still had the third-lowest household income in Rhode Island. It also had the state's third-highest percentage of children under eighteen living in poverty and the city's public school students ranked in the bottom 10 percent in reading and math skills.

But standing in the parking lot of Mount Saint Charles Academy on any school day you would never know you were in one of the poorest cities in the Northeast. The Mount parking lot may not be filled with the Volvos and Lexuses you find in the parking lots of New England prep schools such as Choate and Phillips Andover, but there are plenty of the Ford Broncos and Honda Accords you find in the driveways of middle-class American suburbia.

Once an all-male school founded to educate the sons of the French-Canadian mill workers who lived in Woonsocket and the nearby Manville section of Lincoln, Rhode Island, Mount Saint Charles is now a coed, commuting junior-senior high school with 860 students. These days, only a few Mount Saint Charles students come from the three-deckers of Woonsocket. Most drive to school from their homes in the suburban communities surrounding the city in Rhode Island and nearby Massachusetts.

There are approximately three hundred boys in the high school division and about 20 percent of them play ice hockey. School officials boast about the school's excellent academic programs, and they have plenty to boast about. In 1995, the school was named a Blue Ribbon school by the U.S. Department of Education. Every year at least 95 percent of the graduating class goes on to college. The school also has a highly acclaimed music program: about one-third of Mount students play musical instruments. These are all good reasons why parents pay about $7,000 per year for their child to attend Mount Saint Charles. But the reality is that most of the hockey-playing members of the student body are there because they want to play for the varsity team. It's been that way for two decades now, ever since Bill Belisle began cultivating the modern Mount Saint Charles hockey legend.

Hockey players are a different breed than most young athletes. Most of them started playing hockey before they were in elementary school. But hockey players don't grow up playing on neighborhood fields or courts like their friends who play basketball, baseball, and soccer. Young New England hockey players are driven athletes—they're driven to hockey rinks all over the Northeast.

Youth hockey in New England is a culture unto itself. When I played for the Lions peewee hockey team in Cranston, Rhode Island, as a ten-year-old back in 1956 there were only five or six organized youth hockey teams in the state with players my age. It's likely that fewer than one hundred kids under the age of twelve in the whole state had real hockey uniforms. But that was before Bobby Orr flew through the air after his goal gave the Boston Bruins the 1970 Stanley Cup.

That picture of Orr, his arms raised and his body soaring several feet above the Boston Garden ice, is probably the most famous sports picture in New England. Three decades after that overtime goal gave the Bruins a 4–3 victory over the St. Louis Blues, and their first Stanley Cup in twenty-nine years, you can still walk into family rooms, restaurants, and bars throughout

New England and see Number 4 flying over the Garden ice. The lasting adulation is fitting because no athlete, not even Ted Williams or Larry Bird, changed the fiber of a sport in New England like Orr did for hockey.

For decades prior to Orr's arrival in Boston in 1966, hockey was a Canadian game enjoyed by a dedicated, but small, segment of New England sports fans. Orr brought a sense of creativity and excitement to a sport that had lacked flair. For the most part, HBO (Hockey Before Orr) was a north-south game. A bunch of nondescript Canadians skating virtually straight up and down the rink, chasing the puck. Left and right wings stayed on their side of the rink. Defensemen were in front of their cage, then skated straight up to the opponent's blue line and stayed put. The only players who had any freedom to roam around the ice were the centers. Other than the occasional fistfight, the only excitement in a hockey game came when someone scored a goal—and that usually occurred only a few times a game.

Hockey fans loved the game because it combined the speed of a basketball fast break with the physical contact of football. But for the average New England sports fans there was no verve to the game, no hockey player who roused them by simply carrying the puck up the ice. There was nothing on ice that could rival the excitement New Englanders felt when they watched Ted Williams send a ball into the Fenway Park bull pen or Bob Cousy dribbling upcourt at the Boston Garden. Yet, hockey had a devoted legion of fans for decades. In the early 1960s, despite being the worst team in the six-team National Hockey League, the Bruins drew larger crowds to the Garden than the NBA champion Boston Celtics. But the guy who rooted for the Red Sox in the summer probably didn't pay much attention to hockey in the winter.

Orr changed all that. He changed the geometry of the game. He changed it from a north-south game to an east-west game. Despite being a defenseman, no part of the hockey rink was off limits to him. Rather than taking the puck straight up the ice for a few strides before passing it off to a forward, he would shake off opponents by spinning around in an almost impossibly tight circle and then head up the ice with the puck. That spin-around move, which today is part of the repertoire of every good high school defenseman, had never been seen before Orr started spinning around the Garden.

Just watching Orr move the puck was worth the price of admission. But of course he didn't just skate with the puck. He became the first defenseman to score one hundred points in a season, and he did it for six consecutive seasons. He brought new enthusiasm to the game. His skating was magnificent and he constantly seemed to be devising moves on skates that most people couldn't imitate in a pair of sneakers. As former Bruins teammate Johnny Bucyk once said, "He's athletic poetry in motion—very quick motion. He has sixteen degrees of fast."

Even when he didn't have the puck Orr always seemed to be able to anticipate where the black disk was headed. He always seemed to be a split second ahead of everyone else's move. He was young and handsome and at a time in the sixties when parents of young children were cringing at the sight of long-haired teenaged boys flipping the bird to anyone over thirty, Orr had a brush cut and spoke publicly about how much he respected his parents. Women who never saw any reason to sit in front of the TV to watch a sports event were joining their husbands for the Bruins telecasts on the new UHF Channel 38 in Boston. Little kids were planted in front of the TV set and told to watch Number 4. He was the NHL Rookie of the Year in 1967, and the following year he won what would be the first of eight consecutive Norris Trophies, the award given to the NHL's top defenseman.

Of course Orr wasn't the only reason the Bruins won the Stanley Cup in 1970. The Bruins of the early seventies also had future Hall of Famers Phil Esposito, Bucyk, goalie Gerry Cheevers, Johnny "Pie" McKenzie, and a flamboyant young rogue named Derek Sanderson. Together they formed the Big Bad Bruins and New Englanders loved them. It became known as "Bruin mania."

Little boys, who five years earlier would likely have been bouncing a basketball in their driveways, were now in front of their houses every day playing street hockey. They would rush home from school and without their mothers ever having to say a word would change out of their school clothes and put on their hockey jerseys with the names Orr, Bucyk, Sanderson, or Esposito stitched on the backs. And the kids weren't the only ones who loved the Bruins. It wasn't unusual to drive down a New England road and read a bumper sticker pasted on the car in front of you that proclaimed "Jesus saves, but Esposito scores on the rebound." Parents dreamed of their son becoming the next Bobby Orr, or, if the kid didn't have quite that much talent, another Esposito would be okay.

As Bruins mania spread, hockey rinks with artificial ice surfaces sprouted up all over New England. In the late 1950s, there was only one indoor regulation-size artificial ice surface in Rhode Island. By 1972, there were thirteen rinks in a state with only about nine hundred thousand residents.

The result was an explosion of youth hockey players in New England. In the late 1950s, there were only a few hundred kids playing organized youth hockey in Rhode Island. By the early 1970s, there were more than three thousand. Bob Loeber, a retired pharmaceutical salesman from Cranston, can still remember the time he took his five-year-old son, Bobby, to his first youth hockey practice in 1973. "There were at least two hundred kids on the ice at the same time," he said.

The Orr-inspired hockey rink–building boom and youth hockey explosion was even more prominent in the Boston metro area, where there are several million people. By the midseventies, there were at least ten thousand kids playing youth hockey in New England. In Rhode Island twenty-nine of the state's forty high schools had hockey teams compared with only ten schools that had teams in 1960.

By 1976, a series of knee injuries had started to limit Orr's ice time. During the 1975–76 season he played only ten games for the Bruins, yet despite playing on battered knees he was still one of the best players in the 1976 Canada Cup series. A year later, unable to settle a salary dispute with the Bruins, he accepted a free-agent offer to play for the Chicago Blackhawks. He only played two years with the Blackhawks before retiring at the relatively young age of thirty-one.

"Losing Bobby was the biggest blow the NHL ever suffered," NHL Hall of Famer Gordie Howe said in the *Hockey News*'s special Top Fifty All-Time Great NHL Players edition.

Orr's defection to Chicago and subsequent retirement put a damper on Bruin mania in New England. At about the same time a national energy crisis was making the cost of running some ice rinks prohibitive. Several rinks in Rhode Island and Massachusetts were closed and turned into roller skating rinks or warehouses because of the high operating costs. New England hockey never saw another boom like the Orr era, but the seed had been planted for a new generation of hockey players. By the early eighties, guys who were teenagers during the early stages of Orr-mania were becoming fathers. A few had played hockey, others had been just fans, but they loved hockey and they wanted their sons to be hockey players. It meant a steady stream of young hockey players, and there were still plenty of rinks where their kids could learn to turn on a dime the way Orr did.

And by 1980 it had become almost unpatriotic to not have your son playing youth hockey. That winter, the U.S. Olympic hockey team had performed the "Miracle on Ice" by winning the gold medal over the heavily favored Russian team. Any hockey brownout caused by the energy crunch of the 1970s was reenergized by the 1980 Olympic victory.

Youth hockey isn't just a sport: it's a way of life. Once a game played for the most part on frozen ponds and lakes, by the seventies virtually all organized hockey in New England was played on artificial rinks. A twelve-year-old might be able to walk to a field down the street for Little League baseball practice but it takes an adult to drive a young hockey player to practice at a rink that may not even be in his hometown. Although there are more hockey rinks per person in the Providence-Boston area than any other area in the country, there still wasn't enough ice time for hockey kids to have normal after-school or early-evening practices like their baseball-, basketball-, and soccer-playing friends. Many New England parents found themselves spending early Saturday and Sunday mornings in frigid ice rinks, cups of coffee in hand, watching their kids at hockey practice. What else are you going to do at six or seven o'clock on a Saturday morning in January, ten or fifteen miles from home? There isn't enough time to go back home and do a few things around the house. The shopping malls aren't open yet and even a cold hockey rink is better than sitting in a local donut shop.

It isn't long before parents start critiquing what's happening on the ice. Some of them are former players; others have never taken a slap shot themselves. But it doesn't matter, after a few years most hockey parents assume that they're experts. Some have watched virtually ever step that their kid has taken on skates. They know more about how he can skate and stick-handle than they do about how he can read or figure math problems because they're always at the rink, while they only hear about what's happening in the classroom. It's been said that the definition of a hockey parent is a guy who sits in a rink, drinking a cup of coffee and criticizing every kid on the ice but his own. That may be a little cruel, but there's truth in the image. And it's not surprising that after spending countless hours at the rink that hockey parents become very involved with their kid's hockey careers. It's also not surprising that because they're so accustomed to hopping in the car they will travel wherever and whenever they feel it will make their kid a better player. Long before American soccer parents started taking their kids on the road to seek better competition, New

England hockey parents were packing their cars and headed to hockey tournaments from Quebec to Washington, D.C.

Although ice hockey isn't cheap, it also isn't prohibitive for the blue-collar class. The construction worker or truck driver can't afford the private tennis or golf lessons. But he can afford the money for hockey equipment and team expenses, even though it might mean cutting back on a few other family luxuries. Therefore the lawyer sits in the rink with the truck driver, the doctor sits with the construction worker.

Decades ago, hockey in New England became more than just a winter game. Artificial rinks allowed the sport to be played twelve months a year and hockey parents didn't hesitate to sign up their kids. Spring leagues, summer hockey camps, invitational tournaments—there was never a shortage of opportunities. And with a majority of young hockey players coming from middle-class families funding these trips wasn't a hardship. Vacations for hockey families often consisted of a week in a motel while the family's future Bobby Orr participated in an out-of-state tournament or a summer hockey camp on a college campus.

Most American men will tell you that the first time they bought a bat or baseball glove for their young sons the dream of someday watching them playing Major League baseball flickered through their minds. But for most that's all the dream ever is—a little flicker before reality sets in. There are millions of kids playing baseball in America, but less than a thousand Major League players. There are millions of kids playing basketball in playgrounds and youth leagues around the country, but only five hundred NBA players. It's a real long shot, the proverbial one in a million, for a kid from middle-class American suburbia to make it to the Majors or the NBA. The chances of the kid even getting an athletic scholarship aren't much better.

But it's different for New England hockey players, and their parents. Until recently, youth hockey was a regional game. In the sixties and seventies, the only areas in America where the game was played seriously was the Northeast and some upper Midwestern states such as Minnesota, Michigan, North Dakota, and Wisconsin. So when the NHL began expanding in the late sixties and throughout the seventies greater numbers of American players began showing up on the NHL rosters, and many of those players were from New England. They were guys who had grown up playing in suburban youth hockey leagues, most of them around the Boston-Providence area. It wasn't just the pros. The two most publicized players on the Miracle on Ice 1980 Olympic team were goalie Jim Craig and Mike

Eruzione, the guy who scored the winning goal against the Russians. Both came from working-class Massachusetts families and were graduates of suburban Boston-area youth hockey organizations. Three years later, Mount Saint Charles senior Brian Lawton became the first American-born player to be the number-one selection in the NHL draft. Almost every New England youth hockey organization could boast about at least one of its alumnus that was either playing professional or Division I college hockey. Like Pennsylvania coal-mining burgs and Texas oil towns that brag of all the local kids who've made it to the National Football League, the walls of many New England hockey rinks are adorned with the high school jerseys of local players who went on to the big time. If asked, probably every one of those players would say he could never have made it without dedicated parents who were willing to drive him wherever his game took him.

These days, by the time a young New England hockey player reaches puberty, if he has talent, or at least if his parents think he does, he's probably traveled at least a total of fifty thousand miles to play hockey. With that kind of childhood it's not surprising that when a New England hockey player reaches high school age he's willing to travel wherever he and his family think he will have a better chance of fulfilling his hockey dream. For two decades, the ultimate high school hockey challenge for a southeastern New England kid has been to bring his hockey dream to Woonsocket every day so he can play at Mount Saint Charles.

CHAPTER 2

Joe Cardillo could remember the days when he seriously doubted he still would have been a Mount Saint Charles student on November 20, 1997.

The Rhode Island Interscholastic League is the high school athletic conference in which most Rhode Island high school teams compete and under RIIL rules November 20 is the first day winter sports teams, such as the Mount Saint Charles hockey team, can practice under the direction of their coach.

Like everything about Mount hockey during Bill Belisle's coaching tenure there are some classic tales about the first day of practice through the years.

In 1997, Dave Belisle was beginning his nineteenth season as his father's assistant coach, so no one knows better than he does the agony that his father has caused some teenagers on those opening days.

"Those first days used to be really tough," Dave said. "My father would start the practice, watch some kids skate for ten minutes, then say, 'You, you, and you—get out of here.' Ten minutes later, he'd tell two or three more kids to try out for junior varsity. These kids weren't bad players. They had been playing hockey all their lives and they were being cut in less than thirty minutes. Some kids were so scared they didn't even try out for the varsity, they just waited for the JV tryouts."

It didn't matter if you had been a hotshot youth hockey player, if Bill Belisle didn't like what he saw on that first day, a hockey dream could be finished, or at least put on hold for a year.

It certainly didn't matter who your father was.

In 1997–98, Peter Belisle was an assistant varsity hockey coach at the University of Connecticut, but in 1986, Peter, Bill Belisle's youngest son was just another freshman trying to earn a spot on the Mount Saint Charles varsity.

"My freshman year I was cut after the second day," Peter recalled. "I think the only reason he didn't cut me the first day was because he wanted me to get knocked around for a day by some of the seniors. At least the other kids who got cut could go home and get some sympathy from their fathers, I certainly didn't get any sympathy when I got home."

Just like hundreds of Mount players before him Cardillo had suffered through his share of first-day, stomach-wrenching moments.

"Your first few years, the first day of practice is scary," said Cardillo. "You start off doing simple skating drills, the type of drills you have been doing since you were a little kid. But you're so worried you will do something the coach doesn't like you get scared making a simple turn. You really don't feel comfortable on the first day until your senior year."

Which is why, in the fall of 1997, Cardillo finally was looking forward to a November 20.

He had come to Mount Saint Charles with a dream, but for the first two years it was more of a nightmare. "Hockey player" wasn't the first thing you thought of when you saw Joe Cardillo. He was only five-feet, eight-inches tall, and even though he'd been spending a fair amount of time trying to add physical bulk with weight training, he still only weighed about 145 pounds. But while fate may have shortchanged Cardillo in the size department, it bestowed him with the talent that separates good athletes from average ones. He was one of those players who seems to know where the action is headed a split second before it gets there. Ever since he was a little kid he had been able to anticipate what the other guy was going to do and beat him to the loose puck in front of the cage. He started playing hockey when he was only six and quickly discovered there's something unique about it. Maybe it's the fact that you're on skates creating speed. In a sense, you're always playing on an edge. His quickness made him one of the best players on his team at every rung of the youth hockey ladder.

He lived in Johnston, Rhode Island, a small, semi-blue-collar town of about thirty thousand, ten miles southwest of Woonsocket. Although the town doesn't have its own ice rink, Johnston High, the town's public high school, had fielded a varsity hockey team for about twenty-five years. But with a limited amount of potential hockey players at the 900-student school Johnston never had been a hockey power. In the RIIL, hockey teams are ranked purely according to talent level, and Johnston plays in Division C, the lowest ranked of the League's three divisions. You don't find college coaches scouting Division C games so it's not surprising that youth league all-stars such as Cardillo, who dream about their hockey careers extending beyond high school, don't play Rhode Island Division C high school hockey.

For Cardillo there was only one place he wanted to play high school hockey: Mount Saint Charles. He had grown up hearing stories about the Mount. When he was in elementary school, he had sat in the stands with his father and watched future NHL stars Keith Carney and Garth Snow lead Mount to the 1986 state title. In junior high, it was Bryan Berard, the kid from Woonsocket, who was named the NHL's 1996 Rookie of the Year. There was an aura about Mount Saint Charles hockey, and like hundreds of other Rhode Island kids his age, Cardillo dreamed that some day he would be the star of a Mount Saint Charles team.

In his freshman year, he was cut from the varsity after two days of practice, but that wasn't extremely upsetting. There was a time when most freshmen didn't even try out for Bill Belisle's varsity. Even future NHL players like Brian Lawton, Mathieu Schneider, Carney, and Snow all paid their dues playing junior varsity when they were at Mount back in the seventies and eighties. It wasn't even unusual for a kid to spend three years playing JV before he finally had got his chance to play varsity as a senior.

Cardillo didn't mind spending his freshman season playing on the junior varsity team. Almost every winter school-day morning he was up long before sunrise so he could make it to Adelard Arena for 6:00 a.m. JV practices. He was paying his dues, and he didn't mind because he knew a lot of great players before him had paid the same price.

But it was what happened in his sophomore year that almost ended his career at Mount Saint Charles

Hockey is a team game, but today's young hockey players grow up thinking like individual athletes—almost as much as tennis players and golfers do. Because they've been trying out for all-star travel teams from the time they're eight years old, they become very accustomed to evaluating their competition for team spots.

Cardillo had performed those evaluations before the start of his sophomore season. Ten seniors from the previous year's team had graduated, which left a lot of open spots on the roster. Since he was competing for one of those spots against guys he'd played with the previous year he knew his competition. In his opinion, he was one of the best players. He assumed that he was a sure bet to make the varsity.

He was wrong.

"Today was the second day of tryouts. I was cut," he wrote in his journal on November 21, 1995.

He was in shock, the world as he knew it suddenly made no sense. He had been playing hockey since shortly after he was out of diapers, playing with many of the same guys he was trying out against, and he was *always* one of the best. Now suddenly he was being told he wasn't one of the best.

"I can't understand it," he wrote. "I did awesome today. I skated fast, passed on the mark, and shot great. We did one-on-ones, two-on-twos, and three-on-ones. I did great in every single one."

Apparently Bill Belisle didn't see it the same way.

There comes a time in almost every athlete's career when he discovers that he's not as good as he thought he was. Usually that realization is spread over time. The year he makes the jump from Little League to Babe Ruth and realizes that the overpowering fastball thrown from the Little League pitching mound doesn't have the same devastating effect when thrown from a regulation mount. Or the season he realizes that being one of the tallest kids in his school doesn't make him one of the best basketball players in the state.

But for Cardillo it happened in a split second—and he couldn't understand it.

"The coach read off the names of the kids who were cut. When he read my name I almost fainted," Cardillo continued. "I said to myself, '*No*, this can't be happening.' I told Mom and she went nuts. I can't blame her. If she only knew the confusion that is inside of me she would not ask so many questions."

At fifteen, he felt he was being hit with the slap-in-the-face reality that usually doesn't hit middle-class American kids until they're twenty-two or twenty-three and trying to figure out what to do with that new college diploma.

Every fifteen-year-old is confused; it's the right of the age. But for Cardillo this was more than a simple passage through midteens. This wasn't a girl telling him that she was going to the dance with someone else. This was his hockey dream falling to pieces. For Cardillo hockey wasn't just a game he played for a few hours after school. Hockey was getting up on a New England winter Saturday mornings for a six o'clock practice. Hockey was driving in a car for three hours a couple of days a week when he was ten years old just to play a few games. For him, just as it was for a lot of young players, hockey was more than a game. It was the fiber of their life. And like anything that has that much meaning in your life it can lift your spirits to incredible heights or it can dump you down to depression. For the first time in his life, hockey had dumped on Joe Cardillo.

He was confused and angry—angry enough to consider leaving Mount Saint Charles. If Bill Belisle didn't appreciate his talent, he knew that there were coaches at other high schools who would love to have him. He certainly wouldn't have been the first player to leave Mount because he didn't agree with Belisle's evaluation of his talent.

His parents encouraged him to stick it out, even if they didn't understand why Coach Belisle was causing their family so much anguish. Cardillo really didn't need much encouragement, though. The Mount Saint Charles mystique was still all-consuming.

So he suffered through the anguish of playing junior varsity, of having to practice at seven o'clock in the morning before school while his friends on varsity practiced at prime time after school. He dealt with the inconvenience of having to carry his equipment to school every day while the varsity players left theirs in the varsity dressing room. On certain days, Bill would even instruct him to practice with both the junior varsity *before* school and the varsity *after* school. Almost every day he wrote in his journal, as if putting his feelings down on paper gave him a way of venting his anger and articulating his hopes for better times without anyone asking him questions.

"Dave said he would give me a shot in a varsity game," he wrote one day during his sophomore season.

Eventually his perseverance paid off. By the middle of the season he had moved up to the varsity. Each day after practice he would write about the constant changing of lines. One day he would be on the third line, which meant he would be playing in the game that weekend, but the next day he was dropped back to the fifth, which meant he wouldn't even dress for the game. It was a season of constant uncertainty, a season of trying to understand what Bill Belisle wanted from him. The older players called it "Belisle head games."

Even though he had finished his sophomore year practicing at least every day with the varsity, he was still worried on the first day of practice in his junior year in 1996. One lesson he had learned well in his first two years at Mount was that you never knew what Bill was thinking. Cardillo survived the early cuts, and after the first week of practice it was evident that he was going to be a regular varsity member. But there was always that sense of uncertainty, a sense of insecurity that Bill seems to cultivate in his younger players so that they're always paying attention to what he's saying.

It wasn't until midway through his junior season that he finally felt he had definitely arrived as a Mountie. His play-making skills made him a valuable member of the 1996–97 team. He was one of the team's top scorers with most of his points coming from assists. Dave admired the way he played. In his opinion, Cardillo was the most unselfish player on the team—and he was probably right. Cardillo wasn't flashy, but he never stopped working the corners. He had become an archetypal Bill Belisle player: a kid who had perfected all the basics of his game and would do whatever it took to make Mount Saint Charles a winner.

So after three years, he was looking forward to the first day of practice in 1997. He was no longer scared about not making the team. He was excited about finally getting the season underway. This was going to be his year, the year to be one of the team leaders. But it also was his chance to convince the college coaches who had sent him the perfunctory recruiting letters that they should actively court him. Cardillo was the consummate team player, but he now felt it was time to reap a few rewards for all of his hard work. As he prepared for his final opening day of Mount Saint Charles practice, Cardillo's personal goals were as prominent in his mind as Mount winning another state championship.

Maybe it wasn't his fault. He had grown up in an era when individualism dominates sports. The media loves to follow Michael Jordan and other superstars because they make compelling stories. It wasn't that Cardillo was like some kid from a West Texas oil town whose only chance of escaping the confines of his podunk hometown was by winning a college sports scholarship. No matter how many goals he scored as a high school hockey player, the odds were favorable that someday he would be a college student. He had always been a good student, and he might even have been a better musician than a hockey player. He had taken up the trumpet and alto sax while very young and had established his credentials as one of Rhode Island's outstanding young musicians. His father, who owned a small business, and his mother, who was a school teacher, would somehow find a way to finance his college education.

Of course it would help his parents if he was offered a scholarship. But even without one, hockey might be able to get him into a college that's usually beyond the expectations of the average middle-class suburban kid. He was a good student, but he didn't have the 1,400 college board scores that Ivy League schools and some of the small elite New England schools such as Holy Cross, Amherst, Williams, and Trinity look for. But all those schools make exceptions for athletes, so as Cardillo prepared for his final first day of practice, he couldn't help telling himself that there was nothing wrong about thinking what Mount hockey could do for him rather than just what he could do for Mount hockey. After all, he had paid his dues. Paid them with interest as far as he was concerned.

CHAPTER 3

There are days that leave an indelible mark on a person's mind.

Anyone over the age of fifty remembers where they were when they learned John Kennedy had been shot. Most people over forty remember what they were doing that summer night when Neil Armstrong took "one small step for man, one giant step for mankind."

Tony Ciresi will never forget the afternoon of February 21, 1983.

It was winter break in Rhode Island. Ciresi, then a Mount Saint Charles assistant hockey coach and a teacher, had already been at Adelard Arena for several hours working with the junior varsity when it came time for the varsity practice. Head Coach Bill Belisle had told him to go home because he'd had been at the rink long enough, but Ciresi decided to stay awhile.

If Ciresi had left when his boss gave him the okay, Bill probably wouldn't be alive today.

Ciresi was standing on the side of the rink talking to a player while Bill was on skates in the middle of the ice conducting a drill. In those days, Bill didn't wear a helmet when he was on the ice.

A player sprinting back down the ice after completing a drill suddenly lost his balance and slid toward Bill's back. As he ran into Bill, he took

Bill's skates out from under him. The first thing that hit the ice was the back of his unprotected head.

There was no one in the rink other than the players and Ciresi, who all rushed toward Bill. They immediately saw the blood gushing from his nose, mouth, ears, and even his eyes.

"It was coming out of everywhere," recalled Ciresi.

The fifty-two-year-old had fractured his skull from the back of his head to his temple. He was still semiconscious, however, and his first reaction was to wobble back up on his skates. Ciresi held him down.

"I had taken the first-aid course required for my coaching certification so I knew in the case of head injuries you don't want the person to move because he could go into shock. He was trying to get up and it took me and a few of the players to hold him down. He's an amazingly strong man. If I hadn't been there, the players never would have tried stopping him from getting up," he said.

Ciresi still has the letter sent to him by the paramedics who responded to the emergency call.

"They told me I probably saved his life," he said. "They said with all the bleeding, he would have gone into shock if he had gotten up and he probably would have died."

Bill's fate still was very questionable when he was carried from Adelard Arena that day. He had a sixteen-inch skull fracture.

The rescue squad's first stop was the emergency room of Fogarty Memorial Hospital, a few miles from Mount Saint Charles. The minute the doctors at Fogarty saw Belisle they knew he needed more help than they could give him at their small facility. After doing their best to stabilize him, they laid him in an ambulance and sent him to Rhode Island Hospital, fifteen miles away in Providence. Twice on the way there Bill lost all his vital signs.

Dave was the first family member to reach the hospital, about a half hour after his father had been wheeled in. The attending physicians told him it didn't look like his father was going to live, and that a priest was administering the last rites of the Roman Catholic Church. He should break it to his mother that her husband was close to death.

But Dave didn't immediately inform his mother of the doctor's prognosis. "I was afraid the shock might be too much for her," he recalled. "We were trying to deal with my father's injuries; I didn't also want to have my mother in the emergency room."

When he thinks back to that day now, Dave realizes he was also thinking that despite everything the doctors were telling him he wasn't even sure that a sixteen-inch skull fracture could stop his father.

Dave was right. Bill survived that day. He remained on the critical list for two weeks, but he survived. He had lost virtually all of his memory and he literally had to learn how to walk again. But six months after the accident he was back coaching the Mount Saint Charles hockey team. The determination he demonstrated in his battle to return to coaching helps explain how Mount Saint Charles hockey has become a national phenomenon. Intensity has been a hallmark of Mount teams for more than two decades. Bill Belisle doesn't just preach intensity; he lives it. And that intensity started long before he coached his first high school hockey game.

Legend has it that Mount Saint Charles was the birthplace of Rhode Island high school hockey. It's the story of how Brother Adelard Beaudet of the Order of the Sacred Heart, who had grown up skating on the frozen Saint Lawrence River near his home in Quebec, introduced hockey to the boys of Mount Saint Charles Academy when he arrived at the Woonsocket parochial school in 1924. It appears that Brother Adelard was a missionary of dual purpose: he had been sent to Rhode Island to teach children the way of the Lord, but he quickly included instruction in the art of the slap shot. The legend has it that back then Mount boys couldn't afford hockey sticks, so Brother Adelard sent them to the woods to grab thick tree branches and then had them flatten them into sticks. For pads, they used newspapers and notebooks. He built goals of planks and boards, and set out each winter to teach the game of ice hockey as only a Canadian could teach the game of his homeland.

A few years after his arrival at Mount Saint Charles, he formed a little Rhode Island high school hockey league with another Catholic school and two Providence public schools. A few years later, several other Rhode Island public schools joined the league. Brother Adelard served as the Mount coach and apparently he was a coach well ahead of his time. In an era when the word *recruiting* wasn't even part of the American sports vocabulary, Brother Adelard knew the benefit of having a pipeline to talented players. In those years, Mount Saint Charles had boarding students. Each summer Brother Adelard would return to his native Quebec for a little "vacation" and when he returned to Woonsocket in the fall he would be accompanied by Canadian boys who were eager for a Mount Saint Charles education. It wasn't coincidental that the Canadian students were also sensational hockey players. The good brother wasn't bringing baby-faced fourteen-year-olds back to Woonsocket—Woonsocket old-timers say that a few of Brother Adelard's recruits had actually been quasi-professional players back in Canada. And to make the Canadian boys feel at home Brother Adelard designed the Mount Saint Charles uniforms to resemble those worn by the Montreal Canadiens.

It's not surprising that Brother Adelard's Canadian-laden Mount teams dominated their Rhode Island schoolboy opponents. From 1932 through 1940, Mount teams won 160 games, tied one, and lost only seven. In 1934–35 the Flying Frenchmen, a nickname Brother Adelard had unofficially dubbed his teams, went undefeated in twenty-seven games, had twelve straight shutouts, and won the New England high school title. They even claimed that they were the national high school champions. Of course there never was a national championship game, but then sports legends often are created more by word of mouth than by actual competition.

Brother Adelard never advertised his recruiting techniques and, in the early years, it was easy to hide the Canadian kids among the Rhode Island players. Most of the Rhode Islanders were sons of Canadian immigrants who had come to Rhode Island to work in the textile mills so they had no problem conversing in French with Brother Adelard's imported players. But by the midforties other Rhode Island high schools had learned about the good brother's recruiting methods. In 1946, the state high school league officials ruled that Mount Saint Charles could no longer use Canadians. Once the league shut down the Quebec-to-Woonsocket pipeline, Brother Adelard retired from the coaching business. He never left Rhode Island, however. He died there in 1990 at the age of 106.

The Brother Adelard legend makes for a nice little Rhode Island sports story, but it really is nothing more than that. None of the early Mount players, not even the Canadians, went on to play in the National Hockey League. For thirty years after Brother Adelard was prohibited from using Canadian players, Mount won only two Rhode Island state championships. Even building its own hockey rink in 1963 didn't make the school an immediate high school hockey powerhouse.

That didn't start happening until Bill Belisle became coach in 1976.

Bill certainly didn't fit the description of a typical high school coach. He wasn't a teacher; he was a construction equipment mechanic. He had never gone to college and, at forty-five, his head-coaching resumé consisted of a few years as coach of a peewee hockey team. But he had a passion for hockey and for Mount Saint Charles Academy.

He was a bridge between Mount Saint Charles's past and present. He had been a Mount hockey player back in the 1940s when some of Brother Adelard's Canadian players were still on the team. He had grown up in the French-Canadian enclave of Manville, only a few miles from Mount Saint Charles, and he still lived on the street where he was born. The distinctive Quebecois dialect of his parents still peppered his everyday speech.

Of course nostalgia is great for storytelling; it might even help in a few pregame motivational speeches. But it doesn't turn a losing hockey program into a winner. Belisle did that with a unique coaching style.

From his first day on the job Belisle blanketed his team in secrecy. Old-time Mount hockey fans, guys who had watched Mount practices for decades, were suddenly told they were barred. Parents, for whom sitting in frigid hockey rinks while their sons practiced had become a way of life, were told to wait outside in the parking lot. Practices were closed to everyone except players and team coaches—no parents, no fans, and no college coaches. Bill closed the front door leading into the rink and let it be known that anyone who even stuck his or her head inside that door while practice was going on would be subjected to a verbal assault. He did allow parents to wait in the heated Adelard Arena lobby outside the doors of the rink, but any parent who was foolish enough to open those doors during a practice was greeted with a scream of "Take your kid and get out of here." It wasn't long before most parents didn't even chance sitting in the lobby for fear that they might be associated with some foolish soul who was trying to sneak a peek at practice. They didn't want their kid to pay the price.

Bill could shut out the world outside Adelard Arena from his hockey team because the rink was his, if not literally at least figuratively. In 1974, the year before he was named coach, he'd been persuaded by the Mount principal to leave his job as a heavy-equipment mechanic for a local construction firm to become manager of Adelard Arena. He knew nothing about running a hockey rink, but he wasn't worried about learning how to run and repair the two compressors that keep the ice frozen or the Zamboni ice-clearing machine. He knew that in a matter of time he would become a whiz at fixing a Zamboni just as he was at maintaining a front-end payloader or a two-ton dump truck. But an ice-rink manager needs both mechanical and business skills. One minute he's taking care of the Zamboni and the next he's billing for ice rental. Bill didn't know anything about debits or credits; he never had been good in math. In his family, he brought home the paycheck, but his wife paid the bills. And there was another problem. Taking the manager's job would mean a pay reduction. Even to this day the Brothers of the Sacred Heart are generous with their blessings, but tight with their money.

On the surface it would have seemed like an easy job offer to turn down. Why would any man with four children take a job he wasn't sure he could do for less money than he was making at his present job? To nearly anyone else it wouldn't have made any sense, but for Bill it was a chance to work around two things he loved—hockey and Mount Saint Charles. As a kid growing up in Manville in the late thirties and early forties, he would rush home every winter afternoon from the Catholic grammar school down the street, grab his skates, and head down to the little pond at the far end of the town. There, he and his friends would play hockey until darkness made it impossible even to see the black puck on the white ice.

Bill and virtually all of the other players were sons of Canadian immigrants who had come to America to work in the Blackstone Valley textile mills. The kids would sit at their kitchen tables and listen to their fathers' stories about what it was like playing hockey in Canada. How, unlike in America where hockey was a poor cousin to the national pastime of baseball and even took a backseat to football and basketball, hockey in Canada was king. Otis Belisle, Bill's father, had played a little hockey before coming to the United States, but to him it was just a game. In Otis's mind it was much more important for his son to have good penmanship than a good slap shot. He wasn't fooled for a minute when his fourteen-year-old son told him he wanted to go live with Canadian relatives so he could attend the French Catholic high school in his father's hometown. Otis knew Bill wanted to go to Canada to play hockey. Hockey had always been more important than homework to Bill and there had been more than a few times when he'd found himself in trouble because he was neglecting his schoolwork or chores because he was on the pond. Otis knew that if his son went to Canada he might never finish high school; therefore, instead of sending young Bill to Canada, he sent him to the Brothers of the Sacred Heart.

"He said he was sending me to Mount Saint Charles so the Sacred Heart brothers could straighten me out," Bill now fondly recalls.

The Brothers of the Sacred Heart did set Bill on the straight and narrow, but not exactly in the way Otis had expected. Instead of forcing Bill to choose between hockey and academics, Mount Saint Charles gave him reasons to love both. To this day, Bill recognizes his debt to the brothers. His years at Mount set the standard for the rest of his life. The brothers taught him diligence. He might not have been the best student in his class, but he never missed an assignment. Whether it was fear or respect, he always carried out the brothers' orders to the most minute detail—maybe because he knew if he didn't complete all of his work they wouldn't allow him to skate on the natural ice rink they had set up behind the school. The brothers had crafted the makeshift rink on the field beyond the school from old boards and flooded it with garden hoses. They even strung lights from the trees so that students could skate at night. During the winter, he was at the school from sunrise to sunset, and often well after dark.

In the 1940s, college was rare for sons of mill workers, so when he graduated from Mount, Bill went straight to work as a mechanic. He did, however, continue playing hockey. Even a two-year stint in Germany, after being drafted during the Korean War buildup, didn't diminish his love for the game.

He returned to America to marry Yvette Beaudoin, a girl from Manville he had known most of his life. They began raising a family and Bill returned to his job as a mechanic. It wasn't easy for a blue-collar family man to keep playing hockey around Rhode Island in the 1950s. There was only one artificial ice rink in the state, the former Rhode Island Auditorium in Providence. The Auditorium was home to the American Hockey League Providence Reds, both the Providence College and Brown University hockey teams, and was the venue for all of the state high school games. There wasn't much extra ice time for non-college guys in their twenties. But Bill found a way to play. He and a few other Woonsocket guys would pile into his big Buick and drive thirty miles to Worcester to play in what was basically a semi-pro league. They each received $10 from the money the rink collected for admission. But most nights the cash never made it back to Woonsocket.

"We would go to the bar down the street from the rink for a few beers after the game. By the end of the night the table was covered with beer bottles and we had less money than we came into town with," Bill recalled.

There were times he even had to stretch the truth a bit to play. In the late fifties a team called the Collegiates toured New England playing exhibition games against college teams. The roster was loaded with former college stars, such as the Cleary brothers from Harvard, but there were two team members who had never even been to college: Normand Belisle and

Jack Kirrane. Kirrane was a Boston firefighter who had been a Boston-area high school star and was well known there as an amateur player (he would go on to become one of the stars of the 1960 U.S. gold-medal Olympic team along with the Cleary brothers). People knew Kirrane had never played in college, but they accepted him because he was part of the USA Hockey program. Bill wasn't anywhere as well known in the New England hockey fraternity as Kirrane was but he wanted to play for the team. He therefore decided to embellish his hockey resumé a little. Under college he listed "Providence."

"I played a lot in Providence," Bill said with a sly grin.

His collegiate affiliation wasn't the only thing Bill had to stretch the truth about so that he could keep playing. Although his wife understood how much he loved the game, she also made it clear that he was now a husband with a young family. In the fifties, guys with blue-collar jobs and young families weren't supposed to go off playing hockey against a bunch of young college guys with no responsibilities and nothing to lose if they got hurt. But many nights after eating dinner with his family Bill said he was going back to work for some overtime. He would tinker about the garage for a little while, just about long enough to pick up his hockey equipment, and then head to Worcester or Providence to play.

"I had to make sure when I got back that I put grease on my hands so when I came in the house it looked like I had been working," Bill laughs.

Yvette will tell you now that she knew all along that her husband was sneaking off to play hockey. She knew he had a mistress, but as long as it was a hockey stick and pair of skates she was willing to go along with the scam because as much as he loved hockey he always put his family responsibilities first.

Well into his thirties Bill continued to play against college kids and guys in their twenties, becoming somewhat of a local legend around the Woonsocket area. In 1968, he was named the Most Valuable Player in an amateur tournament at Adelard Arena where most of the other players were recent college grads. Yet there was one thing he wanted to do in hockey that he thought he would never get the chance to do—coach the team of his beloved Mount Saint Charles.

Most American high school coaches are teachers, even at private schools like Mount Saint Charles. In addition to the obvious logistics of teachers' work schedules that make them available for the after-school practices that the average workingman can't make, having a teacher/coach demonstrates the philosophy that high school sports are an extension of the classroom. But Bill wasn't a teacher, and he never would be. The closest he thought he would ever get to coaching at Mount was in the late sixties when Larry Kish, the former Providence College all-American who became Mount head coach in 1966, asked him to be one of his assistants. Bill spent a few years working with the Mount players at practice but in 1971, Kish, who later would become head coach of the NHL Hartford Whalers, left Mount to pursue professional hockey opportunities. Bill was back watching Mount hockey from the outside.

Even when he was asked to be the Adelard rink manger in 1974, he didn't think that it would be a stepping-stone to the Mount coaching position. That chance finally came when, after a few years of losing records under two coaches following Kish's departure, the school administration decided it needed another change. The administration's decision that a new coach was needed was prompted in part by a visit from the hockey team.

"A group of us went to the principal and told him we wanted Mr. Belisle to be the coach," recalls Dennis Plante, captain of Bill's first team in 1975–76.

One of the other players who went to the principal was Bill's son John, at that time a Mount junior. His father had coached his youth hockey team a few years earlier. It was a team that nobody expected would do well in its league, but it ended up winning a championship. A few of the players had gone on to play at Mount and they were now tired of losing. They wanted Bill to do the same thing for Mount that he had done for their peewee team.

The principal listened to the students and asked Bill if he would be interested in the head coaching job. Although it was his dream job, before he said yes he told the principal that the only way he would accept it was if it was okay with the current coach, Steve Shea. Shea had been an outstanding player at Brown University and began teaching at Mount shortly after graduation. Bill didn't agree with Shea's attempt to make Mount hockey a carbon copy of the Russian style that was starting to infiltrate American hockey in the seventies, but he liked Shea as a person. He also didn't think Shea's losing record had as much to do with inadequate coaching as it did with parental interference. As rink manager he had stood in the arena each afternoon watching some of the fathers

31

sitting in the stands at practice criticizing Shea's every coaching move. Time after time he would notice a player look up toward his father when he disagreed with something Shea was trying to teach him. Bill thought to himself that if he ever became coach, the first thing he would do was shut the door to "his" rink.

The principal met with Shea and explained that for the good of the school the administration felt that there needed to be a change in coaching, but they would only hire someone new if Shea agreed. Shea did agree to give up the coaching job, but remained a Mount faculty member for two decades.

Plante, John Belisle, and the other players on the 1975–76 team might have thought they knew what they were getting into when they petitioned for Bill Belisle to become head coach. It didn't take long for them to realize, however, that his youth coaching style was child's play compared to what he was going to do at Mount.

Perhaps Bill was fortunate that he had waited so long for his chance. He knew that at his age this was his only chance, so he was going to do it *his* way. If it worked, great, if not, at least he would never be second-guessing himself. He hadn't been a drill sergeant during his army days, but his coaching style definitely seemed more suited to a boot camp than a hockey rink. Simple hockey drills became daily tests of character and perseverance.

It didn't take long for the rumors about his training techniques to begin circulating. At every Rhode Island hockey rink somebody had a Bill Belisle tale. Of course only Mounties knew fact from fiction—what happened behind those closed doors at Adelard Arena was between coach and players.

"Bryan never told us anything that went on at Mount practices. Maybe he told his brother, but he didn't tell us," Pam Berard, Bryan Berard's mother told me in 1998. "The constant pressure can really foul up some kids. It's not for every kid and it's not for every parent."

Nobody knows better than Pam just how involved some parents become with their kids' hockey careers. She laughs when she thinks about the days when her husband, Wally, was coaching Bryan's peewee team.

"I would be trying to just watch the game but some parents would come up to me with their stop watches complaining that my husband was cheating their kid out of ten seconds of ice time. They've always been there watching out for their kid. They don't know how to handle it at the Mount because they don't know what's happening."

CHAPTER 4

T he Brother Adelard Arena, home of the Mount Saint Charles hockey team, was old the day it opened in 1963.

A few of the small towns around their provincial headquarters in Quebec had built artificial rinks; therefore the Brothers of the Sacred Heart decided that it would be a fine idea to build a rink at Mount Saint Charles.

Of course the good brothers didn't have a lot of money so they bought an abandoned aircraft hangar in Maine for a dollar, had it disassembled, and shipped the parts to Rhode Island. Brothers from throughout North America then spent the summer of 1963 in Woonsocket, transforming the hangar into a hockey rink.

Not much has changed at Adelard since it opened in that fall. The twelve-by-thirty-foot lobby has been modernized somewhat: it's now heated and has sports vending machines and a snack bar. But walk from the lobby through the wooden doors that open to the rink itself and you step back three decades. In most American rinks today, four- to six-foot-high sheets of Plexiglas sit on top of the dasher boards that circle the rink to protect fans in the stands from flying pucks (and bodies). At Adelard, the type of old, gray chain-link fencing that was common in hockey rinks during the fifties and sixties still sits on the top of the boards. The iron girders, which held the airplane hangar together, can still be seen supporting the upper walls of the roof. Exposed beams run only six feet above the corridors. The decor has a definite mid-twentieth century motif. The first few years the rink was open the fans sat on wooden bleachers but in 1965 the Brothers of the Sacred Heart—always on the lookout for a good deal— bought twelve hundred wooden seats that had been used at an exhibition at the 1964 New York World's Fair. Almost forty years later, fans still sit on those sixteen-inch-wide wooden seats. Visitors who don't have a hockey lineage may think Adelard resembles a dungeon, but for the hockey aficionado, it's a classic.

"Every year I try to make one or two pilgrimages over to Brother Adelard Arena. I consider it a shrine of the sport," Tim Taylor, veteran Yale University hockey coach and coach of the 1994 U.S. Olympic hockey team, told me in 1998.

Adelard actually is built on the site of a former shrine. During the 1940s and 1950s the site on which Adelard now sits, a small flat stretch of land about seventy feet down a hill from the school, was occupied by a beautiful flower-laden grotto dedicated to the Blessed Virgin Mary. According to Mount hockey lore, which like a lot of sports stories sometimes doesn't let the truth get in the way of a good yarn, the only structure that the Brothers of the Sacred Heart would allow to replace a shine to the Blessed Virgin was a hockey rink. In reality, however, the brothers never had to make that choice. By the time Adelard was constructed the site had been turned into a junior varsity baseball field because the brother who had been in charge of maintaining the grotto for decades had died in the late fifties.

Once Mount Saint Charles decided to build a hockey rink in 1963 there was never any question that it would be named after Brother Adelard. But sit in Adelard Arena today and you can't escape Bill Belisle's legacy. On the front wall of the rink, facing out to the ice surface, hangs a red, white, and blue banner for each state championship season. There are also four banners for the years Mount was named the number-one high school team in the country. No one has to tell Mounties about the tradition they are responsible for keeping; they see it every day they step on the ice for practice.

But despite tradition dripping from the walls and an ice surface conducive to Bill Belisle's proclaimed Mount style of hockey, it can be argued that the greatest advantage Mount players gain from having Adelard at their disposal is the varsity dressing room.

The Mount varsity room is only a sixteen-by-twenty-four-foot rectangle squeezed under the stands at the far end of the rink. To an unsuspecting eye there's nothing special about it. The walls are cinder blocks painted red and blue. Two of the four walls are lined with permanent benches with shelves overhead for storing equipment. Because the room is located under the bleachers, about midway across the room the ceiling becomes the bottom of the wooden structure holding the World's Fair seats in the area. This section slants down toward the ice, so anyone sitting on the movable benches placed on that side of the dressing room can't stand up straight without moving out toward the middle of the room. All of players' benches sit flush against a wall, even the ones at the base of the sloping ceiling. That way the players are always facing front. There's no way to avoid Bill's piercing glances by sitting off to the side.

Compared to some of the dressing rooms found in modern hockey rinks around the Northeast, the Mount varsity room is antiquated. But the varsity room is the inner sanctum of Mount hockey. Only Mount Saint Charles players, coaches, and managers are granted admittance. No parents, no friends of the players, no other hockey players can step foot in the varsity room at any time. All of the thousands of other hockey players, from peewees to high school players to adults, who use Adelard Arena throughout the season must change into their equipment in one of the six general dressing rooms on the opposite side of the rink. Once the high school season is finished the Mount room is cleared and no one uses it again until the start of the next high school season. Even today's professional athletes have to share their luxurious locker rooms with media members, guests or friends of the owners, team officials, and even their own friends. But Mount players never share their locker room with anyone. You don't even see the president of the school, the principal, or the athletic director in the Mount room. Media members conduct their interviews outside the dressing room door.

The varsity room gives Mounties a luxury enjoyed by few high school hockey players in America. Because most hockey rinks are used by a variety of groups, the dressing rooms are shared, even for high school players. You don't see lockers in hockey rink dressing rooms like you do in high school gymnasiums. Hockey players grow up carrying oversized bags, stuffed with skates, pads, and padded pants from their homes to rinks and back home again. Look in the driveway of a hockey family these days and you'll probably find a minivan, a Ford Bronco, or a Jeep Cherokee. You need room to take hockey equipment on the road.

The agony of every hockey mother is unpacking a bag loaded with sweat-soaked long underwear along with shin pads, shoulder pads, helmets, and gloves that continually absorb sweat into the padding. There's nothing else in sports like the smell of a hockey bag. Most hockey players, or their mothers, know the nightly ritual of emptying the bag so that their equipment can dry out near a furnace or heater. But once a kid earns a spot in the Mount varsity room his days of lugging a hockey bag are finished. Each varsity player is assigned a spot in the dressing room. After practices and games at Adelard, players hang their skates and equipment on hooks above their spots on the bench so they can dry out. They don't even need to worry about bringing a towel for a shower. Clean towels await players every day. It's the kind of treatment usually reserved for college and professional players.

Like a kid's room at home, maybe even more so, the Mount varsity room is a teenager's isolation chamber. It's where Mount players can escape from any problems except perfecting their skating skills and slap shot. It's the one place in their hectic teenage lives where there's a singularity of purpose. It's where Bill's handwritten eight-by-ten-inch paper signs, some yellowed with age, are constant reminders of what it takes to be a champion. For more than two decades, Mounties have been reminded to Think-Quick, Shoot-Quick, Move-Quick.

Each Mount team has prepared for practices and games by blasting music of its generation in the varsity room. Back in the sixties, it was the sounds of the Beatles emanating from a transistor radio, then in the seventies and eighties it was Bruce Springsteen and Van Halen from a cassette tape deck. In the winter of 1997–98, Pearl Jam and a cross section of rap boomed from a compact disc player. Bill doesn't particularly like the music, but he knows it's part of teenage culture so he lets it blast unless he has something to say. Dave can only remember one instance when his father censored the varsity room audio.

"A few years ago one of the kids brought in some rap music that used the word fuck a few times. When my father heard it he went wild," Dave said one afternoon in 1998. "He came in screaming, 'There won't be any of that fuck music in this locker room.' He grabbed a bunch of CDs, threw them on the ground, and started smashing them with his work boots. The problem was he grabbed the wrong CDs. None of the ones he grabbed were the one with the fucks on it. The kid who owned the CDs knew my father had grabbed the wrong ones, but he didn't say anything. He just sat there watching my father smash about a hundred dollars worth of CDs. When somebody told my father what he had done, he went back, grabbed the ones with the fucks, and smashed them, too. The poor kid who lost all his good CDs just sat there looking at the pile of his smashed CDs in the middle of the locker room floor, but never said a word—at least not to my father."

Sometimes you have to pay an extra price to have a spot in the Mount room.

For two decades Mount players have shared the experiences of being a teenage male in the Mount Room without any outside interferences. Even today there's no talk of political correctness. It's one of the most exclusive men's clubs in New England, and most of its members are teenagers.

The advantage of not carrying equipment and having a retreat from the outside world is nice, but the most important thing about dressing in the varsity room is that you practice with Bill Belisle. Only a few showers and a toilet separate the varsity room from the junior varsity room, but in hockey terms the two rooms are worlds apart. If you don't have a spot in the varsity room you carry your equipment to and from practice every day. Worse, while the varsity practices are immediately after school, the junior varsity usually practices before school at 6:00 a.m. For kids who live thirty or forty miles from Mount, that can make for some very early school days for both players and parents.

"One father use to drive his son to practice, then come in and catch a little sleep on the bench in the lobby before he went to work," Dave recalled with a chuckle.

Although prime practice time and the advantage of not carrying equipment home are important, the biggest difference between being in the varsity and junior varsity rooms is that unless you're in the varsity room, you don't practice with Bill, who never works with the junior varsity players. If you don't have a spot in the varsity room you don't get instructions from the guy who gave Brian Lawton, Bryan Berard, Keith Carney, Mathieu Schneider, and Garth Snow the foundations that paved the way for a journey to the NHL.

Dr. Jean Guay has been Bill Belisle's friend since the two were classmates at Mount Saint Charles in the late 1940s. Both men were sons of Canadian immigrants who enjoyed sports. But while Bill would take hockey over homework anytime he was given the choice, Guay was a dedicated student. After they graduated from Mount, Bill found work as a mechanic while Guay went off to college and eventually medical school. By the late fifties, Guay was spending his days operating on broken bones as an orthopedic surgeon while Bill was operating on truck transmissions. But despite their vastly different stations in life, they remained close friends. Guay was pleased when his old friend became the Mount hockey coach in 1976; he knew how much it meant to him. He also had young sons who were hockey players. He could now send them to his alma mater and not worry that he was shortchanging their hockey careers.

Doc Guay is one of Mount's staunchest hockey supporters, both with his time and his wallet. In the early years when Bill needed something that wasn't in the regular hockey budget he turned to his old friend, and Guay usually found a way to get it. Sometimes Guay spent his own money, such as the time he bought a puck-shooting machine. Other times the Doc organized fund-raising efforts. By the early eighties, the Mount Saint Charles hockey program boasted equipment that many college teams didn't have.

But Guay's most valuable contribution to Mount hockey has been his time and his medical knowledge. Right from the beginning of the Bill Belisle era, Mounties had a doctor on call twenty-four hours a day. On his way home from the hospital Guay would stop by Adelard Arena almost daily to check out the players after practice. Many of the minor injuries that so often are left untreated in high school athletes received immediate attention in the Mount locker room. Over a four-month high school season, taking care of those injuries early can make a significant difference for a team.

There's no question that through the years a lot of Mount players were able to get back into a game because Doc Guay was there for quick treatment. And his dedication to the team didn't end when his sons graduated from Mount in the eighties. Although he retired from active practice in the early nineties, he still visits the Mount locker room nearly every day and is always on call for Mount hockey players. He's the only outsider with a free pass to enter the varsity room whenever he wants. Unlike in the early days when he treated almost every injury himself, these days there are greater numbers of doctors specializing in sports medicine—he now hands out more referrals than treatments. But he will still spend hours making up special braces or padding that help Mount players work their way through injuries.

"He's never scored a goal and coached a minute of a game, but without Doc Guay there wouldn't be any title streak," admits Dave.

These days the Mount Saint Charles weekday hockey practices are always after school. There was a time, however, when Bill didn't wait for the end of the academic day to begin his practices. When he took over as coach back in the midseventies, Mount Saint Charles followed the same class schedule every day: Period I was always the first period of the day and Period 6 was always the last. Bill quickly realized that this academic schedule could benefit his hockey program. With a bit of cooperation from the guidance department, each year Belisle made sure that all of his hockey players were scheduled for Period 6 phys ed. Every day during the last period of the school day, rather than report to the gym to do push-ups and sit-ups, hockey players went down to Adelard Arena for their physical education class under the tutelage of "Professor" Belisle.

This schedule gave Bill an extra hour of practice every day—and he made the most of it. That extra hour meant that by the end of the season Mounties were getting at least a third more practice time than any other high school players in the state. Of course, not all of that time was spent on the ice; Bill put his troops through rigorous off-ice conditioning without feeling guilty of giving up valuable ice time. But the off-ice curriculum didn't always sit well with Bill's "fellow" professors.

"I used to have the players dress in their full uniforms with pads and everything, then put on their street shoes and run up and down the hill from the rink to the school parking lot. The other kids in the school would be sitting in class looking out the windows, watching these guys running around in their hockey uniforms. It was a funny sight, but the teachers would get mad because their students were always looking out the window rather than paying attention to their class. Finally, the principal told me we couldn't run around the school anymore."

Of course that didn't change Bill's training regimen; he just altered the running route. Rather than run up the hill to the school, the players ran back and forth through the hilly streets of the Woonsocket neighborhood below the rink, which was out of sight of the school windows.

The gym class practice sessions ended, however, in the late eighties, when Mount Saint Charles changed its daily academic routine from fixed class periods to a rotating schedule. Under the new format, the periods rotate so that one day Period 1 is the first class day but the next day it's the last. The rotating schedule means that Bill no longer can get all of his hockey players together in a last-period gym class. There was a rumor around Mount that a few of the hockey players were among the students pushing for the schedule change so they could avoid Professor Belisle's gym class. But you'll never hear any former Mount player admit that he was part of the conspiracy.

Bill's coaching system is actually built on a contradiction. His goal is to develop self-confidence in his players, yet he never allows that self-confidence to translate into self-absorption. The biggest question in sports may be, "What is teamwork?" Bill's answer is to help his players master individual skills and then transfer those skills into what's beneficial to the team. That can be tough for a lot of young people to understand, especially young hockey players.

"We get good players so they're already accustomed to always having the puck when they get here," Dave said. "That's because in youth hockey they have twice as many games as practices. The coach wants to win so he tells the good players to hold onto the puck because in youth hockey one good player can make a team a winner. We have to break down their games. We have to teach them to think like a member of a team rather than an individual. It's getting tougher every year."

Bill has always been a great spotter of individual faults. Moves that players were allowed to make for years in youth hockey, maybe even encouraged to make because they produced victories, become targets for his wrath when a kid gets to Mount. A crossover step that's lazy, a skating stride that he feels is too short, once Bill spots a fault he's relentless in drilling a player to correct it. For him, the concepts of *hard work* and *paying the price* have never been simply clichés to tape on the locker room wall. It's his way of life, and Mounties have known it for more than twenty years. They see him out on the Adelard ice surface daily, ensuring that the ice on which they skate is smooth and free of any digs. They watch him take the time after practice to clear the snow away from the base of the boards so that there won't be a buildup that could slow down the puck. It's a task he could easily pass on to one of the rink workers, but he wants to make sure nothing is left to chance. The players watch him check the locker room after each practice to make sure everything is in its proper place, from the aspirin bottle being put back on the shelf to making sure each player's equipment is hung so that it will dry properly overnight. To most people these seem like insignificant details that in the grand scheme of things couldn't make much difference. But Bill's whole system, from the locker room to the ice, is built on details. Nothing is left to chance. He knows that it's tougher for players these day to understand why it's all important compared to players twenty years ago. He knows that once today's players leave the confines of Adelard Arena they go back into a world where detail has become secondary. Where the bottom line is the only thing that matters—not how you get there. It's a world of quick answers and instant results. But when they're behind the doors at Adelard, they're in the world of no shortcuts.

"The practices have always been the tests. If you survive the practices the games are the easy part," Tony Ciresi told me one day in 1998.

CHAPTER 5

Y ou can't teach size.

That simple fact of life has been a basic premise of college basketball recruiting for decades, but now it's also the gospel of college hockey recruiting. Once upon a time, size wasn't a major factor in hockey: skating speed, and stickhandling skills were the key attributes that mattered. But for better or worse, the game became more physical over the past few decades and size has become a major factor in determining how far a kid can rise in the hockey ranks. These days, size may determine a young hockey player's fate even more than it does a young basketball player's. There are still plenty of opportunities in big-time basketball for the little guy whose quickness allows him to dribble through a full-court press or who can hit three-point bombs. But unless a young hockey player fits a certain size requirement there's little chance that Division I college coaches or pro scouts will give him a serious look.

Of the 340 defensemen on the 1997–98 preseason rosters of the twenty-six National Hockey League teams, 316 were six feet or taller and 65 percent weighed two hundred pounds or more. In the spring of 1997, the Boston Bruins made Joe Thornton the first pick in the NHL entry draft. At the time, Thornton was a six-three, 210-pound eighteen-year-old.

The Bruins expected Thornton would be up to 230 pounds within a few years, and he's a forward. It's not much different in the major college hockey ranks. It's that lust for size that made Jeff Jillson one of the most sought-after young hockey players in the world in the fall of 1997.

Sports agents first called Jeff's North Smithfield, Rhode Island, home shortly after he celebrated his sixteenth birthday in the summer of 1996. That's what happens when you're six-three, 220-plus pounds, can skate as smooth as silk, play defense, and score goals—a lot of goals. As a Mount Saint Charles junior in 1996–97, Jeff was unquestionably the best high school hockey player in Rhode Island. Despite being a defenseman, he was the state-scoring champion with thirty points in fourteen league games. But he was more than just the best player in Rhode Island. In the summer of 1996, he had been selected as one of the twenty-two players on USA Hockey's National Select 16 team. Selection to the team means, according to the powers that be in USA Hockey, the national governing body for the sport, that you're one of the best sixteen-year-old hockey players in America. It also means an opportunity to play in two world tournaments over a six-month period. Before that age, all-star competition is strictly on a regional basis. The only national competition is on a team basis with team membership being restricted to local USA Hockey districts. But when they turn fifteen, American hockey players no longer have to have a crew of talented teammates to make their mark on the national level. That's when many players, and in most cases their parents, start thinking in terms of individual advancement.

Because the world tournament is the first chance to see the best fifteen- and sixteen-year-olds playing against each other only two years before they're eligible for the NHL draft, it's not surprising the stands are filled with pro scouts, college coaches, and agents. If you make it to the World 16 tourney, you're a prospect. If you play well, you're a hot pro prospect, even if you're only sixteen.

It was as a member of the 1994 USA Hockey's Select 16 team that Bryan Berard, then a junior at Mount Saint Charles, made his first impression on the world hockey scene. At the world championships Berard was named Most Valuable Player in two of four tournament games. Two years later, he became only the third American to be selected first in the NHL entry draft.

As Berard did during the 1993–94 season, Jeff left his Mount Saint Charles teammates for a week during the middle of his junior season in

1996–97 to play for the USA Hockey Select 16 team at the world tournament. He may not have been named MVP as Berard had been five years earlier, but Jeff definitely made an impression. He was bigger than just about everybody on the ice, he could skate with all of them, and he had one of the hardest shots in the tournament.

Under NCAA regulations, a college coach is prohibited from personally contacting a prospective player until after the player's high school junior year. That doesn't mean that college coaches in all sports don't find ways to meet talented young athletes at camps and youth tournaments. But even with those allowances there's at least some sense of control over a college coach's actions. There's nothing, however, that can stop an agent from contacting a young player. In the game of hockey, where talented eighteen- and nineteen-year-olds can make an impact on a NHL team, getting them young is a mainstay of agenting. It's nothing new. Legend has it that Bobby Orr was signed by an agent when he was just fourteen.

So it is not surprising that shortly after he returned home from the world tournament in January 1997, agents started phoning Jeff. He was a sixteen-year-old high school junior, who didn't even have his driver's license, but he had sports agents calling his home telling his parents that they were going to make it possible for them to retire early because of their son's talent.

Most insiders on the Rhode Island hockey scene, including his Mount Saint Charles teammates, didn't expect to see Jeff wearing a Mount Saint Charles uniform during the 1997–98 season. Like every little kid who laces up a pair of skates and actually enjoys the idea of getting up at five o'clock on a Saturday morning to play hockey, Jeff dreamed of one day playing in the NHL. For most kids, it is nothing more than a pipe dream. But by his junior year at Mount, Jeff knew his dream had a strong chance of becoming reality. His performance at the World 16 tournament, coupled with his size put him near the top of the NHL Draft Class of 1998. The *Sporting News* in its 1997–98 Hockey Preview edition listed the top ten candidates for the 1998 draft. Jeff was the only American high school player to make the list. But the so-called experts warned him that if he wanted to stay at the top of the draft list, he had to play the 1997–98 season at a higher level of competition than Rhode Island high school hockey. That's what Berard had done five years earlier. Instead of spending his senior year at Mount Saint Charles, Berard left after his junior year and spent the next season playing for the Detroit team in the Ontario Major Junior Hockey League, one of the top junior hockey leagues in the world. The OHL is considered the best stepping-stone to a professional hockey career. Once strictly the domain of young Canadian kids, greater numbers of American kids have taken their hockey dreams to the OHL and other junior leagues over the past decade. It was Berard's play in his first season of OHL competition that made him the number-one selection in the 1994 NHL draft.

Jeff had options as to which year he would enter the NHL draft. Prior to 1997, players were considered draft-eligible in the year in which they turned eighteen. But because the NHL draft is held in June, a lot of kids who didn't turn eighteen until after June were being drafted. In an effort to relieve concerns that they were exploiting young players, the NHL changed the rule so that a player must be eighteen *when* drafted. They did make a concession, however, to players who might have been planning to be part of the 1998 draft, but would be ineligible under the new rule, grandfathering in any player who would turn eighteen during the 1998 calendar year into the draft. Players such as Jeff, who didn't turn eighteen until August, could have opted into the 1998 June draft. If they chose not to execute their option, they automatically became part of the 1999 draft.

But in 1997, Jeff didn't want to think about waiting until 1999. That was two years away, and when you're seventeen years old and you think you're talented enough to be a pro, two years is a lifetime. He may have been only seventeen, but Jeff had been around the national hockey scene long enough to know the conventional hockey wisdom: if he wanted to be a top draft choice, he needed to prove he could play an entire season against the kind of competition found in the OHL. One of the questions asked about Jeff was whether he was tough enough to play the NHL hard-hitting style. A few observers called him just a big, soft American kid who wouldn't survive against some hard-nosed Canadian kid whose only hope of getting out of Moose Jaw was to show he could bash the head of some hotshot American player who was trying to take over his native game. For although Americans were popping up more often on the rosters of OHL teams, more than 80 percent of the players were still Canadians. Sure, Jeff could dominate against Rhode Island schoolboys who he was bigger, stronger, and faster than, but what could he do in a league like the OHL?

Some hockey insiders had warned Jeff's parents that their son should have left Mount Saint Charles after his sophomore year. Back then, they were saying he should enroll in one of the New England residential prep schools that play games against other prep schools throughout the Northeast. Others said the Jillsons should have followed the example of many other New England hockey parents and send their son out to a place like Des Moines, Iowa, where he could play in one of the lower-level junior programs. Those programs have become popular in the development of young American hockey talent. The American junior leagues aren't as competitive as the major junior leagues, but it's considered a much higher level than high school. But for Joel and Linda Jillson sending their sixteen-year-old son out to live with a surrogate family in Iowa just so he could play sixty hockey games was never a consideration.

"It was more of a family consideration than a hockey consideration," said Joel. "We didn't want our sixteen-year-old leaving his family, and he didn't want to leave either."

"We wanted him to enjoy all the things that go with being a high school junior, like proms and going out with friends," Linda added. "There would be a lot of time for hockey in the future, but you're only a high school junior once."

Joel also figured that Bill's track record of developing great players meant his son's career wouldn't be hampered by spending his junior year at Mount. "I wasn't worried about his hockey development," he said during Jeff's junior year. "We knew the type of discipline Bill Belisle demanded from his players, and that's good for a young player. Bill has had some great players come through here. He knows when he has a stud and he's going to work developing his skills. He wasn't going to change his coaching style for Jeff Jillson and that was good. He didn't change for Bryan Berard so he wasn't going to change for Jeff Jillson."

Jeff spent his junior year at Mount. All through the season, however, his parents knew that in the spring they and their son were going to have to make a decision where he was going to play his senior year. They had wanted to spend the junior year just enjoying watching him play what probably would be his final year of high school hockey, but it was never that easy. The hockey world had been undergoing a dramatic change. When Disney purchased the Mighty Ducks, hockey entered a new sphere of entertainment. NHL salaries were still far from that of professional baseball and basketball, but it was no longer unusual to hear about a millionaire hockey player. With the increased salaries came increased agent interest.

"It was amazing. I was constantly seeing guys I didn't recognize talking to Jeff," Dave recalled about the 1996–97 season. "I would ask Jeff who the guy was and he'd say, 'Oh, just some agent.' It wasn't like that even three years earlier when Bryan Berard was here."

As one of the agents said to Jeff, "I hate talking to somebody as young as you, but I have to because I know other people are going to."

It was distracting, but it also was exciting for Jeff. What sixteen-year-old wouldn't be excited about having sports agents asking him to lunch? The more Jeff though about it during the winter of his junior year, the more he knew he didn't want to spend the 1997–98 season at Mount. He wanted to play in the OHL. He wanted to prove he could be a professional hockey player, and he didn't want to wait two years to do it.

Deciding to play in the OHL, however, is more than just a one-year commitment; it's a lifetime career move taken when you're only sixteen or seventeen. Because OHL players receive a small compensation, the NCAA had declared that once a player plays in the OHL he is ineligible to play American college hockey. For hockey players thinking only of a professional career that's not a major stumbling block. Like a lot of players in other sports whose goals are to turn pro there are more than a few hockey players who will admit attending college is just a way of furthering that goal. They may be listed as Communications or American Studies majors, but their real major course of study is the slap shot and body check. If they're good enough, bypassing college to take the fastest route to the NHL through the OHL is an easy decision.

Jeff, however, was a good student as well as a good hockey player. He was a member of the National Honor Society and he scored close to 1,200 when he took the SATs in his junior year. Neither Joel nor Linda attended college, but they know the advantage of education in today's world. Joel was a fireman in Woonsocket and Linda had just recently opened her own travel agency after years of working for another agency. They were already putting Jeff's older sister through Fordham University in New York and were making plans for how they would afford Jeff's and his younger brother Nick's college tuitions. Now if Jeff wanted it, his hockey ability would give him a free college education.

Jeff may have been a National Honor Society member, but he also was a teenaged hockey player with a dream to someday play in venues such as

Madison Square Garden and the Molson Center. He didn't say anything publicly, but by the spring of 1997 he knew he wanted to leave Mount Saint Charles and play junior hockey.

Linda wasn't saying anything either, but she didn't want her son leaving home before he graduated, and when he did graduate she wanted him to go to college. She had been a hockey mom for a decade and because her husband was a fireman who often worked strange hours, quite often she was the one driving Jeff to 6:00 a.m. practices during his youth hockey days. She spent many mornings perched in the stands of frigid hockey rinks, coffee cup in hand, just like the hockey fathers. She also spent countless weekends traveling to youth hockey tournaments and had become a wizard at organizing fund-raisers for new uniforms or extra ice time. But she never completely bought into the hockey mentality that dictated the lives of so many hockey families. How would spending his senior year in high school away from home enhance her son's future?

For his part, Joel could see the benefits of both sides. He didn't want his son to leave Mount Saint Charles for his junior year, but he was willing to let him pursue his dream and play junior hockey in his senior year.

Had everything followed a normal course Jeff wouldn't have been at the opening day of Mount Saint Charles practice for the 1997–98 season. But sometimes fate can alter a dream, and in Jeff's case fate was obviously on Mom's side.

Shortly after he returned from the World Junior Championships the previous January, Jeff started feeling sluggish. He was tired all the time, even though he was getting adequate sleep. He was still a dominant player against Rhode Island high school competition, but he knew he wasn't playing at the top of his game. He kept blaming it on hockey jet lag, rationalizing that he was still recovering from his two weeks away in Canada. But after a few weeks his parents knew it was something else. They send him to the doctor. In early February, he was diagnosed with mononucleosis.

Mono sidelined Jeff for almost a month. He did return to action for the 1996–97 state playoffs in March and helped Mount win its nineteenth state title, but he was in far from top form in the playoffs. He felt fine, however, so when the high school baseball season began in early April, Jeff, who had been a starter on the Mount varsity since his freshman year, was the Mounties starting catcher. That proved to be a mistake. Playing baseball in what usually is cold, damp New England spring weather, isn't the best way to recuperate. By May, Jeff had a relapse of mono and this time its effects were more severe. Rather than spending the summer improving his physical condition so he would be ready to play the tough style of major junior hockey, Jeff spend most of the summer lying on the living room couch, sleeping his summer away.

His physical condition handed Linda the excuse she needed to delay making any decisions about where Jeff would spend his senior year. From time to time during the summer Jeff would bring up the subject, but she would just say, "Let's wait until you feel better." By late August, Jeff felt he was healthy enough to decide. He started skating a little and told his parents he felt fine, although in reality he still felt weak. He wanted to make plans so he could enroll in a Michigan high school and play for the Plymouth Red Wings, the OHL team that snapped him up in the first round of the league draft in the spring.

But his mother insisted he wasn't yet strong enough to move away from home and play against nineteen- and twenty-year-olds who had spent the summer building up their physiques. "Start school at Mount in September," she said. "Work on building up your strength and in a month or so, which would be before the start of the OHL season, you can transfer to a high school in Michigan." It wasn't what he wanted, but Jeff agreed. After all, another month of home cooking could only help his recuperation. But one month turned into two, and every time Jeff brought up the subject of his move at the dinner table his mother brushed him off with a "We'll talk about it later." Linda always seemed to find a reason why the family couldn't sit down and make a decision.

Linda did, however, agree to take a trip to Michigan to talk to the people running the Junior Red Wings program and visit the high school where Jeff would transfer if he went to Michigan. Jeff hoped that the trip would convince his mother that it was okay for him to go. But his strategy backfired. The trip solidified Linda's opinion that he shouldn't leave Mount.

For Linda, education was the priority—the NHL was always going to be there. Her son should go to college before turning professional. When she met some of the other players on the Michigan team, she couldn't help but feel that education really wasn't that important to them.

"The players on the team were walking out of school at ten o'clock in the morning because they had to leave for a road trip. I asked them how many times that happened and they said sometimes a couple of times a week. That just told me education wasn't a major concern," she said.

The OHL season began in October and Jeff was still in Rhode Island. Before he knew it, he had seen another New England autumn—and he wasn't happy about it. He kept insisting to his mother that he wanted to go; she kept insisting it wasn't the best thing for him. By late October, she was pointing out that he would be at a disadvantage starting to play against players who had already been playing for a month. Joel and Linda discussed the issue, even argued a bit. Joel knew Jeff wanted to go, but his wife was passionate in her belief that the move wasn't the best thing for him. Joel wasn't so sure which was the best route so he went along with his wife's wishes.

Bill and Dave hadn't expected to see Jeff Jillson in Mount uniform for the 1997–98 season. But when October slid into November and he was still at Mount, the Belisles started thinking maybe there was a chance. Then about a week before the start of practice, Jeff called Dave. "Coach, I'm staying," he said.

One of the best high school players in the country had just told him that he would be on his team. He knew Jeff's presence meant Mount Saint Charles was the odds-on favorite to win another state championship. Yet he also knew that in his heart Jeff would have preferred to pursue junior hockey. The Belisles would relish having Jeff leading their team, but coaching a talented player who really wanted to be someplace else can test a coach's patience. Dave knew that his father wasn't all that patient.

CHAPTER 6

"Look at that kid leaning against the boards, we never would have gotten away with that," observed Pat Manocchia. "Back in our day if you leaned against the boards after skating a drill like that kid is, the coach went crazy. He'd have you doing push-ups or he'd throw you off the ice. He's definitely mellowed."

It was the Saturday after Thanksgiving and Manocchia was standing outside the dressing room, watching the 1997–98 edition of the Mount Saint Charles hockey team practice. His black hair, which flowed down to the collar of his black cashmere topcoat, was still wet from a post–alumni game shower. Each year, on the Saturday afternoon following Thanksgiving, the school invites former hockey players to compete between themselves and then attend a reception where they can get together with their families and friends and reminisce about old times. It's all part of the alumni relations/fund-raising efforts that are a staple at every private school in New England.

Manocchia looked more like he should be walking into some tony Manhattan nightspot than standing in a shabby New England hockey rink, which is not surprising because most days that's exactly what he would be doing. Brian Lawton may have been the first American-born player selected first in the NHL draft and Bryan Berard may have been the 1997 NHL Rookie of the Year, but in the summer of 1997 Manocchia achieved a level of notoriety that no other Mount Saint Charles graduate ever reached when he appeared on the cover of *The Enquirer* holding hands with Julia Roberts. Bill Belisle may teach a few smooth moves in his coaching regimen but how to date a movie star isn't one of them. Manocchia, who dated Roberts briefly in 1997, learned that on his own. But Bill played a major role in laying the foundation for a life that took Manocchia from the streets of Providence to the hot spots and executive suites of Manhattan.

Manocchia was captain of Bill's second state championship team back in 1979. Before launching a fitness and sports training facility in Manhattan, he played hockey at Brown University, where he struck up a friendship with fellow student John Kennedy Jr. When Manocchia started his business, Kennedy was one of his first customers. Before long, Manocchia had a client list that included professional athletes, corporate CEOs, and entertainment celebrities such as Roberts and Madonna. Madonna, Roberts, and the CEOs may never have worn a Mount Saint Charles hockey uniform, but in a sense they've became an extension of Mount Pride. Manocchia has applied to his celebrity training programs the concepts of focusing on an objective and taking pride in your work that he learned under Bill's tutelage. It doesn't matter if he's helping Roberts maintain the look that makes her one of the world's most glamorous movie stars or keeping a CEO physically fit so that he can handle the pressures of the business world. Two decades ago in the Mount dressing room, he learned that the secrets to success are simple, if you're willing to work at them.

"He forms the basis for everything you do the rest of your life. Of course, you don't realize it at the time because to you it's just hockey," Manocchia said about his former coach. "He's a genius. Of course, he doesn't know it because he's so basic. I work with a lot of CEOs of major corporations. I'm sure if I put down on paper the basics of how Coach runs his team and showed it to them, they would say, 'Yeah, that's the basic philosophy I use for running my company.'"

By the early seventies, Mount Saint Charles was having problems attracting students. For decades, the majority of its students were descendants of the French-Canadians who had come to America to work in Woonsocket's and Lincoln's textile and rubber mills. French was still spoken as a second language by many Mount Saint Charles teachers well into the early sixties.

But as the ethnic makeup of Woonsocket started changing in the fifties and sixties, Mount Saint Charles's customary source of students began drying up. There were fewer French-Canadian families living in Woonsocket, and the towns around the city transformed into upper middle-class bedroom communities populated by people who grew up in other areas of the state, many of whom were college graduates. To them, Mount Saint Charles Academy was a school behind the times, a school that was stuck in old traditions that were no longer relevant in the educational atmosphere of the sixties and early seventies. Change didn't come easy at Mount Saint Charles because the school philosophy was still set by the Brothers of the Sacred Heart in Canada. Yet eventually one only heard French spoken in a French class. In the late sixties, St. Claire's, the small Woonsocket Catholic girls school that had been a companion school to Mount for nearly forty years, closed, and a few years later Mount Saint Charles went coeducational. But even the change to coed status didn't make Mount a hot commodity on the Rhode Island academic scene. In the early seventies, lack of attendance prompted serious talk about closing down Mount.

But the Brothers of the Sacred Heart don't give up easily. Casting their net beyond the Woonsocket area, they set out to convince Roman Catholics, the largest religious group in Rhode Island, that Mount Saint Charles was a model education institution that also taught the family values of hard work and discipline. Part of their recruiting effort included advertisements in the *Providence Journal*, Rhode Island's only statewide newspaper.

Manocchia's parents came across one of Mount's ads and liked what they read. Their son needed more structure than what was being offered in the Providence public schools. He was also a hockey player, and Mount fielded a hockey team—even though it wasn't a very good hockey team in those days. Hockey might not have been the main reason Manocchia enrolled at Mount, but once Bill Belisle became the Mount hockey coach the sport quickly became central to his life.

Bill was hired in Manocchia's sophomore year, making Manocchia part of the first team that endured Bill's boot-camp training techniques. "I remember one time we were standing on the ice just outside the locker room making little snowballs from the snow along the boards and throwing them at the guys as they walked out of the locker room," Manocchia said. "One of them hit one of the goalies in the face and he couldn't practice. When the coach found out we only had one goalie for practice, he went ballistic. He started screaming, 'Okay if you want to play in the snow, we'll play in the snow.' He made us take off our skates and put on our shoes. Then we went outside wearing our full uniform with all the equipment and starting running. We ran in the snow for miles, up and down the hills. It was freezing and we were slipping and falling all over the place in our shoes. When we stopped he made us do push-ups in the snow, then we went back to the rink and started skating. Nobody ever threw snowballs again."

Whereas hockey had once only been just a game, under Bill's tutelage it became a fiber of Manocchia's life. His character, his very soul was being defined by how he played it. He learned to never let his guard down, to never take it easy, even when he'd finished a skating drill. He learned to push beyond what he thought were his limits.

"Because he locks that door, you're all his," said Manocchia. "There are no outside distractions. You don't have to prove anything to anybody but him. You don't have to satisfy anybody but him."

Manocchia absorbed Bill's sense of dedication and even turned it around on his coach to keep him at the helm of Mount.

"In my senior year, we had some guys who were having some academic problems and the school administration said they couldn't play. The coach got upset because he felt they were picking on the hockey players. One day he said he quit and walked out. I was captain of the team so I went to his home and told him he couldn't quit on us. I said we don't quit on you so you can't quit on us. The next day, he came back."

That incident may have formed Manocchia's special bond with Bill. He comes back every year for the alumni game and it isn't unusual for him to phone Bill to see how the team is doing. He also brings Bill and Dave to New York a couple of times each year and takes them to Rangers games where they sit in the owner's suite because several Rangers players and executives train at Manocchia's facility.

"He's definitely mellowed," Manocchia offered about his former coach as he watched another kid leaning against the boards that day.

"He's sixty-eight," explained Dave. "He doesn't see everything like he used to. These days, he picks his spots."

John Harwood is former Speaker of the Rhode Island House of Representatives. He's also a former Mount Saint Charles hockey star. Harwood was a player in the late sixties, before Bill was hired as coach. As a sophomore in 1968, he led Mount Saint Charles to the state championship, its first state hockey title in twenty years. By the time he finished his high school career he had earned three first-team all-state selections and led Mount to a pair of state titles. He continued his hockey stardom at the University of Pennsylvania. When he graduated from Penn, he pondered a professional hockey career, but he opted instead for law school. He came back to Rhode Island after he finished law school and began both a legal and political career. He's always stayed very close to his high school alma mater, returning almost every year to play in the Saturday-after-Thanksgiving alumni game. Even though in 1998 he was forty-five years old, he still could skate with former Mount players who were fifteen years younger than him.

Some observers say the Speaker of the House is the most powerful political figure in Rhode Island, even more powerful than the governor. By 1998, Harwood had held the office for a decade so around Rhode Island when John Harwood spoke people listened. But one person Harwood would never try brokering a deal with was Bill Belisle. Knowing that he's a former Mount hockey star, through the years a few hockey parents had asked Harwood to speak to Bill on their sons' behalves. He tells them that's one political favor that he can't deliver.

"I would never talk to Bill about a player because I know nobody can influence Bill's opinion about a player, except the player himself," Harwood said.

For most American high school students the weekend after Thanksgiving is party time. They get together with their classmates and their older friends who are back from college. They get together at the Thanksgiving morning high school football games, which are a holiday tradition in Rhode Island and Massachusetts, and make plans for how they will party on Friday and Saturday.

Mount Saint Charles doesn't have a football team, but even if it did it wouldn't matter to its hockey players. If you're a Mount Saint Charles hockey player there's no time for partying during the Thanksgiving break. The hockey team practices the day before Thanksgiving, it practices on Thanksgiving, it practices the Friday night after Thanksgiving, and the Saturday night after Thanksgiving. By the time the school adjourns for the Thanksgiving break, hockey practice has been going on for a week, and usually that's plenty of time for Bill to decide who will wear a varsity uniform. Most years Bill makes his final varsity cuts at the Thanksgiving morning practice, which has made for some very unpleasant Thanksgiving Day dinners. Nobody knows that better than Jo-Anne Fede.

The 1997–98 season was Jo-Anne's eighth year as a Mount Saint Charles hockey mother. Her older son, Frank, was one of Rhode Island's top high school players in 1994 before going on to the United States Military Academy where he set an all-time West Point career-scoring record. The year after Frank graduated from Mount, his younger brother, Paul, entered the school.

His older brother's hockey stardom didn't give Paul any advantage in the quest for a spot on the varsity. It took him three years to become a regular varsity defenseman.

"Thanksgiving morning was always the last day of cuts," Jo-Anne recalled. "If they came walking out of the rink carrying their bag, it meant they had been cut from the varsity because the varsity players leave their equipment in the dressing room. We had a few years like that. As soon as I saw him walking out with his bag, I knew my Thanksgiving dinner was ruined."

But in 1997 it was different. There weren't any ruined Thanksgiving dinners. The parity among the players that year meant it was going to take longer than usual to fill all twenty-five spots in the varsity room. Sixty-five players had been on the ice for the first practice seven days before Thanksgiving. For ten of them, that was the only day they could say they played for Mount Saint Charles.

Most of the activities during the first ninety minutes of the first day's practice are standard hockey drills, drills most of the players have been performing since kindergarten. But that doesn't relieve their anxiety.

"Every year the first drill is the same," said Joe Cardillo. "The coach pulls the cages in a little toward the center of the ice, then, by class, everybody skates around them as fast as they can, starting with the seniors. It's a drill you've done a thousand times, but the first time you do it at a Mount practice you're terrified. All you can think about is: 'What if I fall?'"

No one is told that intensity is part of the Mount Saint Charles practice regimen; it's automatically understood. It has been passed down through two decades of players. Freshmen know before they step on the ice for their first practice with Bill what's expected of them. Sometimes it's what a kid does after he finishes skating a drill that can make the difference between playing and sitting on the bench. After going full speed down the ice, a player doesn't simply glide back to the waiting line, he sprints. And Bill watches his every move. The fact is, he isn't very good with names. He could look at a piece of machinery and within a few minutes determine how it works and how to repair it, but he can see a kid every day for two weeks and still not know his name. What Bill does remember, however, is how he skates and how he shoots. He identifies a player by his skating style, rather than a name or number.

Unlike Cardillo's freshman season, on the first day of practice for the 1997–98 season, no one was cut after ten minutes. There were only five players whose lack of skating talent stood out. Watching them, you got the feeling that the only reason they were on the ice was so they could say they played hockey at Mount Saint Charles—even if it was for only one day. At the end of opening practice, Dave informed those players that they had been cut.

"It wasn't too bad today. I think all of these kids knew they weren't going to make it," Dave said. "But after this it's going to get tough because this year there's a lot of parity. There isn't much that separates a lot of these kids, and they all know it."

On the first day, Jillson, the twelve other seniors, and a few underclassmen who were members of the previous year's team were given the nod to stash their equipment in the varsity room. Each day, for the next three or four days, a few others were informed that they too had made the team. And each day after practice, Bill and Dave met behind the closed door of Bill's little office at the far end of the Mount locker room to discuss what they liked or didn't like about the practice session. The kids still on the bubble, the ones still in limbo in the junior varsity room, kept their eyes on the closed door. Their dreams of wearing a Mount Saint Charles varsity uniform were being discussed behind that door. They moved slowly as they dressed, hoping that if they lingered a bit longer Dave would come out of the room and order them to move their equipment into the varsity room. They were kids who were accustomed to getting their way. Most of them came from middle-class families, families where the kids find most of their wish list under the tree on Christmas morning.

But Bill Belisle will never be confused with Santa Claus.

Only three days into the season, Bill had given a quick refresher course in Mount intensity. The players had just made their way into the dressing room after practice when he came charging in and told them all to pay attention. The young players still in the junior varsity room jumped up and stood in the doorway. Their eyes, along with the eyes of everyone in the varsity room, were glued on Bill, who stood in the middle of the room.

"Don't let this," Bill shouted, pointing to his head, "stop this," he added pointing down to his legs. "Let it all flow. You skate forty-five-second shifts, not ninety-second shifts like you might be used to. You have to think for the team."

He knew he had their minds, now he wanted to make sure he had their souls.

Suddenly, he started banging on the training table in the middle of the room. "You're all one now," he bellowed as he continued pounding his fist on the table.

In any other dressing room the players might have been laughing at a coach going into a tirade after only three days of practice. They hadn't even had an intrasquad scrimmage yet. They were still doing drills and here was a sixty-eight-year-old man banging on a table. But nobody even smiled when Bill finished.

"It means so much to him," Jillson said.

There were still five or six spots available in the varsity room when Dave exited his father's office following a post-practice meeting a few days after Thanksgiving. He walked over to one kid in the junior varsity room and told him to move his equipment into the varsity room. The young player tried acting restrained as he was congratulated with subdued high-fives and pats on the back from the kids standing around him. He tried looking like he knew all along that he would make it, but it was tough hiding his excitement. All around him were his friends hoping they would get the same order from Dave. When it didn't come, they looked like the little boy who gets underwear at Christmas rather than the toy on his wish list. It was a strange feeling for most of them.

"Look at that kid," Dave said as he stood in the hallway outside the junior varsity room, looking back in at a forlorn teenager sitting on the bench looking up at the ceiling. "He's really disappointed. He thought he would be in the varsity room by now. He just missed making it last year, now he's worried he'll miss it again this year."

They have some talent and their selection to all-star teams at each step of their youth hockey careers makes it easy for them to think stepping up to the next level will always be a smooth transition. By the time some of them discover that natural talent alone isn't enough to get you to the highest level of a sport, it's too late. They don't know how to put forth that extra effort because they've never really been tested. They may be only sixteen or seventeen, but they've already established "their game" and they don't want to change it. That's why Bill has been important to the future of so many players. He breaks down their games. He makes corrections that should have been made years earlier, but the youth coaches were afraid to change their stars' games. He makes the corrections that are needed for the kid to have any hope of stepping up to the next level.

Dave knew there was a good chance some of the kids who didn't make the varsity room wouldn't be at Mount Saint Charles after Christmas. For the first two decades of Bill's twenty-five years as Mount coach, players patiently waited their turns to earn a varsity spot. They would spend two, sometimes three years playing junior varsity. But today's young hockey players are different. Patience is not one of their strong points, or at least not their parents'. If a kid doesn't make the varsity his freshman year, or at least by his sophomore year, there's a pretty good chance he will transfer to a school where his parents feel he will play. After all, college coaches don't watch junior varsity games. For a lot of hockey parents getting their son noticed by college coaches is the ultimate goal of playing high school hockey.

That's why it was amazing that there were thirteen seniors on the 1997–98 team. Cardillo wasn't the only member of the Class of '98 who had thought of transferring at some point in his career, but for some reason each of them had stayed. At one time, a team of mostly seniors would have made for an easy season, but both Bill and Dave had the feeling that that wasn't going to be the case in 1997–98.

Bill doesn't care about the parents' agendas. If a freshman isn't willing to spend time on the junior varsity developing his skills and wants to leave, Bill figures let him go. He will make do with the players he has. That's the way it's always been. Dave tends to take a more practical view. He doesn't make any concessions, doesn't make any promises just to keep a player at Mount, but he is willing to sit down, put his arm around a kid, and tell him not to give up. Unlike his father, occasionally he's even willing to talk to parents about their son's hockey career, although he doesn't make a habit of it. He also knows too that these days he and his father might have to put a few really talented freshmen on the varsity roster, just to make sure they stay at Mount. A decade earlier, those freshmen probably would have been relegated strictly to junior varsity for the season just to develop their skills, but Dave knows that the reason they're at Mount is so they can practice with his father. There's no question that they are going to be good players. So these days the varsity roster usually has three or four more players than it did a decade ago. The fringe freshmen will not dress for a varsity game all season, but they practice with the varsity and everybody knows those practices are where the Mount Saint Charles legend is really cultivated.

By the Saturday after Thanksgiving there were still five or six kids battling for a couple of spots in the varsity room—probably the longest Bill had ever gone without finalizing his roster. Each day the kids who still didn't know their status would show up at practice wondering if it would be the day they finally were told to move their equipment or the day they would be told they were being cut. It's that constant sense of uncertainty that Bill has used to keep his players focused for more than two decades.

"Head games, he's always playing head games," observed senior Paul Fede as he stood watching the alumni game before the Saturday practice. "You don't understand until your senior year. You can't really enjoy playing here until your senior year. That's why I'm really looking forward to this year."

CHAPTER 7

Jo-Anne Fede is a public elementary school teacher. It might seem to be a contradiction that the three children of a public school teacher attended a private school, but it became a common occurrence throughout the Northeast during the 1990s because many public school parents and teachers no longer approved of what was happening in some public schools.

In her forties, Jo-Anne is a modern woman with old-fashioned values. Her wardrobe is straight from Liz Claiborne and Ann Taylor, but her idea of how children should be raised is an extension of her Italian Roman Catholic upbringing. Discipline, a deep religious belief, and a willingness to work hard to achieve goals are all part of her philosophy of life as well as her philosophy as an educator.

She's one of those teachers who goes the extra yard, the one who's willing to give her elementary school students more of her time than her teacher's contract stipulates. She's likes to challenge her students, giving them an opportunity to make the most of their educations. That's what she wanted teachers to do for her children—to push them to their limits. She didn't want their teachers to let them take the easy way out. But she was becoming increasingly frustrated that that wasn't the direction public education was headed in the late 1980s. Tough assignments would provoke complaints from parents that she was saddling her young students with too much work. Parents wanted their kids to achieve high test scores, but they didn't want them to have so much homework that they might have to take time out of their busy schedules to help out. Rather than thanking Jo-Anne for challenging their children, they only criticized her. It was as if she was being asked to dumb down the children's education just to make them feel better. She also found she was expending valuable energy just maintaining discipline in the classroom. A small minority of disruptive students were monopolizing her time.

In high school, where students have even more freedoms, discipline and structure begin to fall away completely, so when it was time to consider where her oldest son, Frank, would attend high school back in 1989, Jo-Anne decided to pass on a public high school. For Rhode Island parents, finding a private high school isn't difficult. Within a twenty-mile radius of Providence, the area where 80 percent of the Rhode Island population lives, there are twelve of them. Half are non-secular commuting prep schools where the yearly tuition is between $12,000 and $15,000; the other half are Roman Catholic schools where the tuition is less than half of that. Although they were still as high as $6,000 a year in 1997, which could strain the budget of some middle-class families, it was affordable for many, especially for two-income families such as the Fedes. Therefore, as do one out of every seven Rhode Island high school students, Frank began his freshman year at a private school.

Although it was not an unusual situation, it still came as a shock to Frank that he was going to be spending his high school days at Mount Saint Charles Academy. He had played both hockey and baseball from the time he was about six, but baseball was always his "big" sport, the sport in which he excelled. All through their youth baseball days, Frank and his hometown friends had performed well in statewide competitions, despite living in the small town of Johnston. Frank and his friends boasted that they were going to lead little Johnston High to the state baseball title when they got to high school. In those days hockey was just something Frank played when it was too cold to play baseball.

That all changed when he met Bill during his freshman year at Mount in 1991. He still wasn't extremely happy with his parents' decision to tear him away from his friends and send him to Mount Saint Charles, but he was willing to give it a chance.

Even today Frank isn't sure why he reacted the way he did to Bill's challenge to become a "real" hockey player. Every day was a test of his willingness to push himself beyond what he thought were his physical and mental limits. Most Mount hockey players learn to survive, Frank learned to love it.

Of course when he was at Mount he didn't realize how much he enjoyed it. "You don't realize how much he's going to affect the rest of your life and I don't think he realizes how much he affects his players' lives. He's just teaching them how to play hockey," Frank said one December evening in 1997, while watching a Mount hockey game.

He was then a U.S. Army lieutenant. He had just driven six hours from Fort Drum in New York, where he had spent the night in the field directing his troops in an artillery exercise. After the game he was headed right back to Fort Drum so he could be with his troops the next day. Twelve hours of driving just to see a high school hockey game. Some people would say that borders on insanity, but for a hockey fanatic like Frank it was athletic bliss. He was just glad to be back in the Northeast after spending six months at Fort Silk in Oklahoma.

"The only hockey you see out there is on TV. I really missed being at games," he said.

If you had asked him what he wanted to be when he entered Mount Saint Charles, an army officer wouldn't have entered his mind. But the love of hockey that he developed under Bill's tutelage changed his career plans. He can't tell you exactly when it happened, when playing hockey became more important to him than playing baseball, even though he continued playing baseball throughout his high school career. He can't tell you when hockey began to consume his life or when Bill's teachings became ingrained. It wasn't that he developed a close relationship with his high school coach. For most of his high school career, he was petrified whenever he saw Bill away from the rink.

"We were scared of him. If we were in the lobby of the rink talking before practice and he walked out of his office, we stopped talking. We didn't want him to think we weren't thinking about hockey," he recalled.

He never had dreams of one day earning a million dollars as a professional hockey player. He knew he wasn't the fastest player on the ice. At five-ten, he had decent size, but not pro size. But he took to Bill's challenge of excellence with a passion. He was never afraid to chase the puck into the boards, and he usually came out with it. It was almost instinctive to him, like a good linebacker in football seems to instinctively know how to get to the quarterback. He always seemed to know where the puck was going, whether it was in the boards or in front of the cage. In his four years at Mount, he didn't lose too many battles for loose pucks.

By the time he was a senior at Mount he had become one of the best high school players in Rhode Island. He wanted to take the test to the next highest level and play Division I college hockey, but no Division I coaches were showing any interest. He just didn't have the speed or size needed to play at that level. There was, however, an exception: West Point. Taking on the challenge of the world's most famous military institution was not exactly what Fede had pictured for his college days, but hockey was more important to him than fraternity parties. If West Point was the only college where he would have a chance to play Division I hockey then he was willing to make "Yes, Sir" and "No, Sir" part of his everyday vocabulary.

He would survive the Point for two years while proving he could play at the Division I level and then transfer to another Division I school before he had to make a career commitment to the army in his junior year. But a funny thing happened on the banks of the Hudson. Frank discovered that the atmosphere at West Point wasn't much different than the atmosphere in the Mount Saint Charles locker room.

"There were a thousand Bill Belisles around there. Everybody was always pushing you to give a hundred percent. Always making you try for your best. It was a lifestyle change, but after four years of playing for Bill Belisle I could do it," Frank said.

So he remained at West Point and became an army officer and one of the Academy's all-time best hockey players. In 1995, he set an Army single-season scoring record. He proved he could play Division I hockey and had he been a little bigger and a little faster he might have even been able to take his talent to the professional level. But hockey was really secondary. He became a graduate of one of the most prestigious educational institutions in the world, carrying a diploma that gives him a unique standing among Americans. He's a West Point man, and that will never change. It also never would have happened if he hadn't played hockey for Bill Belisle.

Once Frank had prospered at Mount Saint Charles there was never any question where Paul would go to high school. That was fine with Paul. He had sat in the stands for four years watching his brother add to the Mount mystique. He heard Frank tell the stories at the dinner table and he knew there were other things Frank never even talked about, things that only Mount Saint Charles hockey players experienced. Mount Saint Charles hockey was in his blood even before he stepped through the school doors for the first time as a student in the fall of 1994, the year after his brother had graduated.

Every parent can tell you: no two brothers are alike. They may look alike and it's not even surprising that their mannerisms often are similar, but their psyches are different. It didn't take Dave and Bill long to realize that Paul wasn't his brother's hockey clone. Like Frank, Paul had decent size: he was nearly six feet tall and weighed two hundred pounds by his senior year. But what he didn't have were Frank's natural instincts. With Paul most moves were more calculated. He had to take that split second to think about a move with the puck, when to pass or where the puck was heading before it started going there. In sports, that's often the difference between being good and being great. You can train people to be athletes and the more people with good physical coordination train the better they become. But instinct is the intangible. It's what separated Gretzky and Orr from the other all-stars. It's what separates a college all-American from a college player and high school all-starter from the kid who earns a varsity letter. Paul may not have had natural moves, but he had a natural passion to succeed. He set the bar high for everything he did. He had always been a very good student, mainly because he worked at it. His career goal was to be a doctor, but those who knew him wondered if that's because he had a passion for healing or because medicine is the ultimate academic challenge.

"Sometimes I worry that he expects too much of himself or that too much is expected of him," one of his teachers said. "He's a real nice boy, but things don't come as naturally for him in some subjects like they do for some of the other kids like Jeff Jillson."

But Paul had always been willing to put in the extra time needed to fill his report card with A's. In his view, if it takes thirty minutes longer to do the calculus homework than it does the human calculator who sits next to you in class then you spend the extra half hour. There's always a way to get a good grade if you're willing to work at it. Unfortunately, that's not always the case when it comes to sports. That's why his first three years as a Mount hockey player were so frustrating. He felt he was working as hard as anybody, but it seemed Bill was always finding fault with his play. He called it "Belisle head games." Never letting a player get comfortable. Just when he thinks he's playing well, Bill would find some little flaw with his game. Like his brother, Paul wanted to play college hockey, but he didn't see regular action until midway through his junior year.

But this was his senior year. He and Jeff Jillson were the top two defensemen on the team. His time had finally come. He was being teamed with Jillson, which meant he would be getting a lot of playing time. Finally he would get a chance to show people, especially college coaches, that he was a good player.

He also thought that he finally understood Bill Belisle's head games.

CHAPTER 8

They may talk about political correctness and the importance of individuality, but many Americans nonetheless love a dictator sports coach—as long as he wins. It reminds them of a simpler time, a time before pampered, spoiled athletes on every level, from the high schools to the pros filled American sports.

Bill Belisle *is* a coaching dictator. There's no question about that. But despite all the tales about his dictatorial behavior, his coaching philosophy is built on simplicity more than any thing else. He's never written it down, but his formula for success has always been: Simplicity = Perfection.

Bill's practices have always mirrored his lifestyle. Every detail is covered; nothing is taken for granted. Everything sitting on the shelves over the desk in his dressing room office has two labels, from the aspirin bottle to the videotapes. It's the same way in his practice sessions. Every new drill is explained at least twice. He doesn't want any doubts about what's supposed to be done because doubts create hesitation. If you hesitate in practice, you will hesitate in a game and that can mean the difference between scoring a goal and making an opposing goalie look good. He tries to create a sense of freedom in his players through discipline and simplicity. He knows if they can perfect the basic, little things, everything else will flow. Although the players would probably prefer that he tell them what to do, and then let them try doing it, he doesn't just tell, he shows them. In his herky-jerkey skating style, the seventy-year-old coach skates out every drill himself. He shows them and repeats showing them until he's convinced that they understand it. He evaluates his player's performances by shifts or periods rather than by an entire game. Mount may win a game by five or six goals, but the next day at practice Bill will be yelling about how they played a lazy second period. Everything is broken down to its simplest terms and then built up to create the whole. In the Belisle system, individual performances are evaluated not on the final grand total of points, but on each shift the player spent on the ice. Each player receives a verbal report card from Bill almost every time he comes back to the bench.

"He's all about detail, but he's not anal-retentive," said former Mount star Paul Guay. "He doesn't do things just because he's fanatical about details. Everything he does has a reason. His players usually don't understand the reasons because they're too young, but they do it out of fear of not playing if they don't do it right."

No one knows better than Paul about not understanding Bill's coaching logic when you're wearing a Mount uniform.

If you list the Ten Most Talented Players to ever play for Bill Belisle, Paul Guay would have to be on the list. You may think that the combination of great talent and the fact that he's the son of Dr. Jean Guay, one of Bill's dearest friends, would have spared Paul any periods of consternation during his Mount career, but it didn't. Despite his talent, he didn't play varsity during his freshman year in 1978 and he wasn't even seeing a lot of action at the start of his sophomore year.

"He would come home from practice disgusted because he couldn't figure out why he wasn't playing," Doc Guay recalled about those days back in 1979. "Everybody was telling him he was one of the best players on the team, but he wasn't playing. I told him if the coach thought you were one of the best players you would be playing. He wants to win. He's not going to keep one of his best players on the bench. I told him there must be some part of his game that the coach felt needed improvement, so he just had to keep working. I have to admit, I was starting to wonder myself because everybody also was telling me he was one of the best players on the team and Bill wasn't playing him."

Eventually Paul satisfied Bill's criteria for playing time and become one of the all-time leading Mount scorers. He was a two-time Rhode Island all-state forward and went on to play at Providence College. In the 1982–83 season he scored thirty-four goals in forty-three games. Twenty years later it's still the Providence College record for most goals scored in one season. He left Providence after his junior year to play for the 1984 U.S. Olympic team then turned pro after the Olympics. He played a few years in the NHL before an injury cut his pro career short. He then returned to Rhode Island, started a business career, and also serves as a regional scout for the NHL Scouting Bureau.

In addition to being a Mount hockey great, he's also a good friend of Dave so occasionally he will drop into a Mount practice. Bill doesn't allow parents, agents, or college coaches at his practices, but former Mount players are always welcomed. Once you're a Mountie, you're always a Mountie.

"He's easier on these kids today then he was on us," said Guay as he watched a Mount practice in late November 1997. "He's like a father with five kids. The younger kids get away with more than the older kids did because the parents have seen it all before. But there still are basic things that never change."

Repetition, Confidence, and Pride have been the trinity of Bill's coaching creed since the first day he closed the doors of Adelard Arena to the outside world. He knows repetition builds confidence and confidence builds pride in what you have accomplished. Bill has never taught in a classroom, but his practice sessions are based on age-old academic philosophies. First you learn the basic formulas and then you practice. The more math problems you do the better the math student you become. The more you practice shooting a puck, the better you become at hitting the corners. The more you work on skating techniques, the better the skater you become. But Mount hockey players have never practiced just for the sake of practicing. Time alone doesn't make a satisfactory practice. A one-hour focused practice is twice as valuable as two hours of simply going through the motions. Everything at a Mount practice is accounted for, labeled, identified, and put in proper order. Everything has a reason, even if the players don't totally understand it.

Bill isn't going to change his coaching creed, but he's willing to look for ways to make the mundane, but necessary, aspects of hockey training seem important. Sitting on those shelves above his dressing room office are loose-leaf binders filled with pages of hand-drawn drills. He sits at his desk late at night, devising new ways to teach the same basic hockey skills he's been teaching Mount players for a quarter of a century. Every day is something new, so players must focus on what the coach is saying. It's repetition without redundancy.

"He never does the same drill twice, but he's always teaching the same things," Frank Fede offered about a Belisle practice. "He works on individual techniques. He looks for individual faults."

What Bill does is build confidence by teaching his students to master themselves before they try mastering others. Talk to former Mount players and you know that there's no question, Bill has mellowed over the years, but even as he approached seventy in the fall of 1997, he was still a perfectionist trying to improve on what a lot of people think already is perfection.

That can make for some tough practice sessions.

"Most people don't think he's a very pleasant man, but they don't understand," said Doc Guay. "He loves his players just like he loves his children. But just because you love your children, you don't have to be their best friend. You tell them what they need to do even if they don't want to hear it."

St. Sebastian's School is a private high school located in Needham, Massachusetts. In a sense it's the middle ground between the commuting Roman Catholic high schools that are so numerous in Rhode Island and Massachusetts and the private prep schools where students live on campus. Its campus looks similar to some of the well-known prep schools in the metro Boston area, complete with a modern hockey rink. But unlike St. Mark's or Phillips Andover, there are no dormitories at St. Sebastian's. It's strictly a commuter school, but because it's located only a few miles off Route 128, the highway that circles Boston, it is easily accessible to the six million or so residents of the Boston metro area. Most parents, even hockey parents, want their kids living at home during their high school years. It's therefore not surprising that despite not having dorms students or postgraduate students, St. Sebastian's has always been able to successfully compete against the top prep school hockey teams in New England.

Hockey is very big at the New England prep schools, and it's more than just a love of the game. All you have to do is look at the Northeastern colleges where hockey is popular to realize why the prep schools want good hockey players at their school. Harvard, Yale, Brown, and Dartmouth, and the NESCA schools such as Williams, Amherst, Wesleyan, and Trinity all recruit hockey players. The private prep schools build their reputations on the number of their graduates who go to the so-called prestigious schools. In the bottom line of private education that translates into high tuition and successful fund-raising. Just a scan of the rosters of the Ivy League hockey teams reveals that in most years at least half of the players come from the New England prep schools.

St. Sebastian's may not have been able to boast about having five of its former players in the NHL in the fall of 1997 as Mount Saint Charles could, but the school has had its share of outstanding hockey talent through the years. Mike Grear, for instance, played at St. Seb's back in the early nineties before going on to an outstanding career at Boston University and then moving on to the NHL. St. Sebastian's had another outstanding prospect on the 1997–98 team in Mike Pandolfo. Pandolfo, a six-foot-two, 220-pound forward and the younger brother of an NHL player, was at the top of the recruiting list of most Division I schools that year. Both Jillson and Pandolfo had been among the top Americans in the rankings for the 1998 draft. Jillson had been ranked thirty-seventh among North American skaters and Pandolfo had been ranked forty-fifth.

Every year, a few days after the start of practice Mount travels to Needham to play St. Sebastian's in a control scrimmage. Although in essence it's a regular game, it's labeled a scrimmage because the coaches do the officiating and every so often they'll create conditions in which they can work on their power plays or short-handed situations. These scrimmages don't count against the twenty-four-game maximum Rhode Island high school teams are allowed before the start of playoffs in February. Dave likes to play St. Sebastian's because it's a chance to play a team that is usually stronger than any team Mount will play in Rhode Island, but isn't loaded with fifth-year seniors like many of the New England prep schools. For Mount players still fighting for a spot in the varsity room, it's a chance to show what they can do against challenging competition. Do well against St. Sebastian's and you're usually assured of hanging your uniform in the varsity room the next day.

Even though it doesn't count as an official game, because it brings together two of the better known high school teams in New England, there's always a few hockey fanatics, in addition to the usual array of parents standing around the boards watching the action. But in November 1997, in addition to the regular fans, there were a lot of guys standing around the rink making notations on clipboards or in little notebooks.

When Jillson decided he was staying at Mount Saint Charles it started a feeding frenzy among American college hockey coaches. For several years the tide had been turning against college coaches in their quest to get the top young American players to play in college. Once upon a time the natural progression for a good American player was high school, college, and then maybe a bid to play professional hockey. But the NHL expansion in the eighties started changing that. In the seventies, fewer than 10 percent of the players on the NHL rosters were born in the United States, but by 1997 almost 20 percent of NHL players were American born. The dream of playing in the NHL was no longer something beyond the reality of American kids, and the fastest route to a professional career was through the junior hockey route, especially the major junior leagues. Canadian kids followed that route for decades and now the best young American players were doing the same. But once a player decides to take the major junior route, he automatically gives up a chance to play American college hockey. Where they once only competed amongst themselves for the top American kids, by the midnineties, American college coaches were competing against agents for talented young players.

The coaches have their sales pitches.

For several years, University of Maine coach Shawn Walsh had been pointing out to the top young high school players that the average National Hockey League career is only 4.2 years. That leaves forty to fifty more years for players to do something else with there lives. Walsh would tell them that there was a big difference between what the players with college educations do with those fifty years compared to those who don't have a college education. He also pointed out the social difference between college and junior hockey. In juniors, a player lives with a family in which there is usually no one else his age. In college, a player lives in a dorm with a bunch of his contemporaries. In college, you grow up under the direction of educated people; in junior hockey, you grow up under the direction of guys who may know the fine points of a center-ice trap, but not much about economics or applied psychology. Walsh also pointed out that if a player takes the major junior route he would have to turn pro by the time he was twenty because that's the maximum junior age. Some players aren't ready for pros when they're twenty; they need a few more years to develop. In college, they can have those few extra years, but in juniors their careers are finished by the time they turn twenty-one.

These are all good reasons for playing college hockey, but the coaches know that these days if the kid is really good he's probably going to play major juniors. Hockey is no different than other sports. These days, the top American basketball players are leaving college after one or two years for the pros. If basketball had a junior league like hockey, a lot of the basketball players leaving school early would never even start college. The money in all pro sports has become too tempting. If a kid thinks he has what it takes to make the pros, he wants to take the road that will give him the best chance to get there—and most of them want to get there quickly. For instance, even though Bryan Berard briefly talked about attending college during his junior year at Mount, there never really was any doubt that he was headed to major juniors.

Everyone assumed that that was the route Jillson would also take, even when he started his senior year at Mount. But when he hadn't jumped for juniors by November college coaches took it as a sign that he intended to play college hockey, or at least that the college hockey option was now on even terms with juniors. For the coaches, and even the pro scouts who were still evaluating Jillson for the spring draft, the St. Seb's game was a great chance to see him play against another top player like Pandolfo. It would be the first time anyone other than his teammates and coaches would see Jillson on the ice since he made his announcement that he was staying at Mount. For the first four days of practice he was safely protected behind the closed doors of Adelard, but he was finally going out in public. All eyes were on him, and he knew it. He tried not looking concerned. He tried to take control early, but the lack of any serious competition since the previous winter was showing. It would take time to get his playing edge back, but the people standing behind the cage, especially the pro scouts, didn't want to hear about time. They were talking about the "then and there."

"He should be dominating and he's not," said one scout. "He's going to go down fast in the draft ranking playing like that against this type of competition."

Standing on the Mount bench Bill didn't care about what the scouts were thinking. He had a group of veteran players who were looking like freshmen and sophomores.

"Move it," Bill bellowed in tones that didn't need any amplification to be heard throughout the rink.

"He's the last of his kind," one assistant college coaches offered about Bill to the group of college assistants watching the action from behind the cage. "Belisle is in a class of his own."

A few days after the St. Sebastian's game, Bill and Dave made the final varsity cut. One of the players still sitting in the junior varsity room after the cut was freshman goaltender Tony Ciresi. Ciresi is the son of Tony Ciresi Sr., Bill's former assistant coach and the man who saved Bill's life that day in 1983. Young Ciresi was a talented player. At most Rhode Island high schools, he would have been a freshman starter, but he wasn't quite ready for a spot in the Mount varsity room. Bill owed Tony Ciresi Sr. his life, but that didn't buy his son a spot in the varsity room.

CHAPTER 9

D ave had heard the news on his car radio while driving alone on Route 95 on the way to sales calls in Massachusetts.

"Two Rhode Islanders, Bryan Berard and Keith Carney, are among the players named today to complete the 1998 U.S. Men's Olympic hockey team roster," proclaimed the host of a sports talk show.

Dave couldn't help but flash a satisfied grin that no one could see. Two more former Mount players were going to the 1998 Olympics. The U.S. team would now have three former Mounties on it because Mathieu Schneider had been named to the team back in September. Three players from one little high school in Woonsocket, Rhode Island. The more he thought about it, the more pleased he felt. And why not? High school coaching is one of the closest things to parenting that a human can experience, especially when you take it as seriously as the Belisles do. You spend countless hours with teenagers during a critical development period. You watch them succeed sometimes and sometimes you watch them fail. Throughout it all, you try helping them both with their immediate goals and their future lives. So when former players go on and achieve success it gives a coach a feeling of satisfaction. He knows he played a role in it.

Dave strolled into Adelard Arena for practice that afternoon feeling good, but the euphoria melted away quicker than an ice cream cone on a sunny August afternoon. The team had been practicing for about a half hour and his father was already on a rampage. The passing by the defensemen in the first few scrimmages had been sloppy. Too many intercepted passes, the defensemen had been too slow finding the open man. When the passes did come, they weren't delivered with the authority Bill wanted. He felt his defense was being lazy and now they were going to pay for it. Standing at the blue line he would send the puck down behind the cage and a defenseman would give chase. The defenseman would pick it up at full speed, quickly look to find one of the forwards in the middle of their zone, and feed a pass—all without stopping. If the pass didn't land right on the stick of the moving forward, Bill would start screaming at the defenseman.

Dave knew his father hadn't heard the news about Berard and Carney. Bill doesn't spend afternoons listening to sports talk shows. He can't understand why anybody would be interested in hearing the opinion of some sports junkie who didn't have the slightest idea what it took to be a successful coach. Dave was eager to share the good news, but this wasn't the time. At sixty-eight, Bill didn't have the daily fire that he had back in the seventies and early eighties before his accident. He's always there, always a presence, but Dave is now often the one who sets the agenda and Bill carries out those directives. But there are days, like this one, when the fire in Bill's psyche is restoked because he sees something that he thinks needs correcting. On these days, Dave just stands back and observes.

When the team filed into the dressing room after practice it was Dave's turn to vent his frustration. Like his father he hadn't been excited about what he had seen in the first two weeks of practice and scrimmages. There were too many mistakes being made by a senior team. He had let it go without saying too much, assuming that the older players would start focusing after a few weeks, but it wasn't happening. A few players had already quickly undressed and had started for the showers by the time Dave reached the center of the dressing room.

"Sit down," Dave yelled, catching the kids looking for a fast escape from the dressing room by surprise. "From here on, the seniors will start being told of their mistakes. We're going to get on you."

Around the room, some of the players, especially the younger ones, were sitting upright looking straight at Dave. Most of them were still wearing their complete uniforms. But some of the seniors were just sitting with their heads buried in their hands. Occasionally they would look up with an expression that said, "Sure Coach anything you say. Just finish so I can get out of here. We've been here, done this. We've got places to go."

Dave sensed the inattentiveness and raised his voice. The elation of hearing that three former Mount players would be playing in the Olympics had been wiped from his mind.

Bill had been standing at the far end of the dressing room, watching as Dave spoke. He too sensed the same inattentiveness, but this time shouting wasn't enough for him. Suddenly, in the middle of Dave's speech, Bill charged toward the other end of the locker room, his target senior Mark Esposito. It easily could have been three or four players who really weren't paying much attention to Dave, but unfortunately for Esposito he was the one who caught Bill's eye.

"Take that smirk off your face," he yelled.

"I'm not smirking," Esposito muttered defensively as he tried to sink back on the bench to get away from the charging sixty-year-old.

"Yes you are," Bill screamed as he let loose with an open-hand slap that caught Esposito on the shoulder and sent him flying back against the wall behind the bench.

The coach had the room's attention.

Despite all the tales of physical punishment that Bill had wrought on his players through the years, at least these days, it's rare that he tries motivating a player by hitting or grabbing him. This wasn't the first time a few of the seniors in the room had seen Bill hit a kid, but you could tell by the stunned looks on their faces that it wasn't something they saw often. The blow didn't leave any marks on Esposito's body, but it seriously damaged his ego. A lot of teenager athletes probably would have been mad; Esposito was embarrassed. No teenager likes to be singled out for reprimand in front of his peers. Around the room, twenty other teenagers were feeling sorry for their teammate, but they were also glad Bill hadn't unleashed his anger on them.

Bill didn't say another word; he just walked back to the far end of the room and let Dave finish his speech. The coach had made his point about paying attention.

Maureen Esposito is a hockey mother, but unlike many hockey moms she wasn't content to sit back and watch some guy determine her son's hockey future. There are youth organizations around New England that list women on the board of directors, but for the most part they're there to help with registration and fund-raising. When it comes to coaching and deciding which players will be on the travel teams and the all-star teams, youth hockey is a man's world. But Maureen refused to give up having a hand in her sons' hockey careers just because she was a woman. Mark was the elder of her and her husband's two sons. Her husband liked hockey, but he didn't have a hockey background so he didn't coach in the town youth hockey association where the Espositos lived. Maureen was determined to not let Mark's hockey career suffer just because her husband wasn't a member of the local hockey inner circle. Mark began playing hockey before he was in kindergarten in the Burrillville Hockey Association and attended all the summer camps. In Maureen's opinion, her son was one of the best players in his age group. Other observers agreed. But time after time, it seemed other kids in the association were given greater opportunities to play at the top level. Maureen reasoned that Mark was shortchanged because his father wasn't involved in coaching. She and her husband had become so upset at the local organization that rather than having Mark's younger brother play in Burrillville they were driving him to Massachusetts a few times a week to play in a metro Boston league.

When Mark told his parents that he wanted to go to Mount Saint Charles instead of his hometown high school, they approved. Maureen had heard all the stories about Mount. She'd heard of Bill's reputation as a hockey dictator, but that was okay. Mark's playing time would at least be determined by his ability rather than by whose son he was.

Once Mark was at Mount, Maureen became one of Mount's most enthusiastic volunteers. Whenever there was a fund-raiser, a dinner, or a hockey tournament, she was there helping out. She knew it wouldn't influence Bill or Dave when it came to her son's playing time, but she wanted to be a part of the Mount hockey program any way she could be. At Mount, she was just as involved with the team as any of the fathers.

Like a lot of kids who grew up playing hockey at a high competitive level, Mark Esposito dreamed of someday playing college hockey. By the start of his senior year in 1997, however, he had started lowering his expectations about his college future. He no longer saw himself playing for Boston University or Maine or one of the other top Division I teams. He now hoped that a coach from one of the lower Division I schools might see him play and start showing interest. He'd had little opportunity to play in his first three years at Mount; it had been three years of junior varsity with a little varsity action in his junior year. Finally, it looked like he would be a varsity regular for his senior season in 1997–98. He would get his chance to show he had college potential. But suddenly he had become a target of Bill's scorn. He hadn't been the only one who wasn't paying attention that afternoon. He wasn't the only one who had been wishing Dave would finish his talk so they could get out of the locker room. Unfortunately, Bill was looking his way at the time. He had been singled out and he was embarrassed. But even more important, he was concerned about how much this was going to affect his playing time. Would that one smile cost him a chance to have some college coach put him on a recruiting list?

Maybe it would have helped Esposito's state of mind that day if he had known he wasn't the first Mountie to be caught with a smirk on his face. Of course there was a big difference between Mark Esposito and Keith Carney, both in the way they played defense and in the way they smiled.

"Keith was always smiling," said Dave. "No matter how much my father screamed at him he would still have a smile on his face. You wanted to get mad at him, but you couldn't because he was such a pleasant kid."

Keith Carney could pass, shoot, and play defense as well as anybody who has ever worn a Mountie uniform, but what both Bill and Dave remember most about him was his infectiously pleasant personality.

That pleasant personality, however, didn't prevent him from being one of the toughest, as well as one of the most talented, players Bill ever coached. In his senior year at Mount in 1988, Carney played a major role in what's probably the most memorable high school state title series that has ever been played in Rhode Island. For at least fifty years, the Rhode Island high school state championship has been decided in a best-of-three title series. Under league rules, however, if a game is still tied after two sudden-death overtime periods the game is declared a no contest and replayed in its entirety the next night. In the 1988 series against Hendricken, another parochial school, two games were declared no contests. The result was a unique five-game, best-of-three series.

Mount had lost the first game 7–6 and then came back to win the second game 5–0. But Carney suffered a severe shoulder injury in the second game. The injury was so bad he didn't even dress for the third and fourth games that ended in ties. But he wasn't going to miss the fifth game, even if he could barely move his right arm.

"He was such a tough kid. There aren't too many kids who would have even thought about dressing for that game," said Dave. "Doc Guay made a harness and we strapped Keith into it. He could hardly move his arm. We weren't even sure he could skate with it. So he came to Adelard early and skated with a peewee team that was practicing. He took a few turns around the ice and said he was okay. He didn't even try taking a shot. He couldn't bring his stick back for a slap shot, but he played the whole game and he even scored a goal with quick wrist shot."

Carney was a starting defenseman on three state championship teams from 1996 to 1998. Pretty good, considering he almost didn't make it to Mount.

When he had applied for admission to Mount in the ninth grade he had been put on a waiting list. He also had applied to Hendricken and was accepted so his father sent Hendricken a $100 deposit.

"We figured he was going to Hendricken," said Jack Carney, Keith's father.

But a few weeks before the start of school the Mount Saint Charles admission office called and said there was an opening.

"It was Friday afternoon and they said they needed to know by Monday because if Keith didn't want the spot they would offer it to somebody else," Jack related. "We were going to our beach house for the weekend so I told Keith to think about it. On the way home Sunday night, he said he wanted to go to Mount. It cost me the $100 deposit with Hendricken, but it was worth it."

Like a lot of New England hockey players, Carney's hockey career started on a little frozen pond near his home.

"He would go with me and his three brothers up to a little pond a few miles from our house. Keith was only three when he started, but he loved it and we had a lot of fun," Jack recalled.

Because his older brothers were playing, little Keith was allowed to practice with teams in their hometown Pawtucket youth hockey league before he reached the minimum five-year-old age limit to formally join the league. By the time he became an official player, he was already a peewee hockey "veteran."

"He was the leading scorer in the league when he was five years old because he already had two years under his belt," Jack said with a laugh.

Once he arrived at Mount it only took Carney a little over a year to become a starter on a team, where at the time, most players didn't see substantial playing time until at least their junior years. By his junior year, he was named to the *Providence Journal* all-state team, the team made up of the top six high school players in Rhode Island.

He also established a reputation as somebody who didn't say much, but who was always seeking perfection.

"With Keith, everything always had to be in its proper place," said Dave. "He's still that way. Watch him before every face-off, he adjusts his elbow pads to make sure they are exactly where they're supposed to be, just like he did when he was in high school.

"That's also the way he played the game," Dave continued. "He wasn't the type of player you looked at and said, 'Woo, he's good.' You had to be a college coach or scout to notice what he did well. How he moved the puck, how his shot always was on the net, how he cleaned out in front of the net. Everything always was positional perfect."

One college coach who was happy he noticed Carney was the University of Maine's Shawn Walsh.

"He's one of my favorites," Walsh told me back in 1998. "He's a great guy to be around. He has a radiant smile that never leaves his face. It doesn't matter if you're yelling at him or telling him he's playing great. He always gives back that smile and it's an honest smile."

Carney had opted for a career at Maine despite being drafted in the second round of the NHL draft by the Buffalo Sabres following his senior year at Mount in 1988. He immediately became an impact player in Orono. Despite playing defense he was one of the Black Bears' top scorers in his freshman year and started every game for three consecutive years. In his junior year he earned all-American honors after playing a major role in Maine's drive to the NCAA national championship.

The following year he left school to pursue the dream of every young American hockey player—a berth on the U.S. Olympic hockey team. It looked like he was a sure bet to be a starter on the 1992 Olympic team as he played through the team's exhibition schedule. But a few weeks before the team left for the Olympics the powers of USA Hockey decided that they wanted some older players on the team and added a defenseman who previously had played professional but had regained his amateur status. Carney was one of the last players cut.

It didn't take him long to recover from the disappointment of missing the Olympics. A few weeks after he was cut, he joined the Buffalo Sabres. Unfortunately, that was the year of the NHL players strike so he only played fourteen games. But the following year he became a full-time professional player. He spent one year up and down between the NHL and the American Hockey League, but by the 1993–94 season he had established himself as a valuable NHL commodity. He started that season with Buffalo, but after a few games was traded to the Chicago Blackhawks. His professional game had begun to mirror his lifestyle. Everything had its proper place. Unlike his college days, he wasn't a big scorer in the NHL. His value was as a defensive defenseman. He played perfect-position hockey. He did all the things that coaches love and successful teams must have, but most fans don't notice.

That was fine with Carney, he didn't need fans cheering his every move to have a smile on his face.

Finally in 1998, six years after he had thought his dream of playing for a U.S. Olympic team was dead, the dream became reality. He knew much of his success was because of what he learned back in those practice sessions at Mount Saint Charles.

"He prepares you for all that life has to ask of you," Carney offered about Bill shortly after he was named to the 1998 Olympic team. "If you want to be successful in life you have to give 100 percent and be focused. That's what Coach Belisle teaches you.

"He's always trying to get you to give your best effort and he does it in different ways. A lot of times we didn't understand why we were doing the things we were doing. We would be thinking, 'Why are we doing this?' But it was a sense of accomplishment. 'I'm playing for Bill Belisle.'"

And why was he always smiling during his days at Mount?

"I wouldn't call it a smile, it was more of a smirk. I was too scared of Coach Belisle to smile," Carney said.

CHAPTER 10

fter all the talking had stopped and all the players had showered and left the locker room, Dave finally had a chance to ask his father if he had heard about Berard and Carney.

"Do you hear Bryan and Keith were named to the Olympic team?" Dave asked.

"Both of them. How about that?" said Bill.

The air in the Mount locker room was still thick with the steam from twenty-five teenagers taking showers, just like it had been every day after practice when Mathieu Schneider, Keith Carney, and Bryan Berard were playing for Mount.

"They were three different types of players, but they all were gifted hockey players," Dave said about the three former Mounties who had been named to the 1998 U.S Olympic team.

It's not surprising that Bill remembers them differently.

A kid can have the talent needed to go from Adelard Arena to Madison Square Garden, but Bill will remember more about what the kid couldn't do than what he did well when he was playing at Mount.

"We worked on their minuses," Bill said. "They were good players, but they all had things they needed to work on. At one time Bryan could only spin around one way. Keith was an outstanding passer who became great at moving the puck out of the zone and Mathieu needed work on his skating."

Bill felt Schneider needed so much work on his skating that he moved him from defense to forward in his sophomore year. It was a move that almost caused Schneider's father to have a heart attack.

Don't tell Sam Schneider dreams don't come true.

Sam started dreaming of the day his son would be playing in the NHL shortly after Mathieu went from diapers to big boy pants. So what if he was living in a New Jersey suburb where most of the neighborhood kids didn't know a hockey stick from a cricket bat? So what if the nearest skating rink with artificial ice was the little outdoor rink in New York's Rockefeller Center? Sam dreamed Mathieu was going to be a hockey player and nothing was going to stop him from seeing that dream fulfilled.

A lot of fathers have the same dream; the difference was Sam's dream became an obsession. Because of that obsession, Mathieu has been playing in the National Hockey League for fifteen years. These days the bottom line would have to be: it was all worth it. But there were days when a lot of people were telling Sam that he had lost all perspective about what was best for his son's future. They told him that he was pushing Mathieu too hard. They said that he was the stereotypical Little League father trying to live out his own dreams through his kid.

Nobody can tell you better than Sam that obsessions don't come cheap.

He had grown up in Rhode Island, in the north end of Providence near the old Rhode Island Auditorium. The Auditorium was the home of the Providence Reds of the American Hockey League, and when Sam was a kid in the late forties it was the only artificial ice surface in the state. The kids who lived near the Auditorium were known as "rink rats" because they were always hanging around it. They would watch the Reds practice and then do odd jobs, such as sweeping up the locker room, in exchange for a ticket to a Sunday-night Reds game. In those days, the Reds were the only game in town during the winter months beyond high school sports for a Rhode Island sports fan. Other than the Friday-night fights there weren't any sports on TV. College basketball at schools such as Providence College, Brown University, and the University of Rhode Island was still a game played in little gyms attended by only a handful of students and alumni. The Auditorium was the Mecca of Rhode Island sports from October to April. Almost every Sunday night, nearly all of the six thousand seats would be filled. If you lived near the Auditorium you were automatically a hockey fan.

Like all the rink rats, Sam wanted to be a hockey player, but his parents put an end to that dream at an early age.

"The guys at the Auditorium would leave a few lights on when the building closed after the Reds games so the rats would skate under those few lights after we finished cleaning up. One night when I was only about ten years old I stayed there until two o'clock in the morning. When I walked in the house, I thought my grandfather was going to kill me. Walking in at two o'clock in the morning isn't a good idea for a little ten-year-old Jewish kid. That was the end of my hockey career. My parents said I was hanging around with the wrong type of kids playing hockey. They let me play football, but not hockey," he recalled.

In high school he played football but hockey was still a big part of his life. Like baseball was in the blood of a Brooklyn or Bronx kid who grew up in the forties living a long fly ball away from Ebbetts Field or Yankee Stadium, a kid who grew up near the Rhode Island Auditorium had a natural passion for hockey.

Hockey somewhat slipped out of Sam's life after his high school days. He married a woman from a Rhode Island French-Canadian family and by the midsixties had moved to New Jersey to work as a salesman in the New York electronics industry. But hockey became a focal point of his life once again shortly after Mathieu was born. Mathieu was his first child, and when he was about three Sam began taking him to skate at Rockefeller Center. Might as well get the kid use to performing in front of a crowd before he gets to nursery school.

"There wasn't much ice time around there but Tuesday nights were slow at Rockefeller Center so for $5.00 you could get a meal at the promenade café and a skating session. For another few dollars you could rent a pair of skates. From the first time Mathieu skated he loved it," Sam said.

Sam's obsession had begun. There wasn't an artificial ice surface in every other New Jersey city and town as there was in Rhode Island; he would have to find natural ice. He searched for ponds where Mathieu might be able to skate during the winter. When he found one nearby he called the local fire department. Had they tested the ice? They hadn't—it has been years since anyone had skated on ponds. Schneider was undaunted. He went crawling out onto the ice in his shirt and tie to check for himself. Since he didn't fall in he assumed that it would be okay for his three-year-old. He then bought Mathieu a pair of Bauer Beaver hockey skates, made a uniform out of pajama tops, and bought shin pads that were way too big because they just don't make pads for three-year-olds.

There were no youth hockey programs in their area, but that didn't stop Sam from getting Mathieu started on his hockey career before he was in kindergarten. Some of the older neighborhood kids saw Sam skating with Mathieu on a nearby pond and asked if he could help with their high school club hockey team. Their coach was a gym teacher who didn't know how to skate and knew even less about hockey. Before long, Sam was scheduling ice time for the high school kids at the outdoor rinks of the private prep schools in the area. It was in one of those that a few men had organized hockey clinics for young kids. The kids ranged in age from eight through twelve, but the organizers told Sam if he would help coach, his four-and-a-half-year-old son could participate. Sam became a coach, using Mathieu as his demonstrator. Eventually he started running the Garden State Hockey School. Three nights a week, Mathieu would be skating somewhere in New Jersey and one day was spent doing land practice. Mathieu was just learning his ABCs, but he already knew the intricacies of a backhand pass. Sam's second son, John-Paul, was three years younger than Mathieu and got an even earlier start. Sam had him on skates when he was only eleven months old.

The Schneider family summer vacations were spent back in Rhode Island. Many tourists travel to Rhode Island in the summer to sun themselves on some of the finest beaches on the East Coast or tour the elegant Newport mansions once occupied by the Rockefellers and Vanderbilts. The Schneiders spent their Rhode Island summers in chilly hockey rinks. John-Paul was too young, but Sam took little Mathieu to all the hockey camps that are run by high school and college hockey coaches at rinks throughout Rhode Island each summer. When Mathieu was only five years old, he was sleeping at an overnight camp run by Lou Lamoriello, the current president of the New Jersey Devils who was then the Providence College hockey coach. The next-youngest boy was nine years old.

It went that way for a few years. Every summer the Schneiders headed to Rhode Island and Mathieu would spend several weeks playing against boys two and three years older than he was. Sam insists that it was because he was always a better skater than other kids his age. With the wealth of young hockey talent around Rhode Island at the time it's doubtful

Mathieu was *that* much better. Putting a child into that kind of situation is always a gamble. He could turn off to the game or burn out early. But Sam was lucky. Mathieu persevered.

Sam's dream of his son becoming a hockey star went from a fledgling obsession to an all-out lifestyle in 1981 when Mathieu was twelve and John-Paul was nine. Sam and his wife had divorced a few years earlier and Sam had been granted custody of the two boys. Rationalizing that Rhode Island was where his and his former wife's families lived (and it was important for the boys to have an extended family if they were going to grow up in a single parent household), he left New Jersey. It was more likely that Sam just wanted his boys to have the opportunity to play more hockey.

Sam didn't take any chances that his boys' lives wouldn't revolve around hockey. He rented a second-floor apartment in one of the old tenement houses across the street from Mount Saint Charles, less than one hundred yards from Adelard Arena.

"Me, two boys, and a dog in an old apartment," Sam recalled.

He entrusted Mathieu's hockey development to Bill, a man he had come to know through Bill's coaching at some of the summer hockey camps. Sam liked Bill's no-nonsense style.

"A little taste of Bill is like a taste of reality. I knew it would teach Mathieu how to handle adversity when things don't go right," Sam said. "You know how in the Marines you don't make eye contact with the drill instructor? That's the way it is with Bill. He's tough as nails, but he also has a heart of gold."

Of course, unlike parents of other Mount Saint Charles players who understood that once their sons went with Bill behind the closed doors of Adelard Arena, their influence in their kid's hockey career was limited, Sam never took a reserve roll in Mathieu's development.

From his first day on the job, Bill let it be known to Mount parents that he didn't talk to them about their son's status on the team. For more than two decades, Bill has walked past parents gathered in the lobby of Adelard Arena either before a practice or a game and not been concerned that one of the parents would approach him. They all know the rules. The only exception? Sam Schneider. Pressed on the issue, Bill will admit that there were times when Mathieu was playing that he'd duck out the back door of the rink to avoid running into him.

Sam was tenacious about Mathieu's development. He knew Bill's ground rules, but that didn't matter. The rules were for the other parents.

In Sam's mind, Mathieu was special. Even though he trusted Bill as a coach, he had a master plan for his kid and he had to make sure it was being followed.

Sam's doggedness could have created some problems, but Mathieu was the kind of kid people naturally liked and that likability helped overcome his father's tendency to rub folks the wrong way. Mathieu didn't have Sam's overbearing personality. He didn't have an answer for everything. He was willing to listen to people tell him what to do, especially to Bill and Dave. He loved playing hockey, but he understood that he had a lot to learn. He was also a gentle kid, at least off the ice.

That's why in his sophomore year when Bill shifted him from defense to forward for a little while because he needed to improve his skating, Mathieu didn't argue. Sam wasn't too pleased, however. In his master plan, Mathieu was destined to be an NHL defenseman. He made it clear to Bill that he didn't think Mathieu playing forward was a good idea. His opinion didn't matter to Bill, and Mathieu spent most of the year as a forward.

Somewhere along the line, the father's dream had also become the son's. Was it during the seemingly endless trips to youth hockey tournaments? Or was it when he first put on a Mount Saint Charles uniform? Whenever it happened, by his junior year, Mathieu's goal was to be a professional hockey player.

In his junior year, he was also back at defense. He was good, but he wasn't the best high school defenseman in Rhode Island at the time. He still wasn't that big, but he had an almost natural instinct for how and when to hit people.

"Mathieu was a great open-ice hitter." Dave recalled. "He would just line them up ten or fifteen feet out and there was no way of avoiding it. Even though he was still small when he was here, he was very strong on his skates. He was a smooth skater and he was low to the ice with great balance."

But neither Dave nor Bill envisioned an NHL career for Mathieu while he was wearing a Mount uniform.

"Like any kid with that type of talent, I'm sure he dreamed of playing in the NHL, but when he was here there wasn't much talk of that," said Dave. "Until his junior year Mathieu was just a normal hockey player here. Nobody was talking about the NHL then."

Well, almost nobody. Sam was talking about it, especially to his son.

At the end of Mathieu's junior year, father and son decided it was time to take the next step toward an NHL career. Just like when he was five years old playing nine-year-olds, Sam thought Mathieu's career plan could be speeded up if he played against older and better players than he would encounter in Rhode Island high school hockey. Should Mathieu leave Mount Saint Charles to play major junior hockey in Canada? It was as if Mathieu was crossing hockey's Maginot Line. Not only was it a significant adjustment to leave home at sixteen and live with a Canadian family, it also was a gamble with his future. Once he started playing major juniors he would be ineligible to play college hockey; his life would be geared toward one day playing pro. They took a family vote and it was 3–0 on the side of Mathieu going off to Canada. The dog didn't get a vote.

Sam will tell you now that Bill agreed with him that Mathieu was ready to make the move. That he hugged Mathieu and wished him well. Bill definitely hugged Mathieu because he really liked him, but he wasn't convinced that he was ready. His skating still needed some work and he wasn't big enough yet to take the physical abuse that a young player, especially an American player, would encounter in a Canadian junior hockey league.

"We were shocked when he decided to go to juniors. We thought we would have him for another year. But he felt that was where he could better himself and he earned most of his reputation in juniors," said Dave.

"I have to give Bill credit. Some coaches would have been kissing my feet trying to convince me not to take a player like Mathieu from their team, but not Bill. He just hugged Mathieu and told him 'To be all that he could be,'" said Sam.

Mathieu went through a growth spurt in his first few years, which helped make the transition easier. Although at five feet, eleven inches he will never be big by NHL defenseman standards, at least he had decent size. But it took more than a growth spurt to survive the move from Rhode Island high school hockey to the best junior hockey in Canada. He was no longer playing against kids who grew up in raised ranches in suburban Rhode Island. He now was playing eighteen- and nineteen-year-olds, who grew up hurling bales of hay on Canadian farms, knowing that their only hope of escaping their drudgery was a professional hockey career. Living in a tenement on a hill in Woonsocket rather than a white Cape with a picket fence in some middle-class suburb may have toughened Mathieu, however.

It wasn't as if Mathieu never saw his father, either. Mathieu played junior hockey in Cromwell, Canada, which is about sixty miles north of Montreal. For the better part of three years, Sam was one of the team's most devoted fans. Time after time, in the middle of the winter, Sam drove six and a half hours from Woonsocket to Cromwell, watched the game, slept for a couple of hours wherever he could find a place to lay his head, and then headed back to Rhode Island to get to work on time the next morning. He estimates that during Mathieu's first year he made the trip at least twenty-five times.

Although Sam never doubted that someday his son would play in the NHL, he did ensure Mathieu's future in case something went wrong. In typical Sam Schneider fashion, he worked out a deal with the managers of the Cromwell junior team that if Mathieu never signed an NHL contract, the team would pay for his education at any American college.

But Mathieu never had to tackle English Comp 101. He quickly made a name for himself in juniors. In 1988, after his second year, the Montreal Canadiens picked him in the third round of the NHL draft. A year later, when he was only eighteen, he was playing for them. He played a major role in the Canadiens 1993 march to the Stanley Cup, the last time the Canadiens won it. One of the first things he did when he returned to Rhode Island after the victory was to bring Bill the stick he used in the final game. The stick still occupies a prime spot on the wall of Bill's office. When it came time for him to have the Stanley Cup for a day, as every member of the championship Stanley Cup team does, he brought it back to Rhode Island and threw a party with his family and his old high school coach. Long after he left Mount, he always seemed to have a special relationship with Bill. It was as if he understood that Bill was the counterpoint to his father in his development as a hockey player. He was the one who pushed him to be better. The one who didn't listen to his father about how great he was. The person who wasn't afraid to tell Sam that his kid had some shortcomings that needed work.

Since 1990, Schneider has played for six NHL teams, the Canadiens, the New York Islanders, the Toronto Maple Leafs, the New York Rangers, the Los Angeles Kings, and the Detroit Red Wings. But even though he now plays in venues such as Madison Square Garden, Maple Leaf Garden, and the Molson Center, he will never forget it was in Adelard Arena where he took his first steps toward an NHL career. He still calls Bill regularly and always makes a point of visiting his old coach when he's in Rhode Island.

These days Sam is semiretired and living in Vermont. He doesn't attend all of Mathieu's games like he used to, but he still spends a significant amount of time in hockey rinks, including the Fleet Center in Boston. He will sit at the games watching little kids wearing Bruins jerseys enjoying the game with their fathers. He knows that a few of those kids, and their fathers, are dreaming that one day they too will be playing for the Bruins. He wants to tell the fathers that he's proof that those dreams can come true, but he doesn't. Most people probably wouldn't believe the story of how his son got to the NHL.

CHAPTER 11

In 1990, Mike McShane, then coach of the Providence College hockey team, predicted that "the next great Rhode Island player will be a kid from Woonsocket named Berard." At the time, Bryan Berard was only in the seventh grade.

McShane and a few other Rhode Island hockey insiders knew Bryan was going to be an outstanding hockey player long before he donned a Mount Saint Charles uniform. But it was during his days at Mount that the rest of the hockey world first came to know him.

In a sense he was a natural Mountie, a Woonsocket boy from a blue-collar family of French-Canadian ancestry, a throwback to an earlier generation of hockey players. By the time Bryan started playing hockey in the early eighties, the days of kids learning how to play on the natural ice of frozen ponds was a thing of the past. By the midseventies most young New England hockey players did all of their skating on the artificial ice of indoor rinks. But Bryan was different. He had fallen in love with the game while watching the Boston Bruins on TV with his father before he was in kindergarten. Long before he played his first organized hockey game at the age of eight, he would walk to the field a few blocks from his house that the city of Woonsocket flooded every winter and skate until it was dark. From the time he first started playing organized hockey with the Woonsocket North Stars youth hockey organization, he was surrounded by competent players. His teams won the Rhode Island age-group championships almost every year from the time he was eight. But it wasn't until he was twelve that Bryan really stood out among his teammates.

"I underwent a growth spurt when I was about twelve. That's when my skating really improved. Until then I think I was a little slow," Bryan told me back in 1994.

He was sixteen years old that year, and even if he had been a little slow-skating as a kid, by then he already knew where he was headed.

"I was six years old when I first starting playing hockey and I loved it. I knew right away that I wanted to be a professional hockey player," he said.

A lot of little kids dream about the fame that goes with being a pro athlete these days, but Bryan's dream was never about fame or fortune. Even as a teenager he wasn't fantasizing about fast cars or luxurious homes. He just wanted to be one of the best hockey players in the world.

People outside New England first noticed him when he played in the national peewee tournament at the age of fourteen. From there, it was a steady progression through the American youth hockey system. When he was younger he wasn't flashy, but he was very smooth. A defenseman from his first days in youth hockey, by the time he was a teenager he could make the transition from defense to offense without hesitation.

"The great ones make it look easy," Dave offered about Bryan. "Most young players can only think about one thing at a time, like intercepting a pass. By the time he reached high school Bryan already could think about intercepting a pass and what he was going to do with the puck all at the same time."

Bill has always said Bryan was one of the most self-motivated players that ever wore a Mount uniform. Even when he was only fifteen years old he treated practices as if they were games. At practices, Bill never talks about a player's strengths, but rather his weaknesses, focusing on what will make him a stronger player. This can be discouraging to some teenagers, but it was always okay with Bryan. He seemed to understand that to become a great hockey player he needed to overcome his weaknesses. He never balked at Bill's challenges. Not surprisingly, he was a starter from virtually his first day. In his sophomore year he was one of the six players on the Rhode Island high school all-state team. By the time he was sixteen he had good size, about six feet, one inch and 190 pounds, to go along with his excellent skating ability. It also had become obvious that he had that special gift of being a smooth-skating defenseman with great offensive talents. And he was smooth without being flashy. When he picked up the puck in his zone, his forwards didn't need to look back. They just immediately started breaking out of the zone because they knew he would get the puck up the ice. He also had another characteristic that made him a special hockey player: even at fifteen when he was on the ice he had that little touch of meanness that a player needs if he wants to play professional hockey. Youth sports purists hate to hear it, but that's a reality. If a kid is going to make it at the highest levels of physical sports such as football and hockey he needs a little sports meanness. He has to like to hit people, like the idea of controlled violence. He has to enjoy the feeling that comes with physical contact. Ask any high school football coach why some kids can play offense, but can't play defense and they'll tell you some kids just aren't mean enough to play defense. Bryan never played high school football, but if he did he would have been a great linebacker. He liked contact. But he never carried any meanness off the ice. Off the ice, he was a quiet, easygoing kid, really not all that competitive. When he and his younger brother, Greg, would play street hockey or even monopoly, Greg was the one who always had to win. But once he stepped on the ice, nobody wanted to win more than Bryan Berard.

Making sure that their son had the chance to fulfill his hockey dream wasn't always easy for Pam and Wally Berard, Bryan's parents. They had five other children. Bryan was the middle child and the eldest of the three boys. Wally was an auto repairman and, as the kids got older and money got tighter, he took a second job as a school maintenance man. There was always food on the Berard family table and the kids always dressed well, but certainly not extravagantly. They were a classic blue-collar family who had to work hard to make ends meet. There was never enough money to send Bryan to the college hockey camps during the summer.

Eventually Wally set up his own auto repair shop. He would come home from work in the school department, grab something to eat, and if the boys, Bryan and his younger brother Greg, didn't have a hockey or baseball game, he'd go repair cars. Then one night in 1989, he received a call from the Woonsocket police. There had been a break-in at the garage and all of his tools had been stolen. It had taken him several years and a lot of money to build up what finally had become a fairly complete inventory. He knew he couldn't slowly rebuild his supply if he wanted to continue in his own business, so he and Pam decided it was worth the effort to remortgage their home and take out some extra money to buy new tools. Because of higher interest rates and the extra money, their monthly mortgage payment would skyrocket from $400 to almost $1,000, but by their calculations the proceeds from the garage would enable them to handle the higher payments. They closed on the new mortgage and deposited the money in a savings account at the nearby Marquette Credit Union.

Since it was just before Christmas in 1989, Wally decided to wait until after the holidays to replenish his tool supply. But on New Year's Day 1990, only a few hours after he was inaugurated as governor, Bruce Sundlun closed down every credit union in the state of Rhode Island. Many of the Rhode Island credit unions were insured by a local Rhode Island agency rather than the FDIC. Managers of the Rhode Island agency, many of whom were politically connected Rhode Islanders, were allowing their friends at the credit unions to issue extremely over-inflated real estate loans. The Rhode Island deposit agency didn't have the funds to insure the money the credit unions had lent, especially since the value of real estate in the state was on the decline. Governor Sundlun closed the credit unions until they could secure federal insurance, which several were unable to do. The Marquette Credit Union was one of them. The Berards were one of the thousands of families who had their money tied up in what became known as the Rhode Island Credit Union Crisis. Eventually the Berards and everyone else recouped most of their money through government-funded programs, but it took several years before they received any payments.

Hockey isn't a cheap sport at any level, but especially at the level Bryan was playing by the time he was twelve years old in 1990. For years, Pam and Wally weren't sure how they were going to pay the mortgage, but somehow they made sure that Bryan's dream was never shortchanged because of their financial problems. They had to sell their second car and many years they couldn't afford to take the trips to the New England junior tournaments. Bryan instead traveled with his good friend Brian Boucher and Boucher's family. Bryan may have played with second-hand equipment, but he played in all the USA Hockey regional and national competitions.

Bryan almost left Mount Saint Charles after his sophomore year in 1993. He had gone to Bill after the season and said he felt he wasn't getting enough competition. Bill understood his frustration. Back in those days, the RIIL had only three teams in its top division. The rest of the Mount schedule consisted of games against teams in the lower division. In a state the size of Rhode Island there's a big separation talent-wise between Division I and Division II teams, resulting in crossover games that were embarrassing mismatches, at least when Mount was the Division I team. These games also meant that Mount couldn't schedule non-league games against some of the top teams from Massachusetts and Connecticut and still stay within the maximum limit of games allowed by the RIIL. Bill knew Bryan was right about the competition, but he still didn't want to see him leave. There were still aspects of Bryan's game that he could help improve, for instance, his turning. Like most young players, Bryan favored his strong side and Bill was constantly pushing him to work on the other. For Bryan to reach his full potential he still needed to work on other basics as well, but basics can get lost at a school where the main concern is playing a lot of games.

It's no secret that for a long time some New England prep schools have encouraged top hockey players from commuting high schools to transfer to their boarding schools, even though any active recruiting of transfers is forbidden. In the early nineties, however, the hockey coaching staff at Tabor Academy in Massachusetts launched a very aggressive effort to recruit top players from the New England youth hockey ranks that would make any college program proud. It's not surprising Bryan was one of the Tabor coach's prime targets. In the summer following his sophomore year at Mount, Tabor offered him a scholarship that would make it cheaper for him to live and attend school at Tabor than it would for him to live at home and attend Mount Saint Charles. Bryan was ready to transfer for his junior year. By that time, however, other private New England prep schools were complaining to Tabor about the recruiting efforts of its hockey coaching staff. About a month before the school year commenced in September, Tabor announced that their coach had resigned, undoubtedly under pressure, and the school was dropping to a lower level of prep school hockey competition. It also retracted all of the scholarship offers the former coach had made.

Other scholarship offers came in, but Bryan had had enough of the prep school run-around. He wanted to go back to Mount Saint Charles. But Pam had heard rumors that Bill was so mad that Bryan had planned to leave Mount that he was going to make him pay for his disloyalty. Bryan was going to have to sit out a few games if he came back. The rumors, of course, were totally unfounded. As always, Bill had never said anything to anybody about his team. Although Pam had suspected that that was the case, she wasn't taking any chances.

"Bryan's mom called and said she had heard rumors that Bryan would have to sit out if he came back," Bill said. "I told her I never said that. That I would welcome him with open arms."

So Bryan returned to Mount for his junior year. In some ways he was glad the deal at Tabor never materialized. Sure he would have been playing at a higher level of competition than Rhode Island high school hockey, but he had another year playing with his friends, and he knew Bill would make sure he developed his game.

That December he left the Mount team for a few weeks to compete in the World Select 17 tournament in Canada. The U.S. team did surprisingly well, and in two of the seven games Bryan was named MVP. He also was named to the tournament's twelve-player all-tourney team.

He had made his mark on the world hockey scene, and by the time he got back to Rhode Island his phone number had been penciled into the phone books of several agents. Most sixteen-year-olds would have been distracted by the attention, but Bryan never seemed to lose his focus. Potential can be a burden for some talented young athletes, but he always seemed to love the challenges. He came back and fit right back into the Belisle practice regimen. But he knew it would be his last year at Mount Saint Charles. He had learned all he could playing against American high school kids, and Bill agreed.

"He was the only one I had ever felt was completely ready to leave before his senior year," he would say years later.

When the high school season was finished, Bryan told his parents he wanted to spend his senior year playing major junior hockey. They said it was okay—but only if he graduated from Mount before he left. By the end of his junior year the only credits he still needed to earn his high school diploma was a senior English course and a religion course. The Mount administration allowed him to take a college English course during the summer and complete a special project for his religion course. In August, a few days before he left for Detroit to play for the Junior Red Wings, Bryan walked received his high school degree in the Mount principal's office. To the best of anybody's knowledge he's the only Mount student who has ever graduated nine months ahead of schedule.

Bryan spent the 1994–95 season with the Junior Red Wings, the only American team in the Ontario Hockey League. Although he was only seventeen, in a league with mostly Canadians and an age limit of twenty-one, it didn't take him long to make his mark as the league's top-scoring defensemen. In its 1994–95 midseason scouting report the Central Scouting Bureau ranked Bryan Berard one of the top North American skaters. It wasn't just his skating talents that made him special; it was his competitive spirit. He seemed to like the idea that opposing teams geared their game plans around going after him. He liked them trying to hit him and he loved the challenge of giving it back and making them look foolish. By the time the season was finished there was no question that he was the best player in the world in the 1995 NHL draft class. In June, the Ottawa Senators made him the second Mount Saint Charles player to be the number-one draft selection.

He never donned an Ottawa uniform, however. Ottawa was struggling through tough times in several areas, including attendance and finances. The team needed a boost, something that would create immediate fan interest. Bryan's agent, former NHL defenseman Tom Laidlaw, feared that the Senators wouldn't be afraid to sacrifice Bryan's future for a quick fix. They might not hesitate to throw Bryan onto the ice without any real protection. The NHL was loaded with Canadian guys who would be itching to show that a seventeen-year-old American kid should never have been the number-one pick in the draft just as they did to Brian Lawton a decade earlier.

So Bryan never signed with the Senators. He returned to the Junior Red Wings and played another season of junior hockey. By not signing, he gave up an opportunity to make $850,000 in his first year as a pro. His parents were still struggling to find ways to pay the mortgage and Bryan desperately wanted to help them, but to Pam and Wally their son's long-term career was more important than their immediate financial worries.

"This is all about Bryan's career, not about us," Pam said more than once.

His parents knew Bryan wanted to be a great hockey player, not just a rich one. He had goals that only a select few players can ever realistically envision. He wanted to be the rookie of the year in his first year in the NHL; he wanted to be part of the first U.S. Olympic hockey team that was going to be made up of professional players, and someday he wanted to be an NHL all-star.

Eventually, Ottawa traded his rights to the New York Islanders, a team Bryan and Laidlaw felt would be a much better fit. He made an immediate impact and was named the NHL 1995–96 Rookie of the Year. Two years later, he was the youngest player selected to the first professional U.S. Olympic hockey team. Only four years after he had led Mount Saint

Charles to the Rhode Island state championship, he had already accomplished two of his major professional goals.

In describing Bobby Orr's influence on hockey in its special 1997 Top 50 NHL Players of All-Time edition the *Hockey News* wrote, "Orr begat Paul Coffey, who begat Brian Leetch who begat Bryan Berard." Only three years after he left Mount Saint Charles, the bible of hockey was saying Bryan Berard was an outstanding hockey player headed for a long and special career.

CHAPTER 12

Most American ice rinks are located in suburban cities and towns, places where you find raised ranch houses and shopping malls. But the Dennis Lynch Arena is in a neighborhood of old factories and aged storefronts in Pawtucket. In 1790, Samuel Slater built America's first important textile mill in Pawtucket, and for the next one hundred years Pawtucket was a bustling and prosperous manufacturing city. Unfortunately, not much changed in Pawtucket after the Northeast textile industry collapsed at the start of the twentieth century. Pawtucket isn't pure inner city, but it has its share of inner-city problems. There are residential pockets of the city that could pass for suburbia with neat Cape Cods and well-manicured lawns, but the majority of the landscape is filled with tenements and old commercial buildings mixed in with low-income housing projects and a couple of high-rise elderly housing facilities.

The population of Pawtucket has always been blue collar, working class. Like a lot of working class cities, Pawtucket loves its sports. (The city is the home of the Pawtucket Red Sox, a Triple A baseball team and one of the most successful minor league franchises in America.) Thirty years ago, as did all other New England sports fans, the people of Pawtucket got caught up in Bobby Orr mania. They built a hockey rink in the middle of the city, with a meat-packing plant on one side and a factory across the street. Yet, the city's economics never really allowed Pawtucket the chance to become a hockey stronghold. The city's recreation department has run a comparatively inexpensive Learn to Play youth hockey program for decades, but the cost of equipment and ice time makes even the introductory level of hockey expensive compared to sports such as basketball, soccer, and baseball. Although there have been a few talented hockey players from Pawtucket (Keith Carney grew up there and learned to skate at the Lynch rink), its youth hockey program doesn't have enough of them to continually send all-star teams to regional and national tournaments. Therefore when players like Carney are ready to take their games to the next level they join youth programs outside the city. And it's not surprising that when it comes time for the few good Pawtucket hockey players to attend high school they head for private schools outside the city, just as Carney did.

At one time, both of Pawtucket's two public high schools had varsity hockey teams. But in the early nineties, one of the schools dropped the sport due to lack of interest. For decades, St. Raphael Academy, a Pawtucket parochial high school, was the only one of Rhode Island's four Catholic boys high schools that didn't field a hockey team. But in the late 1980s, St. Raphael's decided to enter the hockey business. It wasn't because the school administrators were avid hockey fans; it was a business decision. Rising tuition costs and a weak Rhode Island economy made it hard for Rhode Island's Catholic high schools to fill their classrooms. With only three parochial teams in the state, St. Raphael's administration determined that there were still more than enough players in the state who wanted to play in the top division to fill another team's roster. That would be twenty-five tuition-paying players. The school therefore formed a hockey team in the early nineties, and within a few years moved up to the RIIL's top division.

Yet, it's not surprising that St. Raphael's hockey experiment has encountered rough times. There aren't too many teenage athletes—or their parents—who imagine themselves as the building blocks of some new dynasty. Today's young athletes, especially hockey players, want to play for established, winning teams. If they can play at Mount Saint Charles, they don't see any reason why they should try to help build a program at St. Raphael's. There had been a few good players at St. Raphael during the 1990s, but most years the school finished either last or next to last in the division. Nothing had changed during the 1997–98 season. The early season outlook was that St. Raphael might not win a game all year, and after three weeks of the season they were living up to the prediction.

"I hate these games," Dave said, dreading the December 13 match-up. "People hate you because they think you're running up the score. The kids pick up bad habits because they start thinking about their stats rather than playing as a team."

Dave knows the only people who usually come to these games are parents. It was a Saturday night and with Christmas only two weeks away it seemed even a few parents had decided to forgo it to finish their holiday shopping. The Mount–St. Raphael game was the second of a high school doubleheader and the first had gone into overtime. That meant Dave's night of agony at Lynch would be longer than he had expected.

"I guess we better start getting them ready," he said as he turned and headed toward the locker room.

Suddenly, his jaw dropped. The last person he expected to see at a Mount Saint Charles–St. Raphael hockey game was Brian Lawton.

It had been sixteen years since Brian Lawton wore a Mount Saint Charles hockey uniform, but he was still instantly recognized by Mount fans, and just about any other Rhode Island sports fan over the age of thirty.

Some people spend their entire lives in sports and never create a lasting mark. Lawton ensured himself a spot in American sports history when he was only seventeen. On a June afternoon in 1983, only a few days after he graduated from Mount Saint Charles, he became the first American-born hockey player to be the first pick in the NHL entry draft.

The list of Mount Saint Charles hockey luminaries is extensive, but if you had to choose one player who has had the greatest impact on Mount hockey it would be Lawton. There had been a lot of talented hockey players at Mount and other American high schools before Lawton, but he was the first American schoolboy to be called the best young hockey player in the world by the National Hockey League. There were no stops in junior hockey or any other level of competition between his playing days at Mount and his draft selection. The day Lawton was drafted first pick was the day Mount Saint Charles became more than just a competent high school hockey team.

At the time of his selection Lawton was a six-foot, two-inch, seventeen-year-old high school forward. To this day, Bill claims he's never seen a player who could skate and pass as smoothly as Lawton did when he was a high school player. It wasn't some inherited family talent.

John Lawton didn't even own a pair of skates when he was growing up in the Bronx in the forties and fifties. A newspaper pressman, he and his wife were raising their young family of four boys in New Jersey when John accepted a job offer from what then was a revolutionary new color printing company in Providence. A few years later, six-year-old Brian Lawton and his two older brothers took up hockey.

John didn't know anything about the game, but he liked the cost. The Lawtons moved to Rhode Island from New York at the height of the Bobby Orr mania. Almost every Rhode Island city and town recreation department had a low-cost youth hockey program.

"Fifteen dollars, that's what it cost for all three boys to play in our town rec league," said John. "We don't know anything about hockey, but it was cheap and all three boys played on the same team. That was important because we only had one car in the family in those days."

Hockey quickly became a way of life. Eventually all four Lawton boys became skillful hockey players. That their Cumberland home was only a few hundred yards from a little pond where the boys would spend their winter afternoons skating helped their development. But it was Brian who stood out.

Bill bristled when he'd hear people say Lawton was just a naturally talented player. "Brian worked as hard as any player I've ever seen," he noted. "People didn't know how much he wanted to play. How he would stand out in the road and thumb a ride to the rink because the family only had one car and his father would need it for work."

It wasn't Lawton's talent alone, however, that assured him a place in American sports history.

Al "Smokey" Cerrone had made a small fortune selling automobiles from an East Providence dealership. But the most impressive sale of his life involved a hockey player rather than a car.

Cerrone had played a little hockey growing up, but it wasn't until his four sons took up youth hockey in the late sixties that the game became his passion. And it's not surprising—Cerrone never did anything in a low-key fashion. His gift for self-promotion was legendary in the Rhode Island business community. While other Rhode Island auto dealers were promoting their products with newspaper advertisements depicting their latest models, Cerrone sold cars by starring in his own TV ads. Those ads made him one of the best-known personalities in Rhode Island during the sixties and early seventies.

When Cerrone fell in love with hockey, sitting in the stands and cheering wasn't enough for him. Instead, he would be a coach, but not just the coach of the local kids team. He put together all-star teams of players from throughout New England and traveled around the Northeast. Brian Lawton was one of his players.

Cerrone quickly made a name in the hockey world, and he wasn't shy promoting his own knowledge of the game. By the late seventies, he knew enough hockey bigwigs that he had become an unpaid scout for a few NHL teams. In those days, scouting American hockey players was not nearly as refined as it is today. The NHL's main source of talent was Canada; teams weren't going to spend a lot of money looking for American players. They appreciated that guys like Cerrone, who knew something about hockey, were willing to work for virtually nothing just so that they could say they were "pro scouts." Selling cars fed Smokey Cerrone's family; selling hockey players fed his ego.

The Minnesota North Stars had joined the NHL in 1967. With Minnesota's venerable high school and college hockey tradition it would seem that professional hockey's success in the state was as certain as Bobby Orr shooting at an open cage. But Minnesotans didn't fall head over heels in love with the pro game and all of its Canadian stars. The North Stars were having difficulty drawing fans in the numbers needed to make the team a financial success. Part of the problem, of course, was that they weren't winning many games.

Because of their poor record the previous year, the North Stars had the first selection in the 1983 NHL entry draft. Smokey Cerrone was their New England scout. When North Stars general manager Lou Nanni told Cerrone the team was hearing favorable reports about Brian Lawton's play in national age-group tournaments and wanted to know more about him, Cerrone saw the potential for the greatest sale of his life.

These days Cerrone, who's now semiretired from the auto business, will tell you he tried convincing Nanni that there were a few other kids in New England who he felt were better pro prospects, such as a goalie Tom Barrasso. He'll tell you he told Nanni as much as he liked Lawton both as a player and as a kid, he wasn't sure he was big enough to succeed in the rough-and-tumble world of professional hockey. But other people who were around at the time will tell you Cerrone threw a Smokey-style pitch to sell Nanni on the idea of making Lawton the first American to be number one in the NHL draft. Nanni was a willing customer. Beyond just getting a good hockey player Nanni was looking to heighten American interest in NHL hockey. Making an American the number-one selection in the draft was one way of doing it. If Lawton was the player he was interested in, Cerrone was too good a salesman to let Nanni start thinking about going somewhere else to find his prize. Every good car salesman knows that once you get the customer in your showroom you don't let him go to another dealer to check out other models.

Cerrone become Lou Nanni's emissary to Brian Lawton. Like everything else about Mount Saint Charles hockey during the Bill Belisle era there are classic stories about the courting of Brian Lawton.

Nanni had decided to travel to Rhode Island to see for himself just how smooth a skater Lawton was. He called Cerrone and asked him if he could watch Lawton practice. Cerrone had known Bill for a long time. He knew all about Bill's no-outsiders rule at Mount practices, but he figured even Bill wouldn't keep an NHL general manager out. So one afternoon in 1983, shortly before Bill suffered his injury, Cerrone strolled into a practice with Nanni. The minute Bill saw the pair walk through the door he bawled, "Get out!" from the middle of the ice. Cerrone's explanation of who Nanni was fell on deaf ears. Cerrone and Nanni left the practice without watching Lawton skate. The NHL could wait for Brian Lawton—at a Mount practice, he belonged to Bill Belisle.

Despite not getting to observe Lawton, Nanni nonetheless bought Cerrone's sales pitch. A strong showing at the U.S. Olympic Sports Festival in the spring of 1983, where he was playing against the other top players in America, boosted Lawton's credibility. In the end, however, the North Stars relieved heavily on a car salesman's opinion that Brian Lawton was the best young player in the world in 1983. They chose Lawton first pick in a draft class that also included Pat Lafontaine (third), Steve Yzerman (fourth), Barrasso (fifth), and Cam Neely (ninth). It was the most impressive NHL draft class in the past twenty years, and a kid from Mount Saint Charles was the valedictorian.

When he was drafted, many observers bet that Lawton wasn't ready to go directly into the NHL—and they were probably right. After all, he was a seventeen-year-old kid who a few months earlier had been playing in a Rhode Island high school league that at the time didn't even allow checking in the offensive zone.

Hockey insiders advised Lawton to spend a year playing for the 1984 U.S. Olympic team. But back in 1984, U.S. Olympic hockey players had to be amateurs, and it was tough for a working-class kid not to jump at an offer of $80,000 to turn pro immediately. Lawton was a valuable commodity for a league that was competing for the attention and dollars of the American sports public.

Lawton's selection was a milestone in the growth of American hockey. It also would become a millstone on Lawton's professional hockey career. Lawton never had the luxury of being just another American hockey player trying to make it in a league that at the time was composed of 95 percent Canadians. He had been ordained American's first hockey superstar, even if he had never been properly trained for the role. The North Stars had proclaimed that he was better than any young Canadian players from places such as Sault Sainte Marie and Moose Jaw, where hockey is as much a religion as a sport. To the Canadians, an American being named the best was heresy. It was bad enough that American-born players had started infiltrating the NHL about a decade earlier; now those obnoxious Yankees, who already thought they owned North America, were bragging that they also had the top hockey prospect in the world.

It didn't make it any easier for Lawton when the North Stars and Lawton's agent thought it would be a great promotion idea for Lawton to wear Number 98, one number lower than the 99 worn by Wayne Gretzky.

"He's going to be the American Gretzky," Lawton's agent told the North Stars.

It was like slapping a bulls-eye on Lawton's back. It was just too much for some of the Canadian players to take. They were determined to prove an American couldn't be that good.

"Even the Canadian players on *his* team would go after him," Bill recalled. "We would meet him after he played a game in Boston and his face would be all cut up, and I knew he didn't get them in the game. He never wanted to say much about it, but he would admit that it was guys on his team that had done it to him during practice."

It's not surprising that after years of being a constant target Lawton developed a reputation of having a "short stick." In pro hockey, having a short stick means you hesitate going all the way into the corners to dig out the puck. Once you get the short stick rep guys go after you even harder. There probably were some nights when Lawton, tired of being a target, might not have gone full throttle into the corners like Bill had taught him.

Yet he still spend ten years in the NHL, playing for five teams and finishing his career with a total of 266 points in 482 games. By normal standards that's an amazing accomplishment for an American-born hockey player in the eighties and early nineties. But Brian Lawton never had the luxury of being judged by normal standards, he was supposed to be the American Gretzky. No one could have fulfilled those expectations.

It was only natural that when Lawton finally hung up his skates he became a player's agent. He may not have had a Hall of Fame NHL career, but moving back and forth between teams during his career taught him the NHL system. Furthermore, some of the guys he played against in the eighties were now NHL managers and coaches.

Lawton hadn't attended a Mount Saint Charles hockey game since his last game as a Mountie in 1983. But in December 1997, there was another kid wearing a Mount uniform whom hockey insiders were saying was one of the best young players in the world. Brian Lawton wanted to sign Jeff Jillson as one of his clients—even if it meant spending a night watching a Mount Saint Charles–St. Raphael hockey game.

CHAPTER 13

By the late nineties, Catholic schools had been dominating high school hockey in Rhode Island and Massachusetts for almost two decades. The parochial school advantage of drawing students without geographical restrictions had become too much for the public schools to overcome, especially in hockey. Even though Massachusetts has almost two hundred public high schools with hockey teams, there were only a few public schools, such as Reading and Arlington, that ever seriously challenged the parochials for the Super Eight (the top division) state title. At the start of the 1997–98 season Catholic Memorial High School of West Roxbury had won eight of the previous ten state championships. Parochial schools dominated even more in Rhode Island. It wasn't only that Mount Saint Charles had won twenty consecutive state titles, the other teams battling for the Mount for the state title were usually two other private schools, La Salle and Hendricken. At one time in the eighties every public school in Rhode Island had given up trying to compete with the parochial schools and dropped down to a lower division than the state Championship Division. For a few years only three teams, Mount, La Salle, and Hendricken played in the Championship Division.

But in the mideighties Mike Gaffney, a former La Salle and Providence College hockey standout, was hired as coach at Toll Gate High in Warwick. Toll Gate is one of three public schools in Warwick, the second largest city in Rhode Island. The geographic area from which Toll Gate draws its students is mainly upper middle class. Gaffney knew if he wanted to keep some of the good players who lived in the Toll Gate district from going to the one of the parochial schools he needed to be playing in the Rhode Island top division. So in the early nineties, Toll Gate moved up to Championship Division.

Gaffney had six sons who were outstanding players at various age levels, which helped him make the decision to play in the top division. Another resident of the Toll Gate area was Joe Cavanagh, a former three-time all-American hockey player at Harvard in the late sixties and early seventies. Cavanagh, a Rhode Island native, had returned to his home state after finishing law school at Boston College to set up a law practice and raise a family. It's not surprising that several of Cavanagh's nine children were hockey players. Between the Gaffney and Cavanagh families alone Toll Gate was assured of a deep supply of hockey talent for a long time, therefore Toll Gate started challenging the parochial powers. Gaffney's early teams were relatively competitive most years, usually posting at least a .500 record against the Catholic schools. But it wasn't until 1996 that a Toll Gate team led by female goalie Sara DeCosta became the first public school in fourteen years to reach the title round of the Rhode Island state playoffs. With DeCosta posting a shutout in the second game, Toll Gate pushed Mount to three games, but eventually lost. DeCosta graduated from Toll Gate in 1996 and went out to become a college star at Providence College and then a member of the gold medal–winning 1998 U.S. Olympic women's hockey team. Even without DeCosta in the net, Toll Gate reached the title series again in 1997, but lost to Mount in two straight games. In eight years playing against Mount, Toll Gate had only won a couple of games. Gaffney's teams always guaranteed Mount a battle, but in the end, Mount usually won.

After the first ten minutes of the Mount–Toll Gate on December 19, 1997, it looked like nothing was going to change. Two days earlier, Mount had played well in a non-league victory over Archbishop Williams High of Massachusetts. Dave had worried that after the solid performance against Williams they might come out flat against Toll Gate. That wasn't the case. Sophomore Chris Snizek scored two goals in the first six minutes, one off a beautiful setup from Jillson. Then Jillson made it 3–0 with a blue-line blast.

Less than ten minutes into the game most of the Mount fans assumed the game was already decided. Dave knew better. It was still early in the season, but he was already getting a feeling that this team didn't know how to put a game away—even when they had a 3–0 lead. They didn't know how to stay focused. That's not unusual with a young team, but this was a team of seniors. Dave sensed that rather than thinking as a team, too many players were thinking more about boosting their personal stats.

It didn't take long for Dave's concerns to prove valid. With a few minutes remaining in the first period, senior goalie Brian Oliver couldn't get a handle on a high floating shot and it bounced off his chest into the goal. He was screened, he claimed at the end of the period, but Bill wasn't buying it. It was just a case of Oliver not concentrating on the play in front of him. In the second period, every Mount player seemed to lose his focus. The defense had problems working the puck out of the defensive zone. Even when the defensemen managed to get the puck up to somebody breaking out of the zone, their lead passes were being cut off at mid-ice. In the defensive zone, Toll Gate forwards were left alone in front of the cage. By the end of the second period the score was tied 3–3.

Dave was the last one into the dressing room for the break between the second and third periods. His father was already in the room quietly talking to a player. Suddenly Dave bellowed a declaration.

"You're living in the past!"

The outburst caught everybody by surprise. If Bill was already in the room and was quietly talking to a player, nobody expected to hear Dave yelling. Dave's outburst even caught Bill by surprise. He immediately stopped talking and turned his attention toward his son.

"You're living on Wednesday's victory," Dave continued. "You stopped playing. You thought they were going to give up when you scored a couple of goals. But they're *not* going to give up. They're *not* scared of you. *You* can't live on yesterday's victories or former Mount teams' reputations. You have to do it. Don't look to anybody else."

He paced around the room as he talked, stopping every few feet to bend down and shove his face a few inches away from a player's. He looked right into his eyes. He didn't want anybody glancing around the room, thinking, "The coach isn't talking about me." He didn't want anyone to think he was talking about someone else. He tried making them look into themselves—there was no opportunity for finger-pointing, as there can be when a coach stands in the middle of a room. It was face-to-face, eye-to-eye evaluation. It was nothing new: it had been a staple of Bill's coaching methodology since his first day on the job. You atone for your own sins on the ice; you don't pass the blame onto teammates. For decades, this has been part of the Mount hockey creed, something that players seem to automatically understand the minute they slip on that shirt with the big M on the front, even though in recent years the Belisles had been finding it necessary to reinforce the concept of personal responsibility.

Years ago, all Bill had to do was make a general criticism and every player immediately began soul-searching. That night, Dave had to spend the break between the periods going eye to eye.

It may have been soul-searching or just plain superior talent, but Mount came out and quickly put the game on ice with three goals in the first eight minutes of the third period. By the time the final buzzer sounded Mount was ahead 8–4.

The first thing Bill does when he enters the Mount dressing room after a victory, whether home or away, is pump his arm in the air and shout "Hip! Hip!" The players respond with "Hooray!" If it's a true triumph there may be two "hip, hips," maybe even three, and each time the Mount players follow with a chorus of "hooray." No matter how upset he is at a particular player or the team in general, Bill always gives the cheer—and then he may start yelling.

In any other team's dressing room it would have been considered corny by a bunch of teenagers in 1998: "Hip, Hip, Hooray" belongs to their grandfather's generation. But it's part of the Mount tradition that Bill has nurtured since 1976. It's a connection between Pat Manocchia, Keith Carney, Bryan Berard, and Jeff Jillson. Anyplace else teenagers would have been embarrassed responding to the chant of an arm-pumping sixty-eight-year-old man. But when Bill pumped his arm and yelled "Hip! Hip!" after the Toll Gate victory twenty-five teenagers gleefully screamed their response.

Chris Snizek had scored two of the eight Mount goals, giving him six goals in the first three league games. The hefty production didn't surprise Dave.

"He knows how to score," said Dave. "He's one of the few on this team that knows how."

111

Snizek was a classic product of New England hockey mania. In December 1997 he was only fifteen years old, but he already had traveled more than a hundred thousand miles with his hockey stick. He wasn't very big, but he was a hockey talent. A player can improve most skills with dedicated practice and capable instruction, but there is also such a thing as natural talent. Snizek was one of those players who had that knack of knowing a split second ahead of the other guy which way the puck or ball is going to bounce. It's called "hockey sense." He also had "soft" hands, the kind that allow him to move a stick with amazing speed when he's trying to deflect a shot in front of the cage or stickhandle the puck past a defenseman. That talent enabled him to make an immediate impact as a high school player. As a freshman the previous season he had been one of the top scorers in the state. He lived in the nearby town of Burrillville, but he had taken his game on the road at an early age. Before he was even a teenager he had played for a variety of youth hockey teams in New England. Burrillville hockey fans said he was playing as many as eighty or ninety games each year as he progressed through the youth ranks.

"I played a lot," Snizek modestly offered about his youth hockey days.

A kid can't play that much hockey without parents who are dedicated to promoting his hockey career. Snizek's parents were more than willing to invest both a lot of their time and their money into his. But they also had a master plan that might not include four years playing against Rhode Island high school competition. Like many hockey parents, they seemed to think strictly in terms of what a team can do for their son's hockey career, not what their son can do for a team.

"He's a good kid. He does whatever we ask and I think he has a lot of friends here. But I don't think he's going to be with us for four years," Dave said.

Dave sat in the little dressing room office after the game that night with a mixed look of contentment and concern. The team had just responded to his challenge and that makes every coach feel good. They were 4–0 overall, including the scrimmage with St. Sebastian's and 3–0 against Rhode Island teams. All they had to do was beat Burrillville, another public school, in a few days and they would be undefeated in League play at the Christmas break.

But only a month into the season Dave knew that this wasn't a team that would allow him the luxury of feeling confident for very long. There had already been a couple of injuries, now it looked like senior D. J. Pelletier would be lost for several weeks.

"He hurt his shoulder in the second period. He's still at the hospital, but I know it's dislocated. It's tough. He's one of the few kids who knows how to score goals. It's tough for us, but I also feel bad for him. He's a senior and he has worked hard to finally be one of our top players. I know he was hoping he would start getting some college interest, and he probably would. Now he's going to miss most of the season."

But Pelletier's injury wasn't the only thing bothering Dave.

"We have to break up Jillson and Fede," Dave said. "Paul is trying too hard. He's trying to show he can do everything Jeff can do and he can't. He's making mistakes because he's trying to do things he can't do. We need to put somebody with Jeff who is willing to be just a defensive defenseman, to cover up when Jeff goes on the offense. I think I'm going to put the sophomore Kasberg up there and move Paul back to the second defense. It will be better for both the team and Paul, but I know he's not going to see it that way."

Bill never could have accomplished what he has if he was coaching at a public high school. It goes beyond the obvious difference that most public high school teams practice at public rinks so that they can't close their practices as Bill does at Adelard. Even, if under some unique situation, a public school coach could keep parents and fans out of his practices, these days he never would be able to conduct Bill's boot camp–type practice sessions without some parent complaining his child's rights were being violated and it probably would be the parent of some kid who wasn't seeing enough playing time. The difference between a public and private high school education is more than just the price tag. Public school education is governed by constitutional law; private school education is governed by contractual law. The parents of every Mount Saint Charles student, and probably students at every private school in the United States, sign a contract that they will abide by the school administration's decisions. If they don't like those decisions their choice is simple: send their child to another school. Parents of a Mount Saint Charles hockey player can't threaten to sue Bill because he is treating their son in a demeaning manner at practice. It wasn't uncommon in the forties, fifties, and sixties for a public high school football coach to try motivating his players with verbal and physical intimidation, but these days their actions are open to scrutiny from everyone from parents to school committee members to the mayor. Bill, on the other hand, answers only to the Mount Saint Charles principal. In the early days, some of Bill's tenacious coaching techniques probably sent shivers up the spines of more than one Mount administrator. A few times through the years the Mount principal called Bill into his office to ask if a rumor he heard was true. Bill always assured his boss that they weren't, and the principal left it at that. Of course the only people who knew the truth were the players—and Mount players never talked about what happened behind those closed doors. There hasn't been one of those rumor meetings in many years. The principals have heard it all and while they certainly would never run their classrooms the way Bill runs a hockey practice, twenty-plus years have proven the good, far, far outweighs the bad. While the majority of Mount hockey parents through the years have entrusted their son to Bill's tutelage because they think he can make the kid's hockey dream become reality, some parents have had additional motives, however.

"You know there's still time to transfer to Bellingham High," Bill jokingly said to one of the members of the 1997–98 team when he overheard a locker-room complaint about how tough practice had been.

"Oh my parents wouldn't let me do that coach," the kid said with a laugh. "They said I was too wild for public school so they were sending me to Mount so Coach Belisle could straighten me out."

"Listen to that," Bill said to Dave and me with a big smile on his face. "What do they think this is, the army? I'm a hockey coach, not a drill sergeant."

No one has to tell Ed Lee how Bill's no-nonsense approach to everything can turn a kid's life around.

Lee grew up in the gritty north-end section of Providence in the seventies. His father was a rough-and-tumble construction worker who always loved hockey but never played seriously. He was determined, however, that his son was going to be a great player, even if he was growing up in an area where basketballs were far more plentiful than hockey sticks. Because of his father's dedication to his career Lee had become a proficient player by the time he started high school, but he was far from a model student.

"I was a tough, inner city Providence punk," Lee offered in 1998 about his adolescent years.

Bill was only in his second year as Mount coach when Lee came to Mount in the fall of 1977. Lee's father didn't know much about him, but he knew Mount had a hockey team and a hockey rink and he hoped that the Brothers of the Sacred Heart could smooth out the rough edges in his son's personality and his academic record.

Lee's chip on the shoulder and "I'll do it my way attitude" didn't sit well with Bill.

"I'll never forget my first day at school in my sophomore year," Lee recalled. "My best friend had been expelled from school that summer. It was 8:00 a.m. and I was looking in my locker, when all of a sudden the entire room went silent. When I turned to see why everybody had stopped talking there was Coach Belisle, standing right in front of me."

The coach didn't mince words.

"I want you to transfer," he told Lee. "You can't handle the academics here and you're never going to make my team. You're too slow."

"He forced my hand that day," said Lee. "Either it was all or nothing. That's the way it was with him. I decided to work harder than ever."

By the time his career was finished at Mount, Lee had become an all-state hockey player, had a 3.85 academic average, and an early acceptance to Princeton University.

But it wasn't easy.

Lee claims that in those early days Bill was "a cross between a rattlesnake and a barracuda. He was ready to bite your head off at any time."

Like a lot of Mount players Lee didn't look directly at his coach until his final year on the team.

"I never wanted to make eye contact with him because I was too scared," he said "Mr. Belisle made sure that every one of us knew there were always fifty JV players champing at the bit to get into the varsity room. The price to get your spot in the varsity room was huge. If you missed a practice, you had to have a great excuse or you were gone. Even if you did have a good excuse you paid for it the next day."

Bill used to tell Lee and his teammates that if you miss one day of practice you lose your skating legs. The inference was if you lost your skating legs you've lost your spot in the varsity room. He scared Lee and his teammates into never missing a practice.

In Lee's days at Mount it wasn't unusual to practice under just the glimmer of the scoreboard lights.

"The time clock was set at 20:00 and the rink worker would operate it," Lee recalled. "We would do length of the ice sprints the entire time in the dark with the coach breathing down our necks, screaming at us."

After twenty minutes, Bill would send the players back to the locker room while the Zamboni cleaned the ice just like in a game. Once the ice was cleaned he'd send them back out for another twenty minutes of the same drills under the same conditions. The only thing they could see clearly was the clock. The only thing they heard was Bill. It was easy to focus on the objective.

Those skating-only practices generally consisted of three of the twenty-minute skating sessions, but sometimes Bill pulled a surprise.

"Usually he would send us back to the locker room after the third period and it was over. But every now and then he'd burst into the locker room and yell, 'It's a tie game, get back out there for overtime,'" Lee recalled. "No pucks, no shooting, no fun."

But Lee and his teammates thrived on the challenges Bill threw at them—even if they didn't always realize it at the time. During his senior year at Mount, Lee was the first Mount player ever selected in the NHL draft when in 1980 he was picked in the fifth round by the Quebec Nordiques. He played at Princeton, and then spent several years in a variety of professional leagues, including the American Hockey League, the International League, and a few European leagues. By 1998, he was back in Rhode Island teaching high school English and coaching hockey at a small private school. He knows that he's never have the Ivy League education, the professional hockey experience, and even his current job if Bill hadn't challenged him that morning in his sophomore year.

"I remember one time I was playing in Germany and I was back home on Christmas vacation. I came up to do a little skating with the team, but Coach made me do everything the team was doing," Lee said. "Even after you graduate he doesn't let you take it easy. But after the practice was over he came up to me and handed me an envelope. When I opened it there was $50 in it and a note that said, 'Have a wiener schnitzel on me.'

"I've had people who have never even met him tell me he's an asshole. Most people don't know him and that's the way he wants it. He loves his family and he loves his players. Nothing else matters."

CHAPTER 14

I t was a few days after Thanksgiving that Peter Capizzo first noticed the traces of blood whenever he spit out the mucus that settled in his throat after he coughed. Sometimes he could hardly detect any blood, but other times the mucus was almost pure red. It had happened a few months earlier and his older brother had noticed it in the bathroom and told his parents, who immediately took him to the doctor. The doctor couldn't find any major problem. "Probably just throat irritation from a cough," he said. In the back of his sixteen-year-old mind Pete knew he should tell his parents that it was still happening, but he knew what that would mean. His parents would say he had to stop playing hockey until a doctor checked him out again. Pete couldn't afford that time away from practice. He was only a sophomore, which for most Mount Saint Charles hockey players means you're still a long way from being a major player in Bill and Dave's master plan, but he could see fate was giving him a chance to fulfill his dream of being a Mount starter a little sooner than he expected. He wasn't going to miss the opportunity because of a little cough.

He was one of three goalies who made the varsity cut. One of the others was senior Jason Catalano. Cat was a great kid, the kind who would do anything to help his team. He was one of the first players in the locker room before practice and one of the last to leave. Making the Mount hockey team had been his dream since he was a little kid. In most average high school hockey teams, he could have been the starting goalie, but he never had the talent to be a starting goaltender for Mount Saint Charles. He was finally given a spot in the varsity locker because he was a senior who had stuck it out through three years of early-morning junior varsity practices. The coaches were rewarding his perseverance. He had paid all his dues, knowing realistically that he would never see much, if any varsity playing time.

Brian Oliver, the senior who had been the number-two goalie the previous season, would be given every chance to become the 1997–98 season's starting goalie. Oliver had also paid his dues, jockeying between varsity and junior varsity in his first two seasons. In his junior year he had appeared in almost half of the varsity games, but the other goalie, a senior, had played in all the important ones. In this, his senior year, the job of starting goaltender was his to lose. But Pete knew there was a strong possibility that's just what Oliver would do. Oliver was a hockey lifer. His older brother had played at Mount and his father had been very involved with youth hockey programs throughout New England for more than a decade. But Brian didn't have that fire in the belly that had characterized Mounties during the Bill Belisle era. His general nature was laid-back, never outwardly emotional, never saying much. He played hockey the same way. At times he looked like he was playing on remote control. Unlike Catalano, he had the talent to play against the top high school competition in New England, but bringing that talent to its utmost level didn't appear to be his major concern. He wanted to be part of the Mount hockey culture, but he wanted it on his terms. It's unlikely that he would have ever played at Mount if his older brother hadn't gone to the school because he never quite seemed to buy into the "Live and Die for Mount Saint Charles" creed.

Pete was the exact opposite. He bought into the Mount creed the first time he walked into Adelard Arena, a year before he was even a Mount student. Like Oliver he grew up in a hockey household. His father Gus played goal for Northeastern University back in the sixties and his older brother had played both high school and college hockey. From a small Massachusetts town about twenty miles from Woonsocket, he's picked up a hockey stick he was only five years old and by the time he was ten he was already entrenched in the metro Boston amateur youth hockey world. Youth hockey in the Northeast is a culture within itself and youth hockey in the Boston area is a subculture within that culture. Kids don't just play for their local organizations. For many of them, by the time they're ten years old they're playing in a metro Boston all-star league that brings in kids from all over New England. Some of the teams in the league hold tryouts where more than a hundred ten- to twelve-year-olds will pay $100 or more just to have a chance to make a twenty-player team. It's the breeding ground for most of the players who eventually go on to play at the Massachusetts high school powers such as Catholic Memorial and Boston College High, as well as the host of prep schools in the metro Boston area.

Gus Capizzo had wanted his youngest son to attend Kimball Union, a small prep school in New Hampshire where Pete's older brother had gone. But when he was in the seventh grade Pete told his father he wanted to go watch some friends playing in a youth league game down at Mount Saint Charles in Rhode Island. Gus had played hockey around New England for thirty years. Long after he graduated from Northeastern he was still putting on the goalie pads once or twice a week to play in men's leagues. He had never played at Adelard Arena, however.

"I thought I knew every hockey rink in New England, but I had to call for directions on how to get there," Gus said.

It wasn't long before Gus knew the route to Mount as well as he knew the route to his backyard barbecue. The minute Pete walked into Adelard Arena that night, he was bitten by the Mount Saint Charles hockey bug. "There was just something about it. Something that's hard to explain in words, but something you feel," he said.

Forget the rounding hills of New Hampshire and the ivy-covered walls of a New England prep school. He wanted the old factories of Woonsocket and the stale smell of Adelard Arena. Most people probably won't understand why he would want Mount Saint Charles. He had grown up in a somewhat privileged life. His father made a good living running a Massachusetts insurance and investment firm. There were always new cars in the driveway of their four-bedroom home that sat on a large piece of land in an upper class Massachusetts suburb. The family spent their summers at their home on picturesque Nantucket Island, where Gus's brother Vito is the legendary coach of the Nantucket High football team.

Pete didn't need to submit himself to the rigors of Bill's hockey boot camp. His parents had worked to make life comfortable for their children. In a sense they were the American dream of the forties and fifties come true. At the age of six, Gus had sailed with his mother and older brother, Vito, from their birthplace in Sicily to America. Like so many other Italian-Americans who grew up in the forties and fifties, Gus's first sight of America came as a little boy standing on the deck of boat as it sailed into New York harbor. A few years earlier, his father had found work in the factories of Natick, Massachusetts. The Capizzo boys, Gus, Vito, and younger brother Frank, who was born a year after Mrs. Capizzo joined her husband in America, learned the values of hard work from their father. Growing up in Natick wasn't luxurious, but it was wholesome. Gus's father wasn't a formally educated man, but he was determined that his boys would be. He made sure that all three went to college. He also didn't know anything about American sports, but unlike many other immigrants who thought sports was just a young boy's excuse for getting out of work, he saw sports as a healthy way to work off youthful energy. He never understood how sports could help his boys get a college education, but he certainly didn't object when college coaches called his house insisting that they wanted one of his boys at their school.

Vito was a hard-as-nails, 160-pound football linebacker and hockey player at Natick High. Because his high school coach had contacts down south he ended up at to the University of Alabama and played football for Bear Bryant. It was not surprising that at 160 he never became a Crimson Tide star, but he did make a contribution to the Alabama football legend. During the summer between his junior and senior year he and a few other players from up North had stayed in Tuscaloosa to attend summer school and work out. One day that summer, Coach Bryant informed Vito that he was putting an incoming freshman, who already was on campus, in Gus's dorm room. The kid was a great player but the word was he had a tendency to be a free spirit. The Bear wanted the older guys to keep an eye on him. So for one summer, Vito Capizzo, an Italian immigrant from Natick, Massachusetts, and Joe Namath, the coal-miner's son from Beaver Falls, Pennsylvania, were roommates. Vito did his job and kept Namath out of trouble that first summer in Alabama, but he'll tell you now that sometimes it wasn't all that easy.

Vito came back to New England after college and began a teaching and coaching career on Nantucket. By the 1997 season, he had become one of the all-time winningest high school football coaches in Massachusetts history. Frank, the youngest of the three brothers, went on to medical school at the University of Connecticut and is now a cardiologist practicing in Barrington, one of the wealthiest communities in Rhode Island.

Gus used that same work ethic and savvy the Capizzo boys learned growing up in Natick to build a prosperous business. After graduating from Northeastern he chose a career in insurance and real estate, working fifteen hours a day, six or seven days a week. There were times when he wondered whether the long hours were all worth it. There were times when it even affected his health, but it enabled him to give his family many of the luxuries that he and his brothers never had when they were growing up. It was the American Dream come true.

As the youngest of three children in Gus and Stephanie Capizzo's family, Peter was the major beneficiary of that American Dream. He had grown up in a beautiful home. He had been chauffeured to and from school and hockey practices in a Ford Bronco or a Mercedes. He spent his summers watching million-dollar yachts sailing into Nantucket harbor, riding his bike around the narrow streets of Sconset, and surfing the waves off Cisco beach. It was a childhood that would seem to lead him toward one of the posh New England prep schools, but he decided he wanted Mount Saint Charles. At first it was all about hockey, all about wanting to wear the Mountie uniform. But the more time he spent at Mount the more he began loving everything about the school. Tough to put into words he would say, but there was something there that just made him feel comfortable about going to school every day.

Of course there was nothing comfortable once the school day ended and he headed to the rink for hockey practice, but he loved that challenge even more. Now he was close to seeing his dream come true. But he was still not feeling well. He was much more tired after practice than he had even been. It was easy to rationalize that it was because he had never gone through the rigors of a Mount varsity practice every day. He had never had to deal with the constant pressure every Mountie faces trying to please Bill. And while it's tough on every Mountie, it's especially tough on goalies. Despite having two of his former goalies currently on NHL rosters, Garth Snow and Brian Boucher, Bill doesn't spend a lot of time working on individual goalie techniques. These days, by the time a goalie gets to him he's already attended a host of hockey schools and clinics where former pros or college goalies have instructed them in a wide range of goaltending techniques. What Bill teaches his goalies is mental toughness. Without ever mentioning the word *focus*, he teaches his goalies to constantly be aware of what's happening around them.

If you're a Mount goalie there's never down time. You never take off your mask during practice, never put your gloves down, even when you sitting on the bench during an intrasquad scrimmage. The goalies never know when Bill is going to spot one of his netminders doing something he doesn't like during a scrimmage or drill and suddenly yell, "Get out of there." On hearing that, one of the other goalies better be ready to skate into action. There's no time to slap on a mask, no time to grab gloves; he just has to be ready to skate full speed into the goal. Unfortunately, the goalies never know when it's going to happen. Bill can go two or three days of practice without saying a word to any of them, and then one day he'll be on them like a dog on a bone for most of practice. Too slow getting up after going down for a shot during a shooting drill, leaving the five-hole open, not talking to their defensemen in front of the cage, there are days when it seems like a Mount goalie can't do anything right. There are kids who just couldn't handle the constant uncertainty, the constant demand. Pete loved the challenge. He had sat on the bench for the first three games of the season, watching as Oliver delivered adequate but far from spectacular performances. There were some great saves, but there also were a few soft goals. Every time the opposition scored, Pete, going through what every kid who sits on the bench for a good high school team goes through, would think that had he been in the goal he would have made the save. He was glad the team was winning, but he'd constantly hope that he'd get a chance to show the coach he could make the victories even more decisive.

He finally got that chance in the fourth game of the season when Dave and Bill decided that the game against Burrillville would be an appropriate opportunity to let him get some varsity experience.

Burrillville is a small rural town in northwest Rhode Island. In the late thirties, a young man named Tom Eccleston, who had played football, hockey, and baseball at Brown University, was hired as a teacher and football coach at Burrillville High. The school didn't field a hockey team, but Eccleston quickly decided Burrillville was a natural place for one. The town, which is located in the highest elevation in Rhode Island, was dotted with little ponds surrounded by trees. Burrillville kids could skate on the frozen ponds near their homes before lakes and ponds in any other part of the state were frozen. In the thirties, forties, and fifties before the days of artificial ice surfaces, that was a significant advantage. It didn't take Eccleston long to develop Burrillville into a Rhode Island high school hockey power. Even after Eccleston gave up high school coaching to become head hockey coach at Providence College in the midfifties, Burrillville continued to be one of the premier hockey programs in Rhode Island. Despite having only a few hundred boys in the school, Burrillville won five of the seven state championships from 1957 to 1963 and also won a couple of New England titles. By the early seventies, however, the abundance of artificial rinks had taken away Burrillville's natural ice advantage. A public school from a small town, without any advantages, couldn't realistically compete with the private school powers that drew players from throughout the state. Burrillville won its last state championship in 1971. By the mid-eighties, it dropped from the top division in the state to Class B—and still couldn't win.

The fortunes of the program took an upturn in the early nineties when Eccleston, who after retiring from a teaching and coaching position at the private Hill School in Pennsylvania, returned to Burrillville and once more took over as coach at the age of eighty. The story of an eighty-year-old guy coaching some of the grandchildren of guys he had coached in the forties even attracted the attention of a few national sports publications, especially after Burrillville won the Rhode Island Division II state championship under Eccleston's direction. In 1994, a few years after Eccleston finally gave up coaching, Burrillville decided to take a major step and move back up to the state's top division with the private school powers, and Toll Gate, the only other public school in the division. The feeling around town was that the only way talented Burrillville hockey players would go to the public school was if the school was playing in the top division. The only games college coaches even scout in Rhode Island is the Division I games and all but one or two of the *Providence Journal*'s end-of-the-season, all-state selection over the previous decade had been Division I players. Burrillville therefore jumped up with the big guys and, although the experience wasn't a disaster, it was far from a roaring success. For the first three years after moving back to the top division, Burrillville had been competitive, but seldom able to beat any of the Division I teams. Things hadn't changed during the first few weeks of the 1997–98 season. In early December, after the first two weeks of the season, Mount St. Charles's record was 3–0 and Burrillville's was 1–3.

According to the form chart, a game with Burrillville should have been an easy night for Mount Saint Charles, which is why the Belisles felt it would be an appropriate game in which to give Pete some playing time. They had told him during the week that he would be starting Saturday night. He was finally going to get his chance to show what he could do. He just wished he felt better. Despite all his efforts to get enough sleep and taking drug-store shelf medications, the cold wasn't going away. That week it even seemed worse than ever. For a few nights he had trouble sleeping because the mucus in his throat constantly woke him up. He would go into the bathroom, spit it out, and notice traces of blood, but he quickly passed it out of his mind. All he could think about was Saturday night, the night he finally would be the Mount starting goalie.

From the outset of the game, it was obvious that most of the Mount players didn't share Pete's enthusiasm. As expected, Mount dominated the action, but they weren't finishing off the plays. They were just going through the motions, not going into the boards with the intensity that Bill preaches relentlessly in practice. Midway through the first period, two Mount defensemen let a Burrillville player beat them for a rebound. Pete didn't have a chance of stopping the shot. Mount continued dominating the action, but it wasn't until 12:44 of the second period that Chris Snizek finally tied the score at 1–1. After two periods, Mount had scored one goal and the score was tied. Nonetheless, no one on the Mount team seemed too concerned. After all, Burrillville had only had a few shots at Pete and other than that one time the defense failed to cover up the rebound, there was nothing testing. Everyone assumed that sooner or later Mount would break the game open. But only four minutes after the start of the third period disaster struck. A Burrillville defenseman had sent a clearing pass toward center ice. The puck found its way past a Mount forward, between two Mount defensemen and began slowly sliding toward Pete. He could see a Burrillville forward a few steps in front of a Mount defenseman, skating full speed toward the puck. The right move was for him to skate out of his cage, beat the forward to puck, and clear it to the side or back out of the zone, a move he had done hundreds of times. If it had been a junior varsity game or some summer league game he would never have hesitated. But this was his first game playing for Mount and his fear of making a mistake overpowered his instinctive reaction. It only took him a split second to recognize his play, but that's all it took for disaster. Assuming that their goalie was going to skate out and clear the puck, the Mount defenseman didn't pressure the Burrillville player. That split second of hesitation gave the Burrillville player the opening he needed. He barely beat Pete to the puck about thirty feet away from goal, and then made a quick move to the left. Pete watched helplessly from the middle of the zone as the Burrillville player skated past and fired home a twenty-foot shot that gave Burrillville a one-goal lead.

Pete was dumbfounded. He slid back into the goal crease and tried not to look toward the bench. Bill would be ripping. It was a stupid mistake on his part—the kind Bill hates. He had thought that this was going to be one of his best nights since the day he'd first tied on a pair of goalie pads ten years earlier. He was finally going to know the feeling of being on the ice when Mount won a game. Now it was coming apart. He tried convincing himself that there was plenty of time for a comeback. One of his teammates would bail him out of the doghouse. But not that night. It wasn't that they didn't try. The goal seemed to shock Pete's teammates out of their lethargy, but even though there were still eight minutes to play it was too late. The Burrillville goalie was good and he was having one of the best nights of his career. Time after time, he came up with dramatic saves. When the final buzzer sounded, Burrillville was still ahead 2–1. For the first time in six years, Burrillville beat Mount Saint Charles.

In the locker room after the game neither Bill nor Dave did much ranting or raving. Dave talked in fairly even tones about taking things for granted. Good teams don't do that—and this team wasn't even good yet.

Bill was more vocal. "My goalie made a mistake, but you guys didn't help him by scoring any goals," he bellowed.

Pete bowed his head. In his mind, the loss was his fault. He had been given his chance and he had failed. Nothing he had ever done in his young life had made him feel that depressed. He hardly spoke to his teammates on the fifteen-minute bus ride from Burrillville back to Mount Saint Charles. His parents picked him up at Mount and tried making conversation but he didn't want any part of it. He didn't sleep very well that night; the play kept running through his mind. Why did he hesitate? It wasn't until the next day that he started thinking about exactly what Bill had said in the locker room after the game. It wasn't "Peter made a mistake" or even "the goalie made a mistake." It was "*my* goalie made a mistake." Bill used the phrase a couple of times as he continued blasting the team for what he considered a lackluster effort. "My goalie needed you to pick him up and you didn't do it," he had said.

Bill didn't offer Pete any direct words of consolation. He didn't worry about repairing a fragile teenage ego with some cliché like, "Don't worry about it; you tried your best." Yet what he did, probably without realizing it because it's comes out so naturally now, is give another young player a crash course in the abstract known as Mount Pride. If you make a mistake, you can be sure you'll hear about it, usually very loudly. But once you put on that uniform, you're one of Bill's boys, an extension of his family. You're no longer just another hockey player. In the coach's eyes, you're "*my* goalie" or "*my* captain." Every kid wants to belong, wants that feeling of being part of something special, something important. Some coaches will use the words for inspiration; with Bill it's actually his belief. Family is more than just a word; it's a state of being. Ironically it took the most depressing moment of his hockey career for Pete to feel as if he was finally a part of the Mount hockey family.

By Monday the anxiety pains had left his stomach, but he knew he was back at square one. He had to prove himself all over again. Nothing was going to stop him, certainly not just a cough. Now, more than ever, he needed to be at practice. Even a day off could ruin his chances of ever getting another start. "It's just a cough," he kept telling himself. It had irritated his throat; that's why it was bleeding, he rationalized. It would go away eventually. He would tell his parents about it, but not just yet. He needed more time to show Bill and Dave that he should be the starter.

CHAPTER 15

I t was one of those mornings that makes living in Rhode Island in the winter so wretched. There had been an overnight December storm that left a few inches of snow on the ground. But by the time Dave drove out of his driveway, heading toward the highway a few miles away, the temperature had already risen, turning the soft white snow into ugly, sloppy slush. For every picture-postcard morning when they can enjoy the beauty of fluffy white snow blanketing the landscape, Rhode Islanders must suffer through twice as many mornings such as this. They're mornings when there's nothing picturesque about the snow, and all Mother Nature has done is make driving slow and hazardous.

He wasn't even out of the driveway before he started mulling over how he was going to fit everything that needed to be done that day into the next five hours. He had several sales calls to make that would take him north of Boston. Usually when he's traveling that far, he would tell his father not to expect him at practice until the last half hour or so. But there were a few things he really wanted to work on that day. The power play hadn't been clicking, and he still wasn't sure about some of the line pairings. He needed to attend the entire practice, but that meant getting back to Woonsocket by 3:30 p.m. Time was of the essence. The last thing he needed was sloppy driving conditions slowing him down.

He was a few streets from his house, still trying to figure out how he was going to get everything done, when he saw her. He couldn't really see her face because it was hidden behind the scarf she had wrapped around her head, but he could tell she was a woman in her seventies, maybe older. She was on the sidewalk in front of her little house shoveling the sodden snow. For most people the shoveling wouldn't have been any big deal, but for an elderly woman, it was a struggle. A few cars in front of him had already passed by without paying much attention. They had their own concerns: the kids had to get to school, they had to get to work. They all needed to be somewhere in a hurry, just as Dave did. And after all, it was just a little bit of snow, he rationalized as he drove past her. He couldn't afford to take twenty or thirty minutes to help a little old lady. He drove to the corner in front of the woman's house and made the turn that would lead him to the highway. He could no longer even see her in his rearview mirror, but he couldn't get her out of his mind. He pulled his van off to the side of the road, trudged back to the woman, grabbed the shovel, and dug into the snow—while dressed in his business suit and dress shoes.

Dave is every bit a man of his time. In December 1997, he was in his early forties. He was college educated and wasn't ashamed to admit that he knew how to party when he was a student at Providence College in the late seventies. He can walk into a sales meeting dressed in a suit and tie and talk about sales quotas, economic projections, and product marketing without missing a beat. Like so many other guys his age with young families, he has to hustle to provide his with a comfortable little suburban home and the amenities of modern life, whether it's clothes from Gap Kids or a Dodge minivan.

Yet there's something uniquely different about Dave from most guys his age. It's a "do unto others as you would want done unto you" philosophy that dictates his daily life.

"I hope somebody would do the same thing for my mother if she was shoveling," he said, explaining why he stopped to help the woman.

Without Dave there wouldn't be any modern-day Mount Saint Charles hockey legend. It would have ended when Bill almost died after his head crashed to the ice that February afternoon in 1983. It was Dave, with help from several other people, especially Tony Ciresi in the few years after the accident, who kept the Mount ship on an even keel while the captain regained his bearings. Without Dave, Bill would never have been able to remain coach of the Mount Saint Charles hockey team. Sure, some other assistant might have been able to handle most of the coaching chores the first year or so after the accident and probably even have led the team to state championships. The 1983 team that included Brian Lawton was so talented they might have been able to win without a coach.

But it took Bill several years to regain his memory, and even after that he would never have been able to handle the day-to-day mental pressures of running a high-caliber high school hockey program or the stress of a one-goal playoff game. Dave's presence allowed Bill to regain his mental strength by concentrating on what he did best as a coach. "Working on their minuses," as Bill puts it.

Bill could still be the practice taskmaster. Dave would then take what his father developed in those practice sessions and turn it into a winning team in games. Since Bill's accident, Dave has handled almost all of the line changes, power plays, and shorthanded alignments in games. Bill stands at the other end of the bench looking for individual faults and corrects them with a scream or a point of his thick finger at the offending player.

As the years have gone by, Dave has assumed an increasingly greater share of the team responsibilities. These days, Bill defers just about all of the final roster decisions to Dave. Bill still offers his opinion, but it's Dave who informs a kid that he's earned a spot in the Mount varsity room or that he's staying in the JV room. Dave also handles all of the scheduling of the games that aren't automatically set by the RIIL. In a sense, he's the bench coach/general manager of Mount Saint Charles hockey.

"Bill couldn't do it without Dave," said Brother Robert Croteau, who in the fall of 1997 was president of Mount Saint Charles. "Bill couldn't have handled all the mental pressure that goes with this job. Dave's being here allows Bill to do what he does best and not worry about the other things. I don't know how Dave does it with his family and his job. It's more than enjoying coaching. He has a real love for his father. He knows how much this means to his father."

When he first became his father's assistant back in 1979, he was very close in age to the players—almost one of their friends. These days he's like the guy with a young family who lives across the street from the players' homes. The players look at him as somebody who's not quite as old as their parents, but not exactly what they consider young. Dave *is* probably as old as some of the parents, but he looks younger than his age, and with two sons under the age of six in 1997 he projected the image of somebody who wasn't anywhere near middle age.

For years Dave was the salve for the mental soreness created by his father's coaching style. If a player had his feelings hurt by Bill's brashness and looked like he was ready to give up, Dave was there to give him a word of encouragement. If players had problems with skating or shooting they talked to Bill, but if they were confused about life, as almost every teenager is, they talked to Dave. Throughout the years, players would confide to Dave things they would never tell Bill, maybe not even tell their parents. But by the late nineties, Dave was sensing a change. As he took on more and more of the team responsibilities he found himself being the one doing the yelling. At times it seemed like the roles had been reversed. He was the screamer while Bill often seemed like the kindly old grandfather.

"My God, I've become my father," Dave said with a mocking laugh.

Dave may have inherited his father's deeply held religious faith and belief in the sanctity of the family, but he will never be his father's clone. If Dave is still coaching at Mount Saint Charles when his sons get there they will never have to go through what their father did during his playing days at Mount.

Dave is the third youngest of Bill's four sons. In many families, a middle child, especially the third of four children, can get lost in the shuffle. But Dave was never lost in the Belisle family hockey shuffle. In some ways it might have been better if he had. By the time Dave was in junior high, it was obvious he was a better hockey player than his older brothers, Bill Jr. and John. Bill Jr., the oldest of the four boys, didn't spend much time playing hockey when he was growing up. Because Bill Sr. was still playing a lot himself when Bill Jr. was young, he wasn't obsessed with his son playing. Bill Jr. didn't even attend Mount Saint Charles. He enrolled at another parochial school in Providence, where he played baseball, but not hockey.

John and Dave were hockey players and both came of age as their father's playing career was winding down. It was John, who's a year older than Dave, and some of his friends who convinced Bill to coach their peewee team when they were about twelve years old. It wasn't so much that they thought he would be a great coach; they just didn't have anybody else who knew much about hockey.

John and many of those same friends were the ones who went to the Mount principal in 1975 and told him that they wanted Bill as coach for their senior year. John was a capable player who went on to play Division III college hockey at Assumption College in Worcester, but he didn't have Dave's talent. He wasn't as strong on his skates and didn't have Dave's hands. But in a sense his talent made Dave a perfect target for his father's coaching obsession. If Bill was going to demonstrate that no player was above his system, then he had to make sure no one felt his son was getting special treatment.

"He was a real asshole to me when I was playing, He was tougher on me that anybody," Dave said.

As he looks back on it now even Bill isn't afraid to admit that maybe he was tougher on Dave than on anyone else. Maybe he was using him as an example—if his own kid couldn't get away with anything than no one could. Maybe it also was a father's pride. Maybe he felt Dave had talent and he could help him develop into a great hockey player. Whatever the reason, there were many tense moments between father and son during the two years Dave played at Mount. The worst came during his senior year. He was having an off day at practice. In disgust, Bill ordered his son to walk home—a three-mile trek. Most of the trip is along a long road at the bottom of a hill that follows the banks of the Blackstone River. It can be a lonely trip any night after dark, but especially on a cold January evening.

When Bill walked into the house that night without Dave his wife immediately asked where he was. Bill gave some off-the-cuff remark that he was still at the rink. Although it seemed strange to Yvette, she didn't say anything—until Dave trudged into the house.

"My mother is a saint. It takes a lot to get her mad, but she went wild when I told her my father made me walk home. She read him the riot act and he just sat there and didn't say a thing," Dave recalled.

Dave might have spared his father the full force of his mother's wrath if he had added the fact that he really didn't walk all that far. Larry Tremblay, his father's assistant coach at the time, had waited at the rink until he was sure Bill was safely out of sight before hopping into his car and picking up Dave alone the road less than a half mile from the rink. But even now Dave admits that he took a little pleasure from seeing his father in the hot seat.

For twenty-six years, until Mount finally lost in 2004, a common Mount hockey trivia question was: "Who was the captain of the last Mount hockey team to not win a state championship?"

The unfortunate answer? "Dave Belisle."

Although Dave was one of the best high school players in Rhode Island during his senior year in 1977, he wasn't good enough to lead Mount to a state championship.

He also wasn't good enough to make an impact at the college Division I level while at Providence College. He was listed on the PC hockey roster in his freshman year but didn't see much action. The following year, Coach Lou Lamoriello recruited a large group of talented freshmen and Dave was cut.

"It was one of the most devastating days of my life," said Dave. "I couldn't believe my hockey career was finished. Lou wanted to stay on my father's good side because he knew he would want to recruit Mount players so he gave him a new pair of skates. Everybody was happy except me."

Dave's hockey exile only lasted a few weeks. After his cut from the PC roster, his father asked him if he wanted to be one of his assistant coaches. Dave harbored serious reservations about working with his father, but he loved hockey enough to put them aside. So two years after he played his final game for Mount, he became a member of the Mount coaching staff. Not surprising, there were some rough spots during the first few years of the father-son coaching combination.

"I remember we were playing a game one night and they started arguing with each other right on the bench during the game," said Bill Dean, a member of the 1981 state championship team. "Dave got so mad he jumped off the bench and went into the locker room. Then Bill followed him and you could hear the two of them screaming at each other in the locker room. We were in the middle of a game and there was nobody there to make the line changes so we made them ourselves. Finally Bill came back and said Dave was taking a little vacation."

Love can overcome a lot of difficulty, even for two headstrong coaches, so eventually father and son learned to work together. The bond strengthened after Bill's accident. By the late nineties, Bill would often say it was Dave's team now, that Dave was the one making the decisions. Many people assume that when Bill finally retires, Dave will simply take over as head coach. But I don't think that's going to happen. Spend time with the Belisles and you can't help but get the feeling that it's more a case of when Bill decides he's had enough, Dave will also leave. For as much as he enjoys coaching, enjoys the competition of matching wits with other coaches,

Dave's greatest satisfaction comes from knowing that without him his father would have had to give up something he still cherishes. Today, the Mount Saint Charles legend is dependent on a middle-aged guy who stops to help old ladies shovel snow and deeply loves a father who once made him walk home in the freezing cold.

CHAPTER 16

It was December 24 and Dave was trying to conjure up the Christmas spirit, but it wasn't easy. At Mount Saint Charles, practice the day before Christmas is always at noontime; every Mountie knows that, or at least Dave thought they did. First there's practice and then there's a party in the dressing room with pizza from the Adelard Arena snack bar. It's been a tradition since Bill became coach. It's not listed on the season schedule, but every parent whose son played Mount hockey for a year or two knows his or her son is going to be busy on Christmas Eve afternoon. It is an important practice, the last one before the holiday tournament starts on December 26.

This year, Dave was looking forward to getting much accomplished. For once he didn't have to worry about rushing to practice from a sales call in Massachusetts. For at least a day he was a full-time hockey coach. He could work on getting the forward lines moving the puck out of the zone more efficiently. He hadn't been happy with the way the forwards were breaking out of the zone: the passes were late, and no one seemed to be anticipating what their linemates were going to do. To do that, a player must feel comfortable with the other guys on his line, instinctually knowing which way the other guy is going to skate. It requires hours of working on drills together. The Christmas Eve practice would afford them those hours. But Dave's plan had been sabotaged because senior Jerry Turcotte wasn't at practice. In earlier years, a Mount Saint Charles hockey player wouldn't dream of missing a practice as long as he was able to walk into Adelard Arena.

"You had two dental checkups a year, and you made sure your parents scheduled one in October before practice started and the other one in April after the season was finished," said Paul Guay. "You didn't want Bill not seeing you skating. He's not very good with names, but he remembers if you do something right in practice. If you impressed him in practice, you might move up on the lines. But if you're not there you couldn't impress him."

But today's kids are different from the kids back in Guay's high school days in the early eighties, even Mount Saint Charles hockey players. It seemed almost every day there was a note on Bill's desk explaining why somebody would be late for or even miss a practice. They were excuses that never would have been offered for consideration a decade or so earlier, such as a college visit or staying after school to make up work. Ten years earlier, every Mount player made sure he didn't have any work to make up so he that he wouldn't be late for practice. But by 1998, missing a practice no longer was considered a mortal sin by some Mount hockey players.

So Dave had become accustomed to excuses, but Turcotte's excuse frustrated him.

"He's having a family picture taken," Dave said. "He's one of the few kids who has ever transferred here, so his mother didn't understand the tradition. She made the appointment for a family picture the day before Christmas because she figured nobody practices on Christmas Eve. The kid didn't want to miss practice, but what could he do?"

Dave was right that Turcotte didn't want to miss practice. Of the twenty-four players sitting in the Mount dressing room, nobody had worked harder than Turcotte to be there. Everyone had to work at playing hockey to wear a Mountie uniform but Turcotte also had to wash dishes to wear it. He was one of only two players on the 1997–98 Mount team who had been raised in Woonsocket. He had grown up spending three or four days a week each winter in Adelard Arena either playing for his Woonsocket North Stars youth hockey team or watching Mount Saint Charles games. He grew up watching Keith Carney, Garth Snow, and Brian Berard and dreaming of the day he would wear a Mount uniform.

But when he was starting high school it cost a little over $5,000 to attend Mount Saint Charles, and his family just didn't have that kind of money. His parents were divorced and although his father was still very involved with his children, his mother was a single parent raising a family. It was a challenge just coming up with the money to pay the utility bills, clothe the children, and put food on the table. There wasn't anything extra for a private-school education.

Turcotte's dream was right down the street from his home. He knew he had the talent to play at Mount, but his mother had to tell him that the family just didn't have the money. For his first year of high school he enrolled at Woonsocket High, instead. Yet, he kept thinking that maybe someday, somehow there would be a way he could attend Mount—a desire his parents knew wasn't going to just fade away. They'd also heard that if he played at Mount it might pave the way for college, possibly even a scholarship, which wasn't going to happen if he played at Woonsocket. After his freshman year they sat down to talk about transferring to Mount. If he was willing to work, both during the summer and during the school year and put his earnings toward paying some of his tuition, somehow his parents would find the money for the rest.

Turcotte never told Bill or Dave why he hadn't started at Mount. The Belisles didn't ask and he never volunteered the information. He also didn't tell the coaches that a couple of nights a week, after finishing two hours of practice, and on Sundays, the only day he didn't have to practice, he worked as a busboy clearing dirty dishes off tables at a well-known family restaurant about ten miles from Woonsocket. Few of his teammates even knew he worked. Working a part-time job is not something most Mounties do. Of course, he would have liked to have been home relaxing as most of his teammates were doing instead of spending Sunday afternoons cleaning dirty dishes. But he never wallowed in self-pity. He was where he always dreamed of being, and if for him the price of wearing a Mount uniform included cleaning dishes, along with the usual tired legs and sweat endured by all Mount players, then that was the way it had to be.

It's never easy for a Mount newcomer. You build your credibility with Bill over time. That's how Bill gets to know you, even if he can't remember your name. That's why at least half of the Mount players over the previous two decades didn't see any appreciable playing time until their senior years. And for all Bill knew, Turcotte was just trying to take a shortcut to being a Mountie. He had talent, but not the Bryan Berard, Jeff Jillson kind that would make him an immediate impact player. He needed to work his way up through the Belisle system, and he had one less year to do it than the other guys in his class. But somehow he did it. In his first year at Mount he played junior varsity. In his junior year in 1996–97, he had seen some varsity playing time on the third and fourth lines. Finally, in his senior year he was determined to be one of the top scorers. Things had been going fairly well the first two weeks of the season. He had two goals in the first three games, but Dave thought he could do a lot more. He needed to work on his focus around the cage. He needed to work on picking his spots better, not rushing shots, but not holding them too long so that the defenseman had a chance to get a stick on the puck. He needed to practice, but instead of practicing that Christmas Eve, he was having a picture taken.

"Something like this never would have happened ten years ago," Dave said. "His mother just doesn't understand."

Mount Saint Charles hockey is not a woman's world. No woman has ever stepped foot into the Mount varsity room, at least not during the season. No woman has ever seen a complete Mount practice.

Yet, if it wasn't for a woman, the Mount Saint Charles hockey mystique might have self-destructed long before Bill became a high school coaching legend.

Yvette Belisle has been the quiet force behind the Mount hockey success for a quarter of a century.

She has known Bill from the time she was a little girl growing up in Manville. A few years her elder, Normand Belisle was one of the older boys in the village who didn't really pay much attention to the girls because they were too busy playing hockey and baseball. But by the time he graduated from high school, Bill knew Yvette Beaudoin was the girl he eventually wanted to marry. Like most kids growing up in the factory village of Manville in the forties, college wasn't really an option for him. He started working immediately after graduating from Mount Saint Charles in 1949. One of his jobs was working for Yvette's father, who ran his own small business and was also involved in local politics. But two years later Bill was drafted in the Korean War build-up. Before he left for the army he asked Yvette if she would marry him when he came home.

Bill's dedication to detail caught the eye of the army, who sent him to Quartermasters Leaders school shortly after he was drafted. He quickly rose to the rank of sergeant and was shipped off to France in 1952. While in France he was offered another promotion to full staff sergeant. It would have been quite an accomplishment for a guy who was only four years out of high school, but it would have meant committing three more years to the army. Bill was comfortable with that, but he figured he better check with the girl he left back home. He sent Yvette a letter telling her about the promotion and asking her how she felt about him staying in the army for three more years.

He didn't have to wait for the mail call to get his answer.

"She sent me a telegram," Bill said. "It said 'The army or me.'"

Bill turned in his uniform and was on a boat back to America a few days later.

By the start of the 1997–98 season, Bill and Yvette had been married for forty-five years. Through all those years, she's been completely dedicated to her husband and her family. She is the one who stayed home with her young sons in the fifties and early sixties while their father kept his love of hockey alive by playing in semi-pro leagues around New England. She's the one who said it was all right when her husband told her he wanted to give up a job as a construction company mechanic to accept a lower-paying job as manager of Adelard Arena because it would get him closer to hockey and Mount Saint Charles. She's the one who nursed Bill back to health immediately after the accident. She's also the person who went through the rough times as Bill battled the effects of the injury and the frustrations he encountered in his drive to prove he could still coach.

"There were some years my father was tough to live with, especially the year after the injury," said Dave. "He was trying to prove to himself and everybody else that he could do it. It was tough for the players, but especially tough for my mother because she was with him every day."

After the accident, Yvette was the person who encouraged Bill throughout his struggle to regain both his sense of balance and sense of being. But she has also always been the person, maybe the *only* person, who knows how to show Bill that there are some things more important than hockey.

These days Mount Saint Charles hockey players don't practice on Christmas, although there was a time when the Mount hockey team did. They might still be if it wasn't for Yvette.

"I remember when Brian Lawton was playing. He and the other guys on the team were hockey nuts," recalled Dave. "That's all they cared about, so they wanted to practice on Christmas. I wasn't married at the time so I said I would run the practice. We practiced from 7:00 a.m. to

9:00 a.m. By the time I got to my parents' house it was ten o'clock and the whole family was there waiting for me to open the presents. My mother was really mad. She wasn't mad at me, she was mad at my father for letting me hold practice on Christmas. She said 'This Mount thing is getting out of control. It's affecting the family.'"

Mount Saint Charles has never had another Christmas Day practice.

For as much as Bill cares about Mount Saint Charles hockey, it has never been more important to him than his family. It's just that once in a while he had to be reminded of what his priorities are. The only person who has always been able to do that is the neighborhood girl he fell in love with fifty years ago.

Two large baking pans of pizza were already sitting on the training table in the middle of the dressing room when the first players came off the ice from the Christmas Eve practice. Within minutes after the players' arrival the pans were almost empty.

"Manager, how they doing with the pizza out in the snack bar," Bill yelled to Josh, one of the mangers. "Go get some more."

Josh looked panic-stricken. He had just returned from the lobby so he knew the next pans were still about ten minutes away from coming out of the one pizza oven in the snack bar. The woman running the snack bar had been a little late putting in the first wave of pies so everything was a little behind schedule. But there was no way Josh was going to tell Bill that he couldn't deliver on the coach's command.

"Slow up a little, will you guys?" Josh quietly asked a few of the young members of the team, making sure Bill couldn't hear him. But it was no use. How do you slow down a group of hungry teenage boys from eating free pizza?

"Manager, I told you to get some more," Bill yelled again when he saw the empty pans.

Josh considered telling Bill about the baking problems, but he decided that it wouldn't be a prudent move. He had only been the team manager for a few months, but he had already learned Bill doesn't want to hear excuses—he just wants results. If you prepare for something the proper way, whether it's a hockey game or a pizza party, you don't have any problems.

Josh headed to the lobby where he would have a better chance of avoiding the coach's wrath than if he waited in the dressing room.

Eventually the pizza arrived and everybody had their fill. Bill was standing in the middle of the locker room and he actually looked like he had a smile on his face. "Coach," Jeff Jillson shouted. "We didn't get a chance to buy your Christmas present, but we'll get it for you in the next couple of days."

The room broke into an uproar.

Every year the team buys Bill a case of Heineken for his Christmas present; it's a Mount Saint Charles hockey tradition. No one asks how a group of sixteen and seventeen-year-old boys are able to secure a case of beer. It just appears every Christmas.

It's no secret Bill likes his beer.

He's no longer the hard drinker sitting with a bunch of guys filling a table with empty bottles the way he and his teammates did when they played in the Worcester Amateur League in the fifties. By 1998, his postgame libation was consumed in his office at Adelard long after the players have left the locker room. In the back of the rink, in a locked room behind where the Zamboni is parked, Bill has a refrigerator that always has at least a six-pack along with the bucket of pucks that he stores in there to keep them hard. He enjoys relaxing with a beer after a game, talking about hockey.

Sometimes Dave or Chris Murphy stay awhile, but usually not long. After a Friday night game, Dave wants to get home because he needs to get up at six o'clock Saturday morning to drive his sons to hockey practice. Chris loves hockey, but in 1998 he was twenty-three years old and single. Even through the second game of a doubleheader might not get over until close to eleven o'clock there was still plenty of time for a guy his age to find something to do that is more exciting than sitting in a sweaty locker room. More than once in 1998, I found myself the willing companion for his postgame beer and conversation. It was during some of those late nights in the Mount locker room that I learned some important things about Bill.

"Do you ever feel sorry about the way you treated your players? Ever think maybe you were too tough on them?" I asked him one night.

"The year after the accident," Bill replied without hesitation.

"It wasn't about the players. It was about me. I wasn't trying to be mean. It was just something inside of me. I was frustrated. I still couldn't remember a lot of things. I still was recovering both physically and mentally. I was trying to prove to people and to myself that I could still do it. I wasn't really sure myself that I could still do it."

"I wasn't fair to the players or their parents. After the accident I couldn't remember anything that had happened during it or before it. My memory came back by people telling me things that had happened. That's what happens when you have a fracture from the front to the back of your skull.

"I remember after a game in Cranston. We won but I didn't like the way they played so as soon as we got back home I told them to put on their sweats and get on the ice. I didn't let them call their parents. That wasn't fair to the parents. Their parents didn't know where they were. We were on the ice more than an hour. The parents were calling the rink, asking if the bus had gotten back because they were worried about their child. Marcel [Bill's assistant rink manager at the time] told them the team was on the ice. It was well past midnight. If I was a parent I would have been mad, but none of them ever said anything to me. I'm not proud of it. I wasn't thinking as a parent."

CHAPTER 17

Joel Jillson knew it was inevitable that people would compare his son to Bryan Berard. Jeff Jillson was Berard's immediate successor in a line of great Mount Saint Charles defensemen. Jeff started his freshman year at Mount in the fall of 1993, three months after Berard left Mount to play major junior hockey. They both had good size, although Berard wasn't as big as Jeff. They also both had that special offensive flare that you don't often find in defensemen. Some hockey fathers might think it was wonderful for people to compare their sons to one of the best young players in the world, but Joel knew it was unfair to Jeff—at least in 1998.

Berard's game was more mature when he was a junior at Mount Saint Charles in 1993 than Jeff's game was in his senior year in 1997–98. Jeff was still discovering how to use his size, and he was only starting to develop that real passion for hockey that Berard had since almost the first day he stepped on skates at the age of six. The first time Jeff tried skating he cried.

Linda Jillson will never forget the vision of her son's first venture on an ice rink.

"I can still picture him. He was this little thing huddled up against the boards crying his eyes out. He was four years old and we put him in a learn-to-skate program, but he didn't want anything to do with it. He came off the ice and said he never wanted to skate again."

But two years later, Jeff changed his mind. Some of his friends had started playing hockey so he told his parents he wanted to put the skates on again. The second time was a charm. Once he started playing again he loved it. He also played soccer and baseball, but hockey became his favorite.

"I just loved everything about hockey," Jeff told me during his junior year at Mount in 1997.

Despite a love of the game he never became a youth hockey zombie. He never spent twelve months a year in hockey rinks while growing up.

"I always put the skates away in the spring and didn't bring them out again until the fall," he recalled. "My parents were firm believers in taking a rest from hockey and doing other things."

Jeff didn't start skating in the high-powered New England high school summer leagues until after his freshman year at Mount. He made remarkable progress during his sophomore and junior years, but his game was still a high-potential work in progress in 1997–98. By his junior year at Mount, Berard knew he wanted to be a professional hockey player and there was nothing that distracted him from that focus. By his senior year, Jeff also knew he wanted to be a pro some day, but there were a lot of other things he also was thinking about at the time. At Mount Saint Charles practices, Berard was like a premed student in a human anatomy class. He knew exactly where he was going and he knew what he needed to study and worked at mastering it. Jeff, on the other hand, was more like a smart high school kid in Chemistry II. The kid knows that someday he wants to be a doctor, therefore it's important to learn the material, but there are a lot of other things swirling around in his life, especially if he's smart. A high school kid isn't always sure what path he should follow to fulfill his dreams. Some days he just wants to be a kid and other days he wants to be a young adult. At times he's brilliant in class, but there also are times when he lets some of the other things in his life take priority over schoolwork.

Smart kids can often get away with neglecting their classes, though. That was Jeff in Professor Bill's hockey class in 1997–98. There were times when he amazed both Bill and Dave with how quick and accurate he was with his shot. The coaches marveled at how well he moved on his skates for a kid his size. Some days he was the hardest worker in practice, but other days he didn't seem to be focusing on the drills. It almost seemed as if he felt that he didn't need to work on some of the basics Bill was practicing over and over again. There were times he made mistakes that infuriated Bill. In his opinion, Jeff had the potential to be a great player, but he still had a lot to learn. Bill was willing to teach him, but sometimes it seemed Jeff wasn't paying attention in class. Nothing upsets a teacher more than a brilliant student who doesn't pay attention.

It probably wasn't surprising that Jeff had become defensive of criticism, even from Bill. Berard had made mistakes in games when he played at Mount, but Jeff's mistakes were scrutinized more thoroughly. The spotlight didn't really start shining on Berard until late in his junior year at Mount. The first in-depth story about him, in any newspaper outside the Woonsocket area, was a piece I wrote for the *Providence Journal* in January 1993, a few months before he played his last game at Mount. Other than the hard-core hockey fans, people didn't start paying attention to Berard until the year after he left Mount and it started looking like he would be the top choice in the 1994 draft. If Berard made a mistake during his Mount days Bill probably was the only one paying much attention. During Jeff's junior year, he had been the subject of a host of stories and TV spots. Everyone knew agents were calling him. Once he decided to stay at Mount for his senior year, Jeff Jillson was in the spotlight from the first day of practice—and he didn't always want to be there. It was more than just observers sitting in the stands evaluating his play. He became the lightning rod for the Mount Saint Charles disdain that exists in Rhode Island.

You don't win as much as Mount Saint Charles wins without creating some animosity. Some Rhode Islanders love to find reasons to cheer against Mount, just like they love to cheer against the Yankees. For decades Bill has been a target of the anti-Mount ravings because of his Spartan coaching style, but he insulates himself from criticism. He lives within his world behind the closed doors of Adelard Arena. As long as his players and his family respect him, Bill doesn't care what anyone else thinks about him—or at least he acts that way. Jeff gave the Mount haters a new target. So what if he was only a seventeen-year-old kid? He was a Mount Saint Charles player whose name and picture was constantly in the paper and there were many people who assumed that that made him fair game for heckling.

There also was a significant difference between the teams Berard played on in his last year at Mount and the 1997–98 team. No one else on the 1992–93 team had Berard's level of talent, but it was a team loaded with gifted players, including Berard's best friend, goalie Brian Boucher. If Berard made a defensive mistake there was a pretty good chance Boucher would cover up for him with a great save in the goal. Jeff didn't have that security blanket behind him. If Jeff got caught up-ice or made a mistake that gave up a two-on-one break there was a good chance the other team would score. Anytime it happened, especially when Mount was playing on the road, the jeers would echo from the stands. "You're never going to be a good as Berard" was one of the favorite taunts thrown at him. That in itself really wasn't an insult to Jeff. Mario Lemieux wasn't as good as Wayne Gretzky, but that doesn't diminish Lemieux's status as one of hockey's all-time greats. But it's tough for a seventeen-year-old kid to make that rationalization. The fact that the jeering seemed to bother Jeff just added fuel to the hecklers' fire. If Berard had ever heard jeering from the crowd, he would have ignored it. Berard grew up in a family of seven children. Kids who grow up in big families learn to be tough-skinned. They learn from their brothers and sisters not to get upset about little slights to their egos. Linda and Joel Jillson didn't necessarily pamper their oldest son, but there's no question that as one of three children in a comfortable, middle-class family, he wasn't accustomed to hearing a lot of criticism, especially not in public.

Joel knew his son's upbringing was a lot different from his own days growing up in the social section of Woonsocket. Jeff hadn't really been hardened against what at times can be a cruel world outside his suburban home. It was one of the things that concerned Joel about Jeff staying at Mount for his senior year. He knew that the spotlight would be directed at him. He knew that there were a lot of people who disliked Mount Saint Charles, and he knew some of them wouldn't hesitate to use his son as a target for their scorn. Only a month into the season, his concerns were proving accurate.

It was going to be a long season for both Jeff and his father.

In baseball it's the Yankees versus the Red Sox. In college football it's the University of Florida and Florida State. But when it comes to American high school hockey there isn't a stronger rivalry than Catholic Memorial and Mount Saint Charles. In a way it's a strange rivalry. Usually high school rivalries are between two schools linked by either geographic proximity or long-standing history of competition. Mount Saint Charles and Catholic Memorial are neither in the same state nor do they have any long tradition of competition. Yet by 1997, Catholic Memorial and Mount Saint Charles had become two of the best-known high school hockey teams in America so therefore anytime the two teams meet it's a hockey happening. Like Mount Saint Charles, Catholic Memorial is a private Roman Catholic commuting high school. It's located in West Roxbury, a Boston suburb. Catholic Memorial had fielded varsity hockey teams at least since the forties, but it wasn't until Bill Hanson became coach in the early eighties that CM became a Massachusetts hockey power. Hanson was a former CM player who went on to play at Boston University before returning to teach and coach at CM. Hanson was more than just a good coach, he also was a great salesman for his program. He also became heavily involved in the USA Hockey's youth hockey programs in the Boston area. It wasn't long before the top young metro Boston hockey prospects were enrolling at CM rather than at some of the other Boston parochial schools. CM won its first state title under Hanson in 1986 and it kept winning. By the 1997–98, season, it had won nine of the previous eleven Massachusetts state titles. And that's in a state that has approximately two hundred high school hockey teams.

The Mount Saint Charles–Catholic Memorial rivalry started a few years after CM won its first Massachusetts state title under Hanson back in 1986. The promotion department of the *Providence Journal*, which had a long history of helping promote high school sports in Rhode Island, decided it would be a good idea to hold a tournament during the Christmas holidays with eight of the top high school hockey teams in the Northeast. There was no question that the feature attractions were Mount Saint Charles and Catholic Memorial. No one was surprised when those two teams reached the championship game in all but one of the first four years of the tournament.

It may have been Catholic Memorial versus Mount Saint Charles, but in essence it was Massachusetts against Rhode Island. It was one of the few times little Rhode Island had a chance to win bragging rights over its much bigger neighbor. Hockey fans in southeastern New England loved the match-up. It was standing room only at Brown's Meehan Auditorium when Mount and CM met in the tournament title game. The rivalry just kept getting hotter as CM kept winning Massachusetts titles and Mount continued its string of Rhode Island championships. When the *Journal* dropped sponsorship of the tournament in 1995, Hanover High in New Hampshire hosted the event for a year, but New Hampshire just isn't the high school hockey powerhouse of the Rhode Island–Massachusetts area. Starting in 1996, Mount Saint Charles hosted the holiday tournament instead. In addition to providing Mount with some exciting nonleague games it would also be a way to raise money for the new Zamboni needed at Adelard Arena.

Mount invited eight of the top parochial high school hockey teams in the country to spend the three days after Christmas in Woonsocket. When they set up the tournament brackets it wasn't coincidental that Mount and CM were on opposite sides. The whole tournament was geared around having a Mount Saint Charles–Catholic Memorial title game.

That's what had happened during the first tournament, and CM won. There wasn't any reason to think that there wasn't going to be another CM–Mount match-up in the 1997–98 tournament final. But before Mount could seek revenge for the loss in the first title game it needed to get past a couple of teams who could ensure themselves of a successful season in just one night with an upset of Mount Saint Charles.

Mount's first opponent was Malden Catholic High of Malden, Massachusetts. Malden had been the runner-up to CM in the Massachusetts state tournament the previous year, but from the outset of the game it was obvious that Malden's strategy was to stop Mount by hitting, legally or illegally. In the first period alone Malden picked up four penalties, but the ploy was doing the job. Despite the four Mount power plays, the game was scoreless after the first period.

The last thing Dave wanted was a chippy game in the opening round. Because the tournament always begins the day after Christmas, the first-round game usually is a little sloppy. The Christmas Eve practice is always comparatively short, and there isn't any practice on Christmas Day, so Dave would prefer to use the first-round game to get the timing and skating legs back after what's basically a two-day break.

Despite the chippiness, by the second period the Mount players seemed to have their skating legs back. With just more than four minutes to play in the second period, Chris Snizek finally broke the scoreless tie. Then, just before the end of the period, Joe Cardillo drilled home a rebound for a 2–0 lead. Yet, even with the lead and a better than a two-to-one shot advantage, Dave was still worried, and not just about the game.

On Christmas morning, Bill's next-door neighbor, a young man confined to a wheelchair, was having trouble negotiating his chair up the icy ramp that led to his apartment. Bill offered his assistance, but couldn't push the chair and the man up the ramp. He tried picking them up—a sixty-eight-year-old man carrying a wheelchair with a grown man in it. He was doing fine until he slipped on a patch of ice, sending the chair, the neighbor, and himself to the ground. The chair and the neighbor were unhurt, but Bill seriously bruised his leg. He was in so much pain that he couldn't even stand and had to sit in a chair all Christmas Day. Doc Guay examined the leg the next morning and advised Bill to stay home. But as long as someone was willing to drive him, there was no way Bill was going to miss the game. By game time, his knee had swollen to the size of a soccer ball.

"That's the blood clotting. He shouldn't be here standing on that leg," Doc Guay noted.

There was no use trying to convince Bill to go home so Guay stayed nearby just to keep an eye on his friend. Bill's leg was so sore and his knee so swollen that he couldn't even step up to assume his usual spot at the far-end bench. He instead parked himself in the alleyway down behind the benches, which start sloping down almost immediately. He couldn't even see what was happening on the ice, but he kept walking back and forth behind the bench patting players on the back and congratulating them for a good shift when they sat down. So what if he couldn't see what was happening on the ice? Dave would take care of that. His team was playing, so as long as he could move, even if it was with a lot of pain, Bill was going to be there.

"Look at him. Most guys hurting that bad would be in the hospital," Jillson had said softly during the break between the first and second period as he watched Bill hobble up and down the alleyway.

No one had to tell Dave about his father's grit, but that didn't stop him from worrying that maybe Bill was pushing it too much. In addition to watching what was happening on the ice in front of him, every so often during the game he would look back to make sure Bill wasn't in too much pain. Of course he knew there wasn't anything he could do even if he thought Bill was suffering too much. His father wasn't going to leave his team.

Dave also had other worries out on the ice. Malden players poked and slashed Jillson all night. They weren't going to try to hit a six-foot-three, 220-pounder head-on, but every time Jillson touched the puck it seemed a stick was up around his hands or upper body. Finally, midway through the third period, a Malden player took a vicious slash at Jillson's wrist as Jillson skated past him. The referee saw the hit and blew the whistle for a penalty. After the whistle, Jillson calmly skated around the back of the Malden cage and headed toward center ice where the offending player was skating toward the penalty box. He wasn't charging toward the Malden player so the officials didn't pay much attention as he continued skating toward the middle of the rink rather than heading to the Mount bench. But when he finally caught up with the Malden kid he dropped his stick and literally picked him up off his skates and flung him to the ice. He then jumped on top of him and started punching. On the Mount bench, Dave couldn't believe what was happening. If he'd any inkling that Jillson had been skating toward a fight he would have screamed to him to get to the bench. But Jillson's nonchalant approach caught Dave completely by surprise. Dave stood on the bench helpless as he watched his star player heading for what he assumed was a certain two-game disqualification for fighting. But after the referees finally pulled Jillson off the Malden player, they merely called a double minor for roughing. Dave was bewildered—if there was ever a high school fighting penalty he had just seen it. Maybe the officials took pity on Jillson because the slash had been so vicious, he thought. Whatever the refs' reasoning, Dave was counting his blessings that Jillson was only sitting in the penalty box for four minutes rather than sitting in the dressing room facing a two-game suspension. The situation brightened further when Hutchins scored a shorthanded goal, increasing the Mount lead to 3–0. That's the way the game ended.

After the game, Dave ordered Jillson into the little dressing room coach's office with him and closed the door behind them. For almost ten minutes the two sat in the office. Not even Bill interfered. There was no shouting; not a sound could be heard through the door. Finally they emerged from the office and Jillson quickly showered and left.

"What happened?" I asked Dave.

"We had a conversation," he said with a little smirk on his face. "Jeff said he's not going to let anybody get away with trying to hurt him."

"What do you say?"

"I told him I understood, but we can't have that. It's going to hurt the team. I tried for humor. I told him if it happens again just look over to the bench. I'll be the one on his knees saying. 'Please, please don't hit him.' I told him to let me take care of it."

"Do you think it worked?"

"Who knows? Tomorrow is another night and another game. We'll see."

The chippiness didn't get much better the next night. St. Joseph High of Buffalo, New York, was hitting even more than Malden had done the previous evening. After two periods, the penalties were far outnumbering the goals.

"All I wanted was for the second period to end so I could get the kids into the locker room and ream them out. Tell them to just skate away from the late hits and the hits after the whistle," Dave said after Mount had eventually pulled out an 8–5 victory with six third-period goals. "I was proud of the kids in the third period. For the most part they did skate away."

The victory over St. Joseph's set up another Catholic Memorial–Mount Saint Charles title game, but Mount fans didn't have much to cheer about that year. Before the start of the season the word was the 1997–98 team could be one of the best Catholic Memorial teams in their history. By the end of the title game the prediction seemed accurate. Leading 3–2 midway through the second period, CM broke the game open with three goals later in the second period en route to an eventual 9–3 victory.

"We played our hearts out, but they're so fast and strong," Dave said after the game. "We have a lot of work to do."

Coach Bill Belisle gives his thumbs-up sign of approval to a Mountie during a game. *(Courtesy Mount Saint Charles Academy)*

Bill and Dave Belisle talk to players during a break in the action. *(Courtesy Mount Saint Charles Academy)*

The 1946–47 Mount Saint Charles hockey team. Bill Belisle is the first player on the left in the middle row. *(Courtesy Mount Saint Charles Academy)*

Mount Saint Charles Academy sits high on a hill above the city of Woonsocket, Rhode Island. *(Courtesy Mount Saint Charles Academy)*

The last thing Mounties see as they leave the Mount varsity dressing room. *(Courtesy Mount Saint Charles Academy)*

Yvette Belisle, former Mount star Mathieu Schneider, Coach Belisle, and the Stanley Cup at a 1993 party after Schneider helped the Montreal Canadiens win the Cup. *(Courtesy Mount Saint Charles Academy)*

The 1993–94 team, which included current NHL players Brian Boucher and Bryan Berard, celebrates after winning the state championship. Boucher is the second player from the left in the front row; Berard is the second player from the right in the back row. *(Courtesy Mount Saint Charles Academy)*

Seniors on the 1997–98 team celebrate after winning the Rhode Island state championship. Top *(left to right)*: Paul Fede, Pat Hutchins, Charlie Ridolf, Joe Peters, D. J. Pelletier, Jeff Jillson. Middle *(left to right)*: Mark Esposito, Jerry Turcotte, Kurt Stokinger, Joe Cardillo. Front: Jason Catalano. *(Courtesy Mount Saint Charles Academy)*

Fans share the excitement of winning a state championship with the players. *(Courtesy Mount Saint Charles Academy)*

Sean Jackson (center), the only junior on the 1997–98 team, served as the 1998–99 team captain and helped Mount capture another state title. (*Courtesy Mount Saint Charles Academy*)

Goalie Pete Capizzo makes a save during the 1998–99 season. (*Courtesy Mount Saint Charles Academy*)

Bill Belisle and Brian Lawton at Adelard Arena early in the 1982–83 season.
(Courtesy Mount Saint Charles Academy)

YEAR	PLAYER	ROUND	SELECTION	TEAM
\multicolumn{5}{l}{**Mount Saint Charles Players Selected in the NHL Entry Draft**}				
1980	Ed Lee	5th	95th	Quebec Nordiques
1981	Paul Guay	6th	118th	Minnesota North Stars
1983	Brian Lawton	1st	1st	Minnesota North Stars
1983	Tom McComb	6th	120th	Minnesota North Stars
1983	Jay Octeau	9th	171st	New Jersey Devils
1984	Alan Perry	3rd	56th	St. Louis Blues
1986	Dave Capuano	2nd	25th	Pittsburgh Penguins
1986	Matt Merten	9th	175th	Vancouver Canucks
1986	Sean Boudreault	12th	249th	Quebec Nordiques
1987	Mathieu Schneider	3rd	44th	Montreal Canadiens
1987	Garth Snow	6th	114th	Quebec Nordiques
1987	Marc Felicio	11th	214th	Minnesota North Stars
1988	Keith E. Carney	4th	76th	Calgary Flames
1988	Jeff Robison	5th	91st	Los Angeles Kings
1989	Keith P. Carney	5th	96th	Minnesota North Stars
1990	Dean Capuano	10th	210th	Boston Bruins
1995	Bryan Berard	1st	1st	Ottawa Senators
1995	Brian Boucher	1st	22nd	Philadelphia Flyers
1999	Jeff Jillson	1st	14th	San Jose Sharks
2003	James Pemberton	4th	124th	Florida Panthers

Brian Lawton meeting the media in 1983 after being named the first American-born player to be selected first in the NHL's entry draft. *(Courtesy Mount Saint Charles Academy)*

Four Mount Saint Charles players who went on to become stars at the University of Maine under the direction of the late Maine head coach Shawn Walsh.
Top row *(left to right)*: Chris Cambio, Keith Carney, Dave Capuano. Front row: Garth Snow. *(Courtesy Mount Saint Charles Academy)*

CHAPTER 18

"We're not in first place," screamed Chris Murphy. "Think about that. Mount Saint Charles is *not* in first place."

Murphy was standing in the center of the Mount Saint Charles locker room. The din of the Zamboni clearing the ice and a near-capacity crowd walking on the stands above the dressing room would have drowned out a soft-spoken person, but the players had no difficulty hearing Murphy.

In a few minutes Mount would play Hendricken for the first time of the season. Hendricken High is another of Rhode Island's parochial high schools. Located in Warwick, the home of the Rhode Island state airport, Hendricken doesn't have the tradition of Mount Saint Charles because the school didn't open until 1960 and didn't field its first varsity hockey team until 1970. But during the eighties and nineties, next to Mount Saint Charles, Hendricken had been the most successful hockey program in Rhode Island. Since 1981, Hendricken was Mount's opponent in ten of the seventeen state title series.

It was January 9, a month into the 1997–98 season, and once again Hendricken was making another push to replace Mount as the best team in Rhode Island. Hendricken was undefeated and Mount Saint Charles had lost a game. Mount Saint Charles was not in first place, and for Chris Murphy that was sacrilegious.

151

Murphy was in his first year as a Mount assistant coach. He may not have been in the NHL, like some other former Mount players, but he was one of the best hockey players Bill had ever coached.

"He was the first player who never played for me on the JV team," recalled Tony Ciresi. "Brian Lawton, Keith Carney, Garth Snow, they all spent time playing JV, but Chris was a varsity regular from the first day of his freshman year."

Murphy played a prominent role in four Mount state championships in the early nineties. In his freshman year in 1989 he scored two of Mount's first three goals in the final game of the state title game against La Salle. If he was three or four inches taller, he probably would have been in the NHL that night, but it takes more than hockey savvy to play big-time hockey these days. It takes size. There aren't too many Division I programs who were looking for a five-seven forward like Murphy.

Murphy attended the University of Connecticut, where he enjoyed an outstanding career playing against Division II and lower-ranked Division I teams. When he graduated he decided he wanted to be a teacher, but he hadn't taken enough education courses at UConn so he returned to Rhode Island to obtain the necessary credits for teacher certification. When he found out Mount needed a freshman hockey coach, who would also serve as a varsity assistant, he jumped at the chance.

He had grown up in Burrillville where hockey is almost a religion. His father was one of the best players ever to wear a Burrillville High uniform, but when it came time to go to high school Chris took his game to Mount Saint Charles. Bill's Mount Pride, that philosophy of never giving anything but your best effort, was ingrained in his psyche.

As a first-year assistant coach Murphy usually didn't say much in the locker room. Occasionally he would sit down next to a player and quietly talk about some individual flaw that he had noticed in the player's game, but that was about it. Speeches were for Bill and Dave.

But that night Murphy couldn't hold back. He stood against the wall listening to Dave implore the team to "play for Coach B." To "go into the boards and if you get hit, don't retaliate because we don't need stupid penalties."

"Sure you will get him," Dave said, "but it will hurt the team. Let them retaliate. Let them get the stupid penalties. That's why we work on the power play.

"They're big, slow, and stupid," he added. "We're fast. We're not smart yet, but we're getting there."

With every sentence his voice rose. "Everything comes from him," he then bellowed, pointing toward Bill. "Everything I know I learned from him. You intimidate them, you poke them, and you jab them, but you don't retaliate."

He stood in the middle of the room without saying anything for a few seconds: a little pause for effect before delivering his final line, probably some cliché such as, "Now get out there and get them." He had no idea Murphy wanted to say anything, but the pause was the opening Murphy needed.

"We're not in first place!" Murphy screamed from his position near the front door of the locker. "Think about that—Mount Saint Charles is *not* in first place."

The sudden outburst caught both the players and Dave by surprise. They stared at Murphy, sensing passion.

Dave knew he didn't need to say another word.

Justin Laverdiere may have been only a freshman, but he didn't need to take a remedial course in Mount Pride. Like Turcotte he was a Woonsocket kid who grew up watching great Mount players at Adelard Arena. There wasn't any Mount family tradition—in fact, his father had played at Woonsocket High School—but Justin had grown up gazing at those banners hanging on the Adelard wall. He started skating there when he was only four years old, and all along the youth hockey route he was one of the better players on the team. Even Bill noticed him.

"I would see this kid skating at the peewee practices and no matter what he was doing, he did it well. I didn't know what his name was but I remember thinking, 'He's going to be a good player,'" Bill recalled.

Now that kid with a lot of promise was one of his players.

"Mount Saint Charles was the only place he ever wanted to go to school," Justin's father said. "He grew up watching Mount games. His dream was to play at Mount."

So despite only having worn a uniform for a few weeks, Laverdiere completely understood what Chris Murphy was saying. Only five minutes after the start of the game, he gave Mount a 1–0 lead as he worked his way into the slot, took a pass from the corner, and fired it home.

Later in the first period, Paul Fede spun around with the puck at the right point and looked for an open man. When he saw no one, he headed into the corner and then passed out to the front of the cage. Too often that would have been the extent of his effort: make the pass and then stand watching to see what developed. It was what Dave and Bill were always complaining about, that he needed to keep moving off the puck, that he couldn't stand around watching things happen. If the play came back his way it was up to him to make them happen. This time he heeded the message. He quickly moved out of the corner after the pass and when the pass was deflected back toward him he was moving at a good clip toward the goal. The Hendricken defense didn't have a chance to stop him and he beat the Hendricken goalie high on the right side.

Six minutes after the start of the second period, Laverdiere struck again giving Mount a 3–0 lead. About less than a minute before the end of the second period, sophomore Josh Venice increased the lead to 4–0. There was still a period to play so Dave didn't want anybody feeling too comfortable, but as the team sat in the dressing room between the second and third period waiting for the Zamboni to finish cleaning the ice, he was feeling good about what he had seen in the first two periods. It was only three days after they had lost to Catholic Memorial and both Dave and Bill still had doubts about this team's character. Although it was a senior-laden team there was little leadership. The Belisles had worried that some of the players would come into the Hendricken game still licking their wounds from the Catholic Memorial loss. They were concerned that rather than focusing on beating Hendricken there would be too many seniors still feeling sorry for themselves, worrying that their play in the tournament title game might have cost them some college attention. But that hadn't happened. They were playing one of their best games of the season. Maybe the team had finally matured.

After talking for a few minutes about needing to work in avoiding odd number breaks, Dave sent them back to the ice with a final mission.

"Let's have a good period. I want to make a statement," he shouted.

Jeff Jillson certainly wanted to make a statement when he hit a Hendricken forward skating across ice-center midway through the third period. Jillson put his whole six-foot-three, 220-pound frame into the hit. He dropped down a little, leaned his shoulder into the player, and then followed through into the player's chest sending him backwards into the air. It was the type of hit you don't see too often in high school hockey.

Standing in his usual spot at the end of the rink, Joel Jillson was pleased.

"Good hit. That's the way they teach them to hit," he said.

But a split second later, Joel's mood turned sour.

As soon as a Mount player touched the puck, one of the referees blew the whistle and called Jillson for high sticking.

"That's disgusting. That was a perfect hit. It's only because it's him. They're looking to call them on him. I wanted him playing someplace else this year," Joel said.

It was one of the few unguarded moments during the season when Joel had allowed his emotions to take control and let it slip out that he really wanted to let Jeff leave Mount Saint Charles. For family harmony, however, he'd backed his wife's desire to keep their son at home.

When the buzzer finally sounded the end of the game, Mount had a 6–0 victory, and sole possession of first place, but a frustrated superstar.

The following night the schedule had Mount playing St. Raphael again, this time at Adelard. Dave wasn't looking forward to the evening.

"How do you get them up for a game against a team they beat 13–1 a month ago?" he asked.

But once again Dave was pleasantly surprised by how the team responded. Joe Cardillo scored only forty-nine seconds after the opening face-off and Pat Hutchins, another senior, made it 2–0, just over a minute later. St. Raphael did manage to cut the deficit to 2–1 late in the first period, but sophomore Chris Chaput made it 3–1 before the end of the period. Then Turcotte, Josh Venice, and Cardillo each scored in the second period giving Mount a comfortable 6–1 lead by the start of the third. As they headed to the locker room for the break between the second and third period Dave and Bill simply wanted to play out the final fifteen minutes without injuries or controversy. For once they were willing to let a Mount team put it on cruise control for a period. But they were learning that nothing was simple this season.

Shortly after the start of the third period, Jillson and a few other players were battling for a loose puck along the boards in front of the visitors' bench. No one could gain control, so the referee blew the whistle. Jillson was backing away from the other players when a St. Raphael player came skating across from center ice and hit him from behind with a cross-check. The hit caught him completely off-guard, sending him flying back on his ass. The St. Raphael kid, who had a reputation for being a loose cannon, was trying to goad Jillson into a fight and for a second it looked like he had succeeded. Jillson was furious. He jumped up and took a few quick steps toward the St. Raphael player. The referees, seeing what had happened, moved quickly to get between the players, but it really wasn't necessary. Jillson suddenly stopped as if Dave's words were echoing through his mind: "Don't retaliate. Let *them* get the stupid penalties."

On the other side of the rink Dave had moved from his usual spot standing on the second row of the Mount bench to the boards in front of it. As soon as he saw the hit, he assumed that Jillson was going to jump up and go after the kid and he was ready to start screaming. But he didn't have to yell; Jillson had showed maturity. He was taking one for the team.

Both Dave and Jillson thought that the St. Raphael kid should get a major penalty, but when the official went to the penalty box he assessed two penalties, one to the St. Raphael kid for cross-checking and one to Jillson for roughing.

Jillson was incensed. He yelled to the referees: "I didn't do anything. What was that penalty for?"

The refs didn't want to hear it. They skated away, telling him to get in the box and shut up. But Jillson wasn't about to quit. He had shown maturity, he had done what the coach said he needed to do, and he had gotten screwed. He kept skating after the officials.

"I'm the captain. I want an explanation."

But the officials had become defensive.

"Get in the box or you'll get a misconduct," one of them told him.

Now Jillson looked toward the Mount bench, expecting to see either or both coaches yelling at the official. But neither Dave nor Bill was yelling. They didn't understand the penalty, but by that time it was a 7–1 game so why get in an argument with officials? There was a good chance that those same officials would be refereeing much more important games later in the season. Why get a bench penalty and have some official develop a bad attitude toward Mount in a meaningless game? Bill and Dave just stood there, complaining to the team members that the call was ridiculous, but not complaining to the officials.

Eventually Jillson went to the penalty box, but he was now more upset with his coaches than with the officials. They hadn't backed him up. He was doing what they said he needed to do if he cared about the team, but when the officials screwed him, they didn't say anything. Ninety seconds sitting in the penalty box didn't temper his resentment. When he came back to the bench after getting out of the penalty box, he slammed his gloves on the floor and muttered, "It's tough when your own coach doesn't stand up for you."

He didn't yell it, but he wasn't hiding his displeasure either. Everyone on the bench heard his gripe, including both Belisles.

Dave was pissed.

Jillson had valid reasons for his frustration—the officials were calling cheesy penalties on him, yet letting people hack at him and not calling anything. But Dave couldn't have Jillson displaying open disrespect for the coaches. He wasn't really worried about himself: it was his father that he felt Jillson was disrespecting.

"Get in the back of the bench and stay there for the rest of the game," Dave yelled at Jillson.

Jillson's gut reaction was to storm off the bench, head to the locker room, and rip off his uniform, but he stayed put.

Of course it wasn't just his displeasure at Jillson's lack of respect that prompted Dave to take Jillson out of the game. Jillson was furious, and Dave didn't want him back on the ice picking up a game disqualification. But he didn't tell Jillson that.

When the game ended, Jillson stormed into the locker room. He dressed, showered, and was one of the first players out the door.

Neither Dave nor Bill said anything to him.

"He's mad. He doesn't want to talk about it," Dave told his father.

Bill didn't care if Jillson was mad. "Tell Jeff to watch his mouth," he said to Fede, Cardillo, and Hutchins after Jillson had left the dressing room.

Dave knew his father was mad, too. Bill didn't really understand what Jillson was going through. If Brian Lawton, Keith Carney, and Bryan Berard could keep their mouths shut, Bill didn't see any reason why Jillson couldn't. Because Monday is a busy day for sales calls, Dave normally doesn't get to practice until the final half hour or so. But on his ride home from the game Dave started worrying that his father might say something to Jillson before Monday's practice that would inflame the situation again. When he got home he called his father, who would still be in his little office in the locker room.

"Don't be too mad at Jeff," he said.

"If he ever says something like that again, I'll throw him off the team," Bill warned his son. "If he wants to talk to me, I'll be here before practice on Monday."

Dave hung up the phone and immediately started rearranging his schedule so that he would be there for the start of practice on Monday.

CHAPTER 19

He's instantaneously recognized by all New England sports fans of voting age. When they see him their minds automatically project the picture of him flying through the air after scoring the winning goal in the 1970 Stanley Cup final. That's what I first thought of when I saw Bobby Orr at Adelard Arena on that January night in 1998.

If I'd had any doubt that we're living in a different sports world these days it was removed that night as I watched arguably the greatest hockey player of all time standing outside a dressing room waiting for a seventeen-year-old Rhode Island high school kid.

"Would you like to go into the locker room?" someone asked Orr that night.

"No, that's okay. I'll wait," he politely replied.

Most seventeen-year-old hockey players would wait in line for hours to get Bobby Orr's autograph. That night, Jeff Jillson had Bobby Orr waiting for him.

Orr now is a professional sports agent. Given his stature in the hockey world, it's not surprising that he has quickly become one of hockey's most influential agents. And he wanted to add Jillson to his client list.

Orr had called Linda and Joel earlier in the week. He wanted to see Jeff play Saturday night against La Salle.

"How do you tell Bobby Orr you don't want him watching your son play?" Joel asked the night before as he watched Mount play St. Raphael's.

But Orr was the only agent the Jillsons were saying yes to those days.

For months the calls had been coming almost daily. Sometimes it was an agent trying to convince Linda and Joel that he was the one who could make their son a wealthy young man. Another time it would be a college coach who wanted to talk to Jeff about scheduling an all-expenses-paid visit to his campus. It was the second week of January and Jillson still hadn't decided whether he was going to opt into the 1998 NHL draft or wait until 1999. The midyear draft forecasts had come out that week and Jillson had dropped to thirty-three among North American skaters. He was the top American high school player, but there was no question that his standing in the 1998 draft had seriously slid because he had decided to stay at Mount. But that didn't stop the agents and it made the college coaches more insistent because they knew the possibility of Jillson opting for college rather than a direct pro route had become more likely.

"It's getting out of control in our house. We have to put a stop to it," Joel complained. "We need to get an advisor."

It had become the season of hell for Joel. He no longer enjoyed the simple pleasure of watching his son play a high school hockey game. Every time he watched, he now worried that he was endangering his son's future by not purchasing an insurance policy covering a career-ending injury. But a policy like that was going to cost at least a couple of thousand dollars— and that kind of money wasn't in the Jillsons' normal budget. Should they go into debt or take a chance? If Jeff was definitely going professional in the spring they could sign with an agent and the agent would pay for the policy. But signing with an agent would immediately make Jeff ineligible to play in college. Of course there are some agents who are willing to lend a family the money for the policy with only a gentleman's agreement that the player would eventually sign. Under NCAA rules, that's illegal. But as long as nothing was signed who would ever know? Joel was getting a fast lesson about the slime that coats professional sports these days, but he didn't want anything to do with it. So on most nights that Mount played at Adelard Arena, he stood behind the boards near the front of the rink and mixed the joys of watching his son play a sport he loved with the fear that he might sustain an injury that could jeopardize his future.

The night before Orr's appearance Mount had played its second game in eight days against St. Raphael. Once again it was a total mismatch. By the middle of the second period Mount was ahead 6–0 and Joel was worrying.

"That's a stupid penalty. He's trying to prove he's tough. He sees the rankings and it bothers him," he said that night when Jeff was called for a charge. "That's an uninsured player out there. I worry about him every time he plays now, but especially in games like this. Games like this are when stupid things happen."

Joel had been careful not to tell many people that Orr was planning to attend Saturday's game.

"The big guy is coming tomorrow, but do me a favor and don't say anything," Joel told me Friday night. "They don't want a sideshow."

It's tough not having a sideshow when Bobby Orr is in a New England hockey rink. To avoid a commotion in the lobby, Joel arranged for Orr to enter through the back door near the Zamboni. Orr tried being inconspicuous, sitting alone with Joel and Linda in the seats at the far end of the rink. But it wasn't long before word spread around the rink that Orr was in the house. Fathers handed their children scraps of paper and told them to go get his autograph. By the second period almost every time there was a break in the action, one or two little kids wearing hockey jackets would rush over to Orr and timidly hand him a piece of paper. Orr graciously fulfilled every request. He seems to understand that his standing as one of the greatest hockey players carries an obligation. These little kids are the future of the game, and the bottom line is Orr loves the game. After years of signing close to a million autographs he must get tired of it, but that night he signed every slip of paper. Here were his roots. It wasn't a card show with collectors pushing color photos and hockey sticks in front of him so that they can profit from selling Bobby Orr–autographed items. This was little kids wearing hockey jackets in a rink with wire screening on top of the boards. It was about as pure as it gets in today's sports world.

Occasionally Orr even got to watch some of the game.

"He's bored out there," Orr offered about Jillson. "He should be playing someplace else, but he's living in a house divided. It's tough on him and his parents. He wanted to play someplace else and his father wanted to let him, but their family is important. It will work out."

Mount was struggling on a night Dave knew shouldn't have been. After two periods the score was tied 1–1 and in his opinion it was because too many of the players weren't focusing on the task at hand. It was Saturday night, which meant that there was a good chance several of them had been out partying after Friday's game, especially the seniors.

As soon as the team filed into the dressing room, waiting for the ice to be cleared between the second and third period, Dave started pacing the room, lecturing about keeping focus. With every step he took his voice seemed to raise a few octaves. He was facing the players in the corner near Bill's office when suddenly from behind him Jillson let loose with a loud fart that echoed through the room and left its distinctive odor. A fart usually sends a roomful of teenagers into uproarious laughter. But Dave wasn't laughing; he was infuriated. He didn't even look around to see who the offender was.

"If one more guy gasses while I'm talking, he's out of here," he screamed. "If you can't control yourself while I'm talking that shows you don't know how to focus."

He scanned the room, challenging any one of them to laugh. No one did, but it wasn't easy.

Whether it was Dave's criticism or Jillson's gastric interlude, Mount came out flying in the third period. Cardillo banged home a rebound off Jillson's shot from the point during a power play early in the period. A little later, Chris Lentini caught the La Salle goalie going the wrong way and gave Mount a 3–1 lead. La Salle scored with twenty-eight seconds to play, but by then the Mount victory was secure.

Everyone was already seated when Dave walked into the locker room after the game. You could see the look of satisfaction on his face.

"I guess they'll have to make more phone calls," he said sarcastically as he walked into the locker room.

It was a rare shift for Dave from his usual stoic approach toward people who were always trying to steal Mount Saint Charles players.

"They're always trying to get our kids," he complained.

The "they" is the other three parochial schools playing in the RIIL.

"The calls start coming as soon as we finish our tryout. The kids who don't make the varsity get the calls telling them they should transfer. There are three kids on that La Salle team that started here at Mount," Dave said.

The calls don't come from the coaching staffs at the other schools. That would be illegal under RIIL rules. The calls are made through the parental pipeline or some youth hockey coaches. It's always the same message: You're never going to play at Mount Saint Charles, so why don't you transfer? Quite often it's not the player who thinks transferring is the only answer, it's his parents.

"I remember one year we had this kid on the JV whose parents were upset that he wasn't playing varsity," Bill said. "One day he walked out without saying a word and the next day I found out he had transferred. He knew he was transferring, but he didn't want to say anything. Maybe he was embarrassed. Maybe he felt bad about leaving. I don't know because we don't even call our kids trying to keep them."

Somebody came in the back door and told Jillson Orr was waiting for him outside.

"I'll be there in a few minutes," Jillson said.

Let the legend wait.

"Coach do you want to talk to Mr. Orr?" Jillson asked Bill as he stepped into the little office at the far end of the locker room.

"No, he wants to talk to you," Bill replied.

Jillson took a few steps to the door, but he stopped abruptly and turned to Dave. "Coach, I'm sorry. That was me who farted. My stomach was just hurting."

The confession caught Dave by surprise. If he had known at the time it was Jillson breaking wind he might not have made the threat of kicking the next guy out. Even Dave or Bill doesn't throw out a superstar for an ill-timed fart.

"That's okay," he told Jillson, "I didn't know it was you. Haven't you noticed some guys aren't paying attention when I'm talking? It takes away from the focus. But they took the criticism and went out and did a good job."

The Saturday-night meeting with Orr was the climax of what had been a hectic week for Jillson. On Wednesday, University of Maine coach Shawn Walsh had traveled to Woonsocket. He didn't come on the weekend to see a game, he came during the week because he wanted to observe Jillson at practice.

"Everybody works hard in a game," Walsh said. "I want to see how they work in practice."

That Walsh had been sitting in Adelard that week watching a Mount practice shows that Bill has mellowed a little since the day back in 1983 when he threw Lou Nanni out of a practice when he came to see Brian Lawton. But the new attitude wasn't a carte blanche invitation for any coach to visit a Mount practice. At that time Walsh was the only collegiate coach who had ever witnessed a complete Mount practice. Bill figured he owed Walsh something because Walsh had taken more of his kids than any of the other big-time American college coaches. Walsh took a chance on Garth Snow when nobody else was interested. He also recruited Keith Carney and a few other Mount players. It was mutual admiration between Walsh and Bill.

"I like to get the Mount Saint Charles kids," Walsh told me that year. "You get guys with a good understanding of the game; kids who are coachable and can handle an intense coach. Not every player can handle an intense coach."

In the general sense there isn't a lot of diversity in hockey. In the mid-nineties, the NHL began an effort to bring diversity to hockey by helping fund inner-city youth hockey programs and assisting in the construction of inner-city hockey rinks. In the long run the programs probably will change the face of hockey somewhat, but for the immediate future the cost of playing hockey makes it a white, middle-class game in America. But the lack of extensive ethnic diversity doesn't mean there aren't a lot of different kinds of American kids playing the game. Other than sharing a passion to play hockey at Mount Saint Charles, Joe Peters and Charlie Ridolf were as different as two middle-class white kids could be.

Joe Peters was a play-by-the-rules teenager whose life seemed rooted in old-fashioned American values. He grew up in a family of four: himself, his mother, father, and younger brother. He started playing hockey when he was six years old and almost every year his father would take him to the state high school tournament. He became fascinated with Mount hockey watching guys like Keith Carney, Mathieu Schneider, and Garth Snow lead Mount Saint Charles to state championships. He would go home and fantasize that someday he would be playing for Mount in the state tournament. But his parents were never completely part of hockey culture. To them hockey was just a sport their son played. He would play high school hockey, but it didn't really seem to matter where as long as it was a good school with a good hockey program. When it came time for Joe to start high school, it only made sense to his parents that he go to Hendricken, which was only about a few miles from their home rather than Mount Saint Charles, which was almost forty miles away. Joe had told them he would like to go to Mount Saint Charles, but he wasn't the kind of kid who would mount much of a protest against his parents' wishes. He therefore enrolled at Hendricken as a freshman, hopeful that once he made new friends and started playing sports, his fascination with Mount Saint Charles would dissipate. It didn't. His year at Hendricken only heightened his desire to play for Mount Saint Charles. At the end of his freshman year he begged his parents to let him transfer to Mount and they agreed., even though there were no guarantees that he would ever play at Mount. He hadn't been a youth hockey superstar. He had decent size, but he didn't have great speed or the quick hands that enable players to convert rebounds into goals. But he had a dream.

Charlie Ridolf had a dream, too. He dreamed that someday he would play big-time college hockey. He also dreamed that someday he would be riding a Harley. But unlike Joe Peters, who knew the only way he would realize his dream of playing at Mount was by becoming a blue-collar, "bring you lunchpail" kind of hockey player, Charlie assumed that his talent would be his ticket for a joyride to the big time. He thrived on the excitement of hockey, but the rink wasn't the only place he went looking for excitement. Ever since he was young he always pushed the envelope, testing any sense of authority.

"He scares me," Charlie's father admitted about his son one day in 1998. "I have three sons and he's the youngest, but he's the one who worries me the most. He always seems to be doing things on the wild side."

Charlie began playing hockey in Rhode Island when he was a small child, but then he moved with his divorced father to Long Island. Long Island isn't exactly known for its youth hockey programs, but his father made sure Charlie's hockey career didn't suffer because of his residence. A long-distance truck driver, Charlie Ridolf Sr. would drive young Charlie wherever it was necessary to make sure he was playing against the best youth competition in the Northeast. When it came time for high school, Charlie moved back to Rhode Island and lived with a relative so that he could attend Mount Saint Charles. Every weekend during the hockey season his father would drive up to Rhode Island and stay in a motel so that he could see his son play.

Ridolf definitely had talent. He was only about five-feet, nine-inches tall, but he had quick acceleration on his skates and good hands around the cage. But his proclivity for walking on the wild side often hindered his hockey development. When he was fifteen years old he had been invited to the tryouts for the USA Hockey's National 15 team. After the first few days, he was right on the bubble of making the team, which would have been a big step in his hockey career. But just before the team was selected he and three other players were caught with beer in their room. They all were thrown out of the tryouts.

He came back to Mount and completed an outstanding junior season in 1996–97. He was one of the top scorers in the state and earned first-team all-state honors along with Jillson. But that spring he jeopardized his hockey career once again with his off-ice antics.

Although Ridolf preferred "not to talk about it," the word was he and a few other students violated a school code at a school function and were suspended from all extracurricular activities for the first semester of their senior year. Charlie would miss half of his senior hockey season. He had thought about transferring, but he really didn't have many options. His father couldn't afford to send him to one of the high-priced boarding prep schools, and even if he could Charlie probably would have had a tough time getting accepted. He was only seventeen but he had already developed a reputation within the New England hockey scene. Charlie had no choice but to return to Mount for his senior year and wait until he could resume playing in mid-January.

Ironically, Joe Peters, the kid who followed all the rules, found himself in the same predicament as Charlie Ridolf in 1997–98, although for entirely different reasons.

Joe's classroom performance was similar to his hockey game. He wasn't an academic whiz, but he had always studied hard enough to get satisfactory grades. But in the spring of his junior year an emotional one-two punch floored him. First, his mother underwent tests for an illness that the doctors couldn't seem to pinpoint. Although she was eventually diagnosed with the early stages of Parkinson's disease, the initial fear was cancer. Then, at about the same time, Joe's girlfriend broke up with him. Between worrying about his mother's illness and nursing his broken heart, he didn't pay much attention to his schoolwork. Although he didn't fail any of his classes, his grade point average for the final quarter of his junior year slipped below Mount Saint Charles athletic eligibility requirement. He was declared academically ineligible for the first semester of his senior year, and like Charlie he could not play until January.

It wasn't surprising Charlie and Joe approached their ineligibility differently. Charlie didn't seem the least bit embarrassed by his suspension. Although he couldn't skate with the team, he was a frequent visitor to the

Mount locker room before and after practices. Sometimes he would even get to the rink early and do a little skating before the team took the ice. Joe, on the other hand, never appeared at the rink; there was no question he was mortified. He had played mainly junior varsity in his junior year, but Dave had told him after the season, if he worked hard, he could be a varsity starter in his senior year. Now he had missed almost two months of the season because he hadn't done his schoolwork. He hadn't played a role in any of the previous state championship drives and nobody was really expecting that he would be a key player on the 1997–98 team, but in Joe's mind he had let down the team.

Although Joe usually avoided the rink he did, however, work out on his own. By the time he was able to join the team in early January the season was half finished. Some kids would have said it was too late, but not Joe. He still had two months to fulfill that dream of helping Mount win a state championship. It was a picture that had been in his mind since he was a little kid sitting in the stands watching guys like Keith Carney, Garth Snow, and Mathieu Schneider. You don't give up your dream just because it's late in the game.

CHAPTER 20

On the morning of Friday, January 16, 1998, there were only two American high school hockey coaches who had won at least 600 games, but by the end of the day there were three.

Ed Burns had won 695 games in forty years as coach of the Arlington, Massachusetts High before he retired in 1997. Willard Ikola won 616 games at Minnesota's Edina High in a thirty-three-year career that spanned from the late fifties to the early nineties. When Bill was hired as Mount Saint Charles's coach in 1978, Ikola was already an American high school coaching legend. He had directed Edina, a public school in a small city near Minneapolis, to eight state titles in the famous Minnesota state high school tournament. Ikola was the standard by which Bill measured success. Bill even tried setting up a series between Mount and Edina in the mideighties, but the Minnesota high school association wouldn't allow its schools to travel as far as Rhode Island for a game. So Bill never had a chance to coach against Ikola, but on that January night he was about to join his idol in the elite 600 Club.

The victory over La Salle the previous Saturday night was Bill's 599th in only twenty-three years of coaching. A victory over Toll Gate on January 16 would raise his tally to 600. He may have trailed both

Burns and Ikola in total victories but he had a far better winning percentage than both men. In fact, the .900 win percentage that he had amassed by January 1998, was one of the best winning percentages among veteran American high school coaches in any sport. For example, at the start of the 2001–02 season Morgan Wootten, the legendary coach of Maryland's DeMatha High basketball team had won 1,276 games, a greater number of victories than any other American high school basketball coach. But Wootten's win percentage over his forty-five-year career was "only" .870.

There was no question that Bill would eventually score his 600th victory, but Dave was worried that too many people were taking for granted that it would be that night. The headline on the front page of the *Woonsocket Call* sports section that day proclaimed "Another Milestone Moment Lies Ahead." The crowd was unusually large for a regular-season Friday-night game and the school president had arranged for a special ceremony at the end of it to present Bill with a memento of the evening.

But Dave knew that just because Mount had beaten Toll Gate 8–4 a month earlier didn't mean the second meeting would be an easy victory. He knew Toll Gate would pack in its defense around the cage in the defensive zone so as not to give Mount any rebounds. That meant Mount had to stay focused, be patient, and not get frustrated. Toll Gate wasn't going to out-skate Mount for forty-five minutes, but they had a few good players who were always ready to take advantage of any Mount mental lapses. Unfortunately, mental lapses had become regular occurrences for that year's team. It had also been exam week at school, the only time Bill holds optional practices. Years ago, the fact that practice was technically optional didn't make any difference to the team. Mounties didn't use the two hours that they could be at practice for extra study time. If they needed extra time, they burned a little more midnight oil. But these days, a few players will take advantage of the free pass from practice—not many, but a few. Dave was therefore a bit concerned as he stood watching the pregame warm-up.

"He will be embarrassed if we lose with all the hype and all these people here," Dave offered about his father. "I don't want that."

He also didn't want his father's milestone to become a distraction to the team. He wanted to get it out of the way quickly. If there was one thing this year's team didn't need, it was somebody creating a distraction for them. They were proficient enough at doing that themselves.

But apparently the 600-victory milestone also meant a lot to the team. Freshman Josh Venice gave Mount a 1–0 lead only 4:52 after the opening face-off and senior Pat Hutchins made it 2–0 before the end of the period. The game also was memorable for Charlie Ridolf. After sitting in the stands watching the team play for almost two months, he was finally eligible again. He had been practicing for a few days, but the comeback hadn't been going smoothly. His timing was off; everybody seemed to be on a different wavelength. Last year he had been one of the stars, one of the go-to guys. Plays were geared around him. He thought it would be the same way when he got back this year, but it wasn't. Some of the other seniors now had their own priorities. They had been doing okay without Ridolf for the first two months of the season. He wasn't Jillson. Everybody on the team knew they probably couldn't win without Jillson, but Ridolf was a different story. Having him might make them a better team, but he wasn't so good that anybody was willing to subjugate their game to his. Bill never said as much, but he agreed with his players. Ridolf wasn't his type of player. Sure he had talent, but in the past he had been undisciplined at times. Now in his senior year, when Mount players traditionally are expected to prove leadership, he seemed to be more out of control than ever. Bill didn't want to hear about how the kid was struggling to live up to his own expectations; he wanted a disciplined hockey player who was willing to work for the success of the team. Right now, Ridolf wasn't that player.

Dave, on the other hand, felt having Ridolf at the top of his game was very important to Mount's hopes of winning another state championship. It wasn't going to be easy, but he needed to get Ridolf under control.

In the second period, Ridolf showed how much he could mean to the team as he scored with a nice move. Later in the period, Jillson increased the lead to 4–0 with a blast from the blue line. Even Oliver seemed especially focused. In each of the first two periods he came up with a couple of good saves and didn't give up a goal until late in the third period. When the final buzzer sounded Mount had a 4–1 win and Bill had his 600th victory.

They held a little ceremony near the Mount bench and the president of the school presented Bill with a small plaque commemorating the event. Bill was all smiles, but Dave wasn't.

"Look at that little plaque. What kind of an award is that for 600 victories?" Dave grumbled as he walked into the dressing room.

There were times when Dave felt the Brothers of the Sacred Heart didn't fully appreciate what his father had done for Mount Saint Charles.

Mount was a school in trouble back in the midseventies. It was a Cjatholic school in an old city at a tough economic time in Rhode Island. Few people outside the area even know about Mount Saint Charles, and Woonsocket no longer could support a Catholic high school. Mount needed to attract students from outside the area, but it wasn't easy. Sacred Heart Academy, another school run by the Brothers of the Sacred Heart in another old Rhode Island factory city had closed in the early seventies because of low enrollment. A lot of people were thinking Mount would suffer the same fate.

The success of the hockey team certainly wasn't the only reason Mount started making a revival in the eighties, but it was one of the main reasons. People like to be associated with a winner. The hockey team's success made a lot of non-hockey parents curious about the school, even those who came from outside the Woonsocket area who'd never have considered Mount Saint Charles for their children if the hockey team hadn't put the school in the media spotlight. They didn't send their kids to Mount Saint Charles only because it had a stellar hockey team, but it was the hockey team that gave the rest of the school an opportunity to show what it had to offer.

Dave felt the Brothers of the Sacred Heart owed his father a great deal for all he'd done to promote their school. They were never going to pay him a high salary—that just doesn't happen at a New England Catholic high school, even if you win 600 hockey games. But he though at least they could have shown their appreciation with an impressively sized plaque.

The size of the plaque disturbed Dave a lot more than it did Bill. Bill was all smiles as he walked into the locker room, clutching the plaque and pumping his arm for his customary "hip, hip," postgame cheer. A few minutes later, someone dimmed the locker room lights and within a few seconds Jillson, still in full uniform with his skates on, tottered through the front doorway with a big sheet cake topped with burning candles. There weren't six hundred of them, but there were enough to light up the entire dressing room. Dave's sour mood evaporated. His father was happy and that was all that counted. Sure, somebody's mother had baked the cake, but for Bill it meant his boys cared about him.

These days, no Mount hockey parents would dare directly challenge Bill's coaching moves. They might question what the coach is doing during family discussions at the dinner table or while parked in the stands at Adelard, but after twenty-five years there are no secrets about what it's like to be a Mount hockey parent. No one asked them to send their children to Mount: it was their choice, and their son's. Parents may not think their son is getting enough playing time, but they're not going to question Bill because they know what his answer is going to be.

"If you don't like it, take your kid and get out of here," he'd say.

It's easy for a coach who has reached the legendary status that he now enjoys to take a hard-line approach, but for Bill it's been that way since the beginning. One of the main reasons he has become a coaching legend is that he was never willing to compromise his coaching philosophy for any player—or any parent.

One of the best goalies who ever donned a pair of pads at Mount was Allen Perry. Perry was already a youth hockey star when he enrolled at Mount as a freshman in 1981, only four years after Bill had become coach. Rhode Island fans predicted that he would step right into the starting spot at Mount in his freshman season. Bill didn't see it that way, however. Perry wasn't seeing as much playing time as his father thought he should in his freshman year so he expressed his dissatisfaction to Bill one day before practice. Bill didn't even give Mr. Perry an answer. He simply walked back to the varsity room, grabbed a plastic trash bag, and piled all of Allen's equipment into it. He then walked out to the lobby, deposited the bag at Mr. Perry's feet, and told him to take his kid and get out.

"Allen was the best goalie I had even seen at that age and Bill was telling his father to take him and get out," said Tony Ciresi. "That's the thing with Bill. There's never been any compromising."

Perry never left Mount. By his sophomore year he was getting more than enough playing time. He was a first-team all-stater in both his sophomore and junior years before leaving Mount to play junior hockey and eventually moving on to a minor-league professional career.

On the same night Bill was earning his 600th victory in Woonsocket, fifteen miles away at the Providence Civic Center, another former Mount goalie, Brian Boucher, was taking one more step toward fulfilling his dream of playing in the NHL.

There have been many Mounties through the years who didn't let a little adversity stop them from achieving a measure of success, but few were more determined to fulfill his dream than Boucher.

Boucher and Bryan Berard grew up riding their bikes together through the streets of Woonsocket and conjuring up visions of themselves as professional hockey players. But while Berard had taken the fast track to the NHL and was a pro star only three years after he played his final game for Mount Saint Charles in 1994, Boucher's journey to the NHL was taking a much slower route.

Boucher had always seemed to get lost in his best friend's shadow. The two had started playing together in the Woonsocket North Stars youth league when they were both five years old, skating around the rink. But when he was six, Boucher opted to become a goalie so that he could play with older kids.

"The mite team needed a goalie so I asked my father if I could play goal. He didn't want me to be a goalie, but he finally agreed," Boucher told me back when he was at Mount in 1994.

Boucher suited up as the goalie for a group of Woonsocket area kids who were some of the best young hockey players in New England for their age. With Boucher in the goal, Berard at defense, and several other talented players, North Stars teams won New England championships at almost every age-group level as they were growing up. When it was time for high school, Mount Saint Charles was the obvious choice for most of them. Just like Berard, Boucher enjoyed the challenges presented by Bill's coaching style. He was a tall, thin kid who didn't say much, but he wasn't afraid to take anything Bill dished out to him. Yet, the problem for Boucher was that his Mount Saint Charles teams were too good. His goal against average in both his sophomore and junior year was below 1.00, but nobody gave him much credit for the impressive stats. The consensus was that he was the beneficiary of a great defense, led by Berard, and an offense that outscored the opposition better than two-to-one. Berard was a first-team all-state selection in both his sophomore and junior years, but Boucher's only postseason honor was a second-team all-division selection in his junior year.

He had discovered what many Mount Saint Charles goalies had learned for decades before him. Mount goalies are the Rodney Dangerfields of New England high school hockey—they get no respect. In truth, without some clutch goaltending performances through the years, Mount never would have set the national record for most consecutive state high school hockey titles. Nonetheless, Mount has had so many teams that dominated its Rhode Island opposition that it's easy to understand how Mount goalies get no respect.

That didn't discourage Boucher. It would have been easy for him to think that the doubting Thomases were right when he didn't make it past the first cut at the tryouts for the USA Hockey National Select 16 team in the summer before his junior year at Mount. Berard, of course, became one of the team's stars. But Boucher kept working. Finally in the summer of 1994, some other people started recognizing his potential. He was selected for the USA Hockey Select 17 team and his play in a tournament in Mexico convinced him that he could compete at a higher level than high school.

Berard already had made plans to head to Detroit to play Junior A hockey, but Boucher had planned to return to Mount for his senior year. Instead, he packed his bags and headed to Canada to play for the Wexford Raiders of the Metropolitan Toronto junior hockey league, a second level junior league. Only a few months later, however, his seventeen-year-old world began unraveling. The coach of the Wexford team was fired and the promises made to Boucher about his living conditions—among other things—weren't being fulfilled. Yes, the competition was at a higher level than what he would have been facing playing Rhode Island high school hockey, but he was only practicing two days a week, far less than he would have at Mount. He was five hundred miles from home and he had a lot of spare time on his hands. It was a perfect prescription for homesickness.

It would have been easy to just call his parents and tell them he was coming home but he knew if he really was serious about playing professional hockey he needed to head in the opposite direction. Rather than traveling five hundred miles east to Woonsocket, he moved twenty-five hundred miles west to Kennewick, Washington, to play in the Western Junior Hockey League, a major junior league. It was more than just moving three thousand miles from home to live with a family he had only spoken to on the phone and to play at a level in which he wasn't quite sure he could compete. Players in the Tier-II Metropolitan Toronto junior league are still eligible to play American college hockey. But like the Ontario League where Berard played, the Western League is classified a major junior League. Under NCAA regulations, if you play in the Western League you are ineligible to play American college hockey.

Only nine months earlier, observers were saying Boucher wasn't even good enough to be a Rhode Island high school all-stater, now he was taking a chance that he could prove he was good enough to play in the NHL. Somehow he did it. By the end of the season he had become a legitimate pro prospect. That June, he was a first-round selection of the Philadelphia Flyers in the 1995 NHL draft, the twenty-second selection overall.

But even on what was the biggest day in his hockey career to that point, he still was living in the shadows of his best friend. The same day Boucher was the twenty-second selection, Berard was the number-one.

Even though he was a first-round selection, Boucher knew he was still a long way from the NHL. He played another year of junior hockey in 1996 and then played in a western Canadian professional league. He was constantly working to improve his game, even when he was supposed to be home on summer vacation. The day that I went to Adelard Arena the previous summer to talk to Bill and Dave about spending the season with the team, Boucher was on the ice with Peter Belisle. It was a beautiful, sunny summer day and Boucher was in a chilly, dim ice rink having somebody take shots at him.

Sports dreams usually aren't cultivated under bright lights.

On that night of January 16, he was in Providence playing for the Philadelphia Phantoms of the American Hockey League in a game against the Providence Bruins. His performance helped Philadelphia post a big victory that night. The word around Philadelphia that winter was that the Flyers were projecting him as one of their future stars. His dream of becoming an NHL player was becoming clearer.

Only a few players were still in the locker room celebrating Bill's 600th victory when Sean Jackson walked into the little locker room office.

"Coach, what am I doing wrong?" he asked, looking for an answer from either Bill or Dave.

He was the only junior on the team and at times he felt like he was existing in a no-man's land. He couldn't share the bond that has always existed among the seniors on the team, yet he felt he was too old to share the uncertainties that go along with being a freshman or sophomore. It was the only time in two decades that there was only one junior on the team. Three years ago, he'd had a couple of classmates on the team with him, but both of them left Mount, one for academic reasons and the other because he wasn't getting enough playing time.

He was constantly being changed from one line to another. To him it seemed that Bill was singling him out more than the others. There was some merit to his assumptions. Bill tends to treat the seniors as a group and he always gives freshman and sophomore some slack, especially early in the season. He allows them time to learn his system. That leaves the juniors as the players who traditionally receive most of the attention—and some of it is unwanted attention. They are the guys Bill thinks have been around long enough to know what they should be doing, but haven't earned the "security" of being seniors. When there are five or six juniors on the team serving as whipping boys isn't too bad; at least the lashings are spread around a bit. But in 1997–98 there was no other junior to share the burden with Jackson.

Ask the average Rhode Island sports fan why Mount Saint Charles has won so many state championships and you'll probably hear that it's because they've had so many gifted players. There's some truth to that answer. You don't win twenty-one consecutive state championships, as Mount had by 1998, even in a state the size of Rhode Island, without players like Brian Lawton, Bryan Berard, and Keith Carney. But even with nineteen NHL draftees on its alumni list, the key to Mount's success may be its marginal players more than its superstars. For every Brian Lawton, Bryan Berard, and Keith Carney there have been at least five or six Sean Jacksons. They are talented hockey players compared to the average American high school player, but at the level at which Mount Saint Charles competes, they're only marginal. The key to Mount success is that at practice the marginal players get just as much attention as the superstars. That can be a problem for players like Jackson, though. Bill expected as much from him at practice as he did from Jillson. That made for some long afternoons for Jackson because things didn't come as easily for him as they did for Jillson. But Bill believes that's how his marginal players learn how to play and how to accept pressure. They may not be in the spotlight during the season, but if their time comes, they'll be ready. Almost every year at least one of those "no-name" players plays a significant role in Mount's title drive. Sean Jackson knew the history, knew that someday it might be his day to shine. But on that night in 1998, he wasn't sure he could survive until that day.

CHAPTER 21

Pete Capizzo knew he was late for practice as he burst through the locker room door the Monday afternoon following the Saturday-night Toll Gate game. Everybody else was already on the ice, and even from inside the locker room Capizzo could hear Bill shouting. Officially he knew he had a good excuse for his lateness. He had gone to see a teacher about making up the work he had missed because he was out of school sick one day the previous week. The teacher had written him a note explaining where he had been, which might keep him out of Bill's doghouse, but it wasn't going to get him another chance to prove he should be the starting goalie. The only way that would happen was if he was on the ice. Even though he wasn't feeling great, he had played well in a couple of junior varsity games and with Oliver's up-and-down play you never knew when Bill was going to blow up at him. If he did, Capizzo needed to be there, ready to jump when Bill yelled, "Give me another goalie." The last thing Capizzo needed was for Bill to think he didn't care enough to be at practice on time. A note from the teacher would never make up for a missed opportunity.

He nervously rushed to get into his bulky goalie equipment, every second seeming like a minute. To make matters worse, he was suddenly hit with a coughing fit. It had been a few weeks with only a few minor coughing bouts, which made him think his health was improving. Then a few days earlier, the coughing had started again and there was more blood than ever. He sat on the bench coughing and trying to put on his goalie pads at the same time. Mucus had filled his mouth but he was in too much of rush to walk over to the toilet between the varsity and JV room. He instead spit into a white towel that was laying next to him on the bench. Just then, Doc Guay walked through the locker room on his way to Bill's office. The coughing caught his attention and when he glanced over at Capizzo he noticed the bloodstained towel.

"How long have you been coughing up blood?" he asked.

"About a week," Capizzo said, trying to play down the situation.

"Take your stuff off. You're going to the hospital for X rays."

"Sure Doc, right after practice. I can't miss practice."

"You're going right now," Guay fired back. "I'll tell Coach Belisle not to let you on the ice."

Capizzo didn't know it at the time, but his season was finished and his life would never be the same.

A few days later Bill came rushing through the locker room heading for his office where his skates waited for him. Practice was scheduled to start in about five minutes. Half of the team was already on the ice, but the others were still sitting on the benches putting on their equipment. Bill looked around as he kept walking toward the office. "You better be ready," he said to anybody who was smart enough to take the warning.

Bill wasn't happy with the way practices had been going that week. On Monday, Doc Guay had informed him that he was taking Pete Capizzo to the hospital for X rays because he thought the kid had pneumonia. Capizzo hadn't been in school since and nobody knew what the story was. Bill was concerned about his player's health and he also hated not having him at practice. Of course he never said anything to Capizzo, but Bill admired the kid's competitive spirit. He knew without Capizzo at practice, Oliver wouldn't feel challenged no matter what he did or said. To make matters worse, Jillson hadn't been at practice either Monday or Tuesday because he was on a recruiting trip to Maine. Bill wasn't happy about Jillson missing practice, but he understood that it's unavoidable at times. He puts up with it because Dave tells him that's the way it is these days. Bill also knew that missing two days of practice wasn't all Jillson's fault. He'd planned to fly to Maine Monday morning and then fly back on Tuesday morning in time to be back at Mount for practice. But it had snowed in Maine on Tuesday and his flight had been canceled so he ended up spending an extra day in Orono. He had called Bill on Tuesday morning, so at least he knew that Jillson was still thinking about the team, even if he wasn't going to be on the ice. But Jillson's absence on Tuesday just made Bill more irritable and by Wednesday he was downright cranky. Monday's and Tuesday's practices had been sloppy. Did the other guys think that if the team captain was taking a couple of days off then they also could take it easy? Or because it was the week after midterm exams did they think that they deserved a few days of easy practices after all the long hours they had put in the previous week studying?

Bill thought otherwise.

To Bill's way of thinking, on November 20 his players make a commitment for the season, which means that every day there's a practice they arrive ready to work. Practice begins the split second he blows his whistle. That's the players' cue to begin skating in a circle from center ice around the back of the cage, taking the turns at half speed and then sprinting down the straightaways. Sometimes Bill doesn't even wait until he's on the ice to blow the start whistle. He will blow it while he's still walking through the locker room and everyone on the ice better be listening and start skating immediately. A decade ago, he would blow his whistle and then just stand in the JV dressing room. The *whoosh* of the skates on the ice told him that the players were sprinting down the sides. Nobody dared not sprint because the coach wasn't there.

"These days I have to be on the ice, or they will take it easy," said Bill.

There's a reason that the whistle means the immediate start of practice. When the referee drops the puck for the opening face-off, the game begins. It doesn't begin two or three minutes later. There are workers who walk into their offices at the exact minute they are scheduled to report to work and then sip a cup of coffee while they read the paper before they start their day's assignment. That's not the way Mount Saint Charles hockey players start their workday. They don't take one more warm-up shot at the cage and then go leisurely to collect the pucks. Mount players do their stretching and get their equipment ready before Bill blows that whistle.

Every Mount Saint Charles player over the past twenty years can probably tell some horror story about not being ready for practice.

"People are always saying, I made my players skate in their underwear. We never skated in our underwear," Bill said one day with a laugh.

But he does remember one day when the players were afraid they were going to practice in the nude.

"A bunch of them had been slow getting dressed," he recollected. "When I blew the whistle at three for the start of practice, they still were warming up. So I told the whole team to go back into the dressing room and strip down to their birthday suits. What a sight it was when I went back into the room. There were a lot of peckers hanging around there. They must have thought, 'This guy is weird.' I took out my watch and told them they had five minutes to get dressed and get back on the ice. Then I went back on the ice and waited. I actually gave them eight minutes, but I had guys coming out with pads hanging off, skates loose, and shirts on backwards. I didn't say what would have happened if they weren't there in time, but I guess they didn't want to find out."

"Why do things like that?" I asked.

"Because they're spoiled, but they don't realize it," he replied. "They have the rink and they have their own dressing room. They don't have to bring their equipment home like every other high school player does. They walk out of here after practice and don't have to worry about anything because the managers take care of everything for them. But sometimes they take that for granted. Sometimes I have to remind them of it."

Jillson was back for Wednesday's practice, but even then there were more distractions.

Jillson had been selected to be the *Sports Illustrated* Old Spice Amateur Athlete of the Month. It was a new advertising promotion the magazine had launched that year. Each month it selected an outstanding amateur athlete and featured his or her picture and bio in a full-page Old Spice advertisement. The *Sports Illustrated* photographers who were shooting the photo had arrived at Adelard about an hour before the start of practice so they could set up a mini studio in the lobby. They needed a posed shot of Jillson in uniform and on skates, but they didn't want to try shooting it on the ice so they set up backdrops, lighting, and rubber mats in the lobby.

When they first arrived and had checked in at Bill's main lobby office to ask where they could set up, Bill couldn't have been more gracious. He welcomed them into his office, sat down with them, and answered all their questions. He then asked them what they needed and made sure they got it. The photographers couldn't get over what an amiable, cooperative gentleman he was. Because Jillson didn't arrive until just before the start of practice, the photo shoot meant he was going to miss some of the it.

"No problem," Bill told the photographers.

"Hurry up Jeff, you don't want to keep these people waiting," Bill advised Jillson as they headed toward the locker room.

Changing into or out of his equipment quickly was not Jillson's strong suit. The two photographers were still standing in the lobby waiting for him when they heard the team starting practice inside. Rather just stand around in the lobby, they walked through the doors to watch. They weren't in the rink more than thirty seconds when they heard a shout from the far end of the rink.

"Get out, get out," Bill bellowed as he skated toward them. To the photographers, he looked like a sixty-eight-year-old raging bull with a helmet on his head and a hockey stick in his hands, waving his arms and screaming, "Get out!" They couldn't believe that this was the same guy who fifteen minutes earlier couldn't do enough to help them.

"Let's go. We'll get this done fast," they said to Jillson when he finally arrived in the lobby.

"Sorry," Jillson said "I didn't know you were in a rush to get out of here."

"We're not in a rush," one of the photographers said. "But I'm not getting your coach mad at me for keeping you out of practice. Is he always like that at practice?"

"Most of the time," Jillson said with a laugh.

Even *Sports Illustrated* wasn't going to disrupt Bill Belisle's practice.

Dave had been tied up with sales calls longer than he expected on Wednesday afternoon so there was only about a half hour left in practice when he finally hit the ice.

"I don't need you," Bill yelled.

Ten years earlier that type of outburst from Bill would have probably provoked a shouting match between father and son. Bill was annoyed that Dave wasn't at practice when the team needed a lot of work. Dave was upset that his father didn't understand the problems he has trying to balance his work schedule with practice and spending time with his family. A decade ago they probably would have argued, but these days Dave just smiles. It's no longer a battle of egos. Dave is comfortable with his father's emotional tirades. In a way he likes to see Bill get energized. It shows that he still has the spark in him. There are times when Dave worries about his father. He worries that the old brain injury may affect Bill as he gets older, but it certainly wasn't affecting him that day. So Dave skated off to the boards near the bench and stood watching the drills, occasionally offering words of encouragement to players as they skated past.

Dave didn't realize that about thirty minutes earlier, his father had been showing more of the Bill Belisle of old. In the middle of a drill he spotted Jackson doing something he didn't like. He went charging up to Jackson and starting screaming in his face. Rather than simply listening, Jackson made the mistake of asking, "What am I doing wrong?"

Bill wasn't in the mood for questions.

"Get out of here," he yelled.

Jackson was frustrated, but he knew better than to continue the debate.

At least he understood the routine. Although Bill had thrown him out of practice that day the next day he could return with a clean slate. Bill's grudges never last more than a few hours. For two decades, Mount players have been thrown out of practice with the command, "Get out and don't come back." But they always came back the next day.

At least most of them did.

Brendan Whittet was a star defenseman for Mount in the early 1990s. He was also an outstanding student who went on to Brown University. But when Bill screamed at him one day to get out and don't come back Whittet took him at his word.

For three days Whittet went home right after school worrying that his career at Mount was finished. Yet within a few hours after he had thrown Whittet out of practice, Bill forgot about it. When Whittet missed practice the next day, Bill assumed that he was sick. When he missed another day, he asked one of the other players what was wrong with him.

"You threw him out, Coach."

Bill phoned the Whittet's home that evening.

"His father told me I said he was no good and to get out and don't come back. I said I didn't really mean that. I think he was the only one I had to call and tell him it was okay to come back," he said with a chuckle.

The practice session might have ended, but Bill wasn't finished. Usually he remains on the ice and circles the rink clearing the snow from the bottom of the boards so there won't be piles of ice building up around them. But this day he followed the players into the locker room.

"Sit down. Don't anybody shower," he yelled.

Then his rant started.

"You don't care. Instead of being in here getting ready for practice, instead of working out in the weight room you're outside in the cars with the coochies" (Bill's nickname for girls).

He then proceeded to pace the room, stopping now and then to confront a player. With his face less than a foot away from the player's he then pointed his finger. "You don't care," he screamed and then hopped over to another player and berated him for not skating back at full speed after a drill. He worked his way along the bench on one side of the locker room, jumped over to the other side of the room, and lit into the players sprawled on the bench below the bleachers. As a finishing flourish, he grabbed the twenty-gallon trash bucket that sits on the floor next to the training table and hurled it against the wall. Either he was lucky or he carefully planned his toss, for the barrel didn't hit any players en route to the wall. But those sitting on bench next to where it hit, popped from their seats to avoid the ricochet. Bill didn't say another word. He just stalked out the door and headed back to the rink to clear the edges.

Dave had been sitting in the little locker room office taking off his skates and watching the episode unfold.

"He's got their attention," Dave said with a little smirk.

CHAPTER 22

When you looked into Kurt Stokinger's eyes in late January, you saw an angry young man. Some people might say it was frustration, but there's a difference between frustration and anger in a teenager. If you looked into Stokinger's eyes and the eyes of a few other players who weren't seeing as much playing time as they would have liked you knew the difference.

Stokinger was one of the team's four senior defensemen. On the first day of practice he was sure this was going to be the year he joined the legion of Mount players who came out of obscurity in their senior years to play a major role in the team's drive to another state championship. The season had started out well. He was seeing regular shifts at defense and he even scored Mount's first goal of the league season in the opening game against La Salle. He assisted on another goal in the season's second game, but since then he hadn't scored another point. Halfway through the season it had become obvious that his value to the team had been diminishing rather than increasing as the season progressed. At about five-feet, eleven-inches tall and 180 pounds he had good size and he certainly had played enough hockey. He was from a blue-collar South Boston family and had spent his youth hockey days playing eleven months a year in the crazy world of the metro Boston leagues. His parents were divorced and he came to live with his father in a southeastern Massachusetts town so that he could go to junior high at Mount Saint Charles. He then had planned to apply for admission at Catholic Memorial, but he liked Mount so much that he stayed for high school.

He had some talent, but not as much as he thought he did. That's not unusual for young hockey players, but Stokinger's bigger problem was that he didn't have discipline, at least not Mount Saint Charles discipline. He considered himself a tough kid and apparently he had decided if he couldn't be the team star then he was going to impress college coaches by being the team enforcer. He was going to show them that he wasn't afraid to hit guys and didn't back down from anybody. Bill and Dave, however, felt that too often he went looking for trouble. He'd make a good play, but then he'd pick up a penalty. That doesn't fit with Bill's simple philosophy of disciplined hockey. Every year Mount is one of the least penalized teams in Rhode Island. You're not going to do a lot of scoring if you're always killing off penalties. But that hadn't stopped Stokinger. When Jillson got into a shoving match with a Catholic Memorial player in the holiday tournament title game, Stokinger jumped right into the fracas.

"Somebody had to help Jeff out. You have to protect your teammates," he said, sounding like a true NHL enforcer.

Mount ended with two penalties, however, while CM only received one because the referees charged Stokinger with being the first man into the fight. To Stokinger, he had defended his teammates; to Bill and Dave, he'd given CM the advantage with a stupid penalty.

At the start of the season, Stokinger thought he was going to be one of four defensemen in the regular defensive rotation. He wasn't better than Jillson or probably not even Fede, but he assumed that he'd be number-three on the depth chart. He was bigger than Esposito and had a better shot from the point, and he had a lot more experience than the sophomore and freshmen defensemen. But by midway through the season, it was obvious to him that the coaches pegged him as their fifth defenseman. He thought he should have been playing ahead of Esposito, but even though Bill was constantly finding fault with Esposito, both he and Dave felt Esposito wasn't going to hurt the team as much as Stokinger. It also had become obvious that the Belisles liked sophomore Matt Kasberg. Ever more frequently they had been sending Kasberg out with Jillson rather than Stokinger. Kasberg complemented Jillson. He was young, but he knew his role was to cover up when Jillson went on the offensive.

Stokinger had missed about a week of practice in early January with an injury, which didn't help his cause. Now with the season moving into the final push toward the playoffs he was only getting spot time as the fifth defenseman and he wasn't happy about it. Stokinger never understood that on a team such as Mount's you have to adjust your game to the team's needs.

"He's a little loose; you never know what he's going to do," Dave noted. "I feel sorry for him sometimes because I think he has problems that go beyond the hockey rink. He once told me his father would hit him after a game if he didn't play well. You don't know if it's true or he's just trying to get sympathy."

A lot of high school athletes in Stokinger's position would have just quit. They weren't going to sit on the bench in their senior year. But Stokinger would never quit; hockey meant too much to him. Being part of this team was his life. So the anger kept building in his eyes. Each game he came hoping it would be the night he'd get the opportunity to show how he could help the team. If they would give him a chance, he would make a statement.

He probably would have made a statement, but it wasn't the kind of statement the Belisles wanted issued from a Mount Saint Charles hockey player.

These days Bill usually doesn't say much before a game. He might have a few one-liners about playing with focus or keeping your head even when an opponent antagonizes you, but it's usually Dave who runs through the game plan. Dave's the one who dissects the Mount films and decides what, if any, special defensive strategies need to be deployed against the opposition. But before the second game of the season against Burrillville on January 23, Bill was standing in the middle of the dressing room with his own four-page game plan. He was amazingly calm. His voice didn't rise at all as he went through the notes on each page and then tossed it into the trash barrel in the middle of the room. Bill never worries about the other team: that's Dave's job. Bill figures if his players play the way they have been taught, they'll win regardless of what the other team does. To him, it's all basic hockey and for a few weeks he had felt some Mount players hadn't been paying attention to the basics.

"After you pass, let your teammate know where you are," he said, then quickly went on to next rule in Belisle Hockey 101.

"One forward covers the two defensemen, go from side to side, force him toward the boards. If he shoots from the boards, my goalie can see it. If you make him shoot from the boards, it's tougher for them to get the bodies in front of my goalie. If you let him go to the middle, my goalie can be screened."

Once again it was "my goalie." Oliver felt better hearing Bill say, "Give my goalie help," rather than, "Give Oliver help." You're *his* goalie, you're *his* defenseman, you're not just some name on a roster. You're part of his family and no one wants to let his family down.

Dave stood off to the side. There was nothing he needed to say. Mount never should have lost to Burrillville a month earlier. They shouldn't need any special game plan to win this game. If everybody played the way they were capable of it should be an easy victory. This was one of those nights that his father could be the only person giving instructions, just like it was in the old days.

Dave only had one thing to say after Bill had thrown his last slip of paper into the trash barrel.

"No stupid penalties. Any stupid penalties and you're out of there. It's your game. It's not for coach and it's not for me. I shouldn't have to say much."

Chris Murphy had one more thing to add, however. "I believe in revenge," he shouted as Jillson started leading the parade out of the dressing room.

Apparently Murphy was absent the day his religion class at Mount Saint Charles studied "Blessed are the Forgiving."

The game was starting to follow an all-too-familiar pattern. Mount dominated the action, but produced no goals. Most of the time the puck was in the Burrillville zone, but nobody was finishing off plays. To Dave, that meant either a lack of focus or a lack of effort. Everybody was waiting for the other guy to give that extra push needed to finish off plays because the Burrillville goaltender wasn't going to give up any easy goals.

Chris Snizek finally scored late in the first period to give Mount a 1–0 lead. But only twenty-nine seconds after the start of the second period, Esposito couldn't handle a loose puck near the Burrillville blue line, allowing Burrillville to break out with a two-on-one against Jillson. Jillson made a nice slide to try and keep a pass from getting across the ice in front of the Mount cage, but somehow it found its way under his six-three frame and the Burrillville player slammed it home for a goal.

Halfway through the second period the score was tied 1–1 and Dave could see another nightmare in the making. His disposition didn't even improve after Hutchins and freshman Chris Chaput scored goals within twelve seconds of each other giving Mount a 3–1 lead. Burrillville cut the deficit to 3–2 a few minutes later, but Snizek scored again, giving Mount a 4–2 lead by the end of the second period.

If you hadn't looked at the scoreboard you would have thought Mount was losing from the atmosphere in the dressing room between periods. Dave was looking for senior leadership—and he wasn't finding it. Ridolf was all over the ice. His main concern seemed to be showing his stickhandling skills rather than setting up scoring opportunities. Fede wasn't thinking. He was taking shots from the point that didn't have any hope of getting past Burrillville defenders. Jillson, meanwhile, seemed more concerned about complaining to the officials about his opponents grabbing and slashing him than he was about getting shots at the Burrillville cage.

"It's not your game anymore, now it's ours," Dave screamed. "Now I'm going to make some changes. We have some young players here who want to play. My father is asking me what I'm doing. Fede, you have taken eight shots and only one has gotten through. Jillson, why aren't you shooting?"

Despite the threat, the coaches didn't make any wholesales changes in the third period, but maybe they should have. Oliver, who had made a few good saves in the first two periods, seemed to fall asleep in the third period. He let up a soft goal on an easy mid-range shot about three minutes after the start of the third period. About nine minutes later, he didn't cover up a rebound giving Burrillville a chance to tie the score with four minutes to play in regulation. After forty-five minutes of regulation play, the score was tied 4–4. Mount Saint Charles had taken sixty shots, Burrillville had taken thirty, but the score was even.

In Bill's twenty-three years as head coach, Mount Saint Charles had never lost two games to Burrillville in one season. Now, one bad play in the sudden-death overtime and it would happen. That had to be on the mind of some Mount players, especially the seniors, but Jillson knew they couldn't worry about losing. Once a team lets the fear of losing rather than the desire to win take over its collective psyche, it's doomed.

"Don't be afraid to lose," Jillson yelled as the team stood in front of the Mount bench waiting for the start of the overtime.

Finally, he was starting to sound like a captain.

The overtime didn't take long. Less than a minute in, Ridolf picked up a loose puck about twenty feet out from the Burrillville cage and fired a backhander into the upper left corner for the winning goal. Mount had survived the unthinkable.

But Bill and Dave's night of frustration was far from finished.

A crowd of Mount students in the stands near where Ridolf scored the goal went wild when the game ended. Ridolf was so excited that rather than celebrating with his teammates on the ice he skated over to the boards, jumped up over the wire fencing, and hugged the fans in the stands. It was the type of reaction you might see in some pro game, good stuff for the late-night TV sports highlights. But jumping into the stands wasn't something you ever saw a Mount Saint Charles player do: that's undisciplined, that's out of control.

Dave went ballistic at Ridolf's move. To calm down, he headed to the back of the runway behind the Mount bench. Meanwhile Bill was still planted in his usual spot near the far right end of the bench.

"I've never seen anything like that," Bill screamed in a mixture of amazement and anger.

"Get in the dressing room," Dave shouted as the players filed off the ice. Their gleeful expressions quickly evaporated. No one needed to be told why Dave was so upset after a victory. They knew what Ridolf had done was against every tenet of Mount Saint Charles hockey law.

Once they were all seated Dave launched into his tirade. Surprisingly, Ridolf's transgression wasn't his first topic.

"You stunk out the place," he berated the whole team. "You didn't play position. Too many people behind the cage."

He didn't say it specifically, but there was no question that the next statement was a warning to a few of the seniors.

"If you are going to pout when I change lines and put different people in there then get out of here. I got young guys here who want to play and are working hard," he said pointing to freshmen Dustin Demianiuk and Graham Johnson. "I was a good guy and it almost cost us. That's not going to happen again. I have guys on the JV team who want to be here and are willing to work to get here."

Finally he turned his displeasure toward Ridolf.

"We don't jump into the crowd after scoring goals," he screamed as he moved across the room toward Charlie. "*These* are your guys," he said pointing around the room as he stood virtually on top of Charlie. "You celebrate with *them*."

No outsiders are allowed admission into the Mount hockey psyche. Fans can watch it from afar, they can get excited by it, but they can't be part of it. Mount players suffer together in practice and celebrate together in victory. It's them against everybody else.

"I'm sorry," Ridolf said first looking into Dave's eyes and then looking around the room to his teammates.

Charlie Ridolf said he was sorry. That apology may have been more important than the victory.

An hour after the Burrillville game the dressing room was empty except for Dave, Bill, and me sitting in the little office.

"We have a team of all centers," Dave commented. "Everybody wants to be all over the place. They're all trying to impress people."

On a hockey team the center usually is the only player who has the freedom to skate anywhere on the rink. The center is the player the fans notice because he's always around the puck. But for every center on a forward line there needs to be two wings who are willing to do their job without constantly taking the spotlight. Midway through the season, Dave was still trying to find players who were more concerned about making contributions than making headlines.

But as much as he was worried about finding people who would play their position, he was more concerned about Jillson's health.

"I think Jeff still has some physical problems. He seems weak all the time. Plus he didn't practice all week. He can't do that and still be sharp for games," Dave said.

Every game seemed to be more frustrating for Jillson and he had been taking his frustration out on officials. There was no question he was being hacked and held more than any other player in the league. At the professional level, officials tend to protect the stars, but here the officials seemed to be allowing opponents a little more leeway when it came to playing against Jillson. They may have judged that his size gave him such an advantage over most other high school kids that he should be able to handle the holding and slashing that would have been a penalty if perpetrated on any other player.

Jillson was taking more than his share of physical abuse from opposing players and unfair verbal abuse from some opposing fans. Even from his spot on the Mount bench that night, Dave could hear a small group of Burrillville kids sitting in the far corner across the ice yelling such slurs as, "Jillson, you're fucking ugly." No high school kid should have to hear that, but unfortunately for Jillson it was one of the prices of stardom. His time in the spotlight also made him a target for the hordes of Mount Saint Charles haters throughout the state.

"Nobody has ever gotten as much attention as he has during their career here," Dave pointed out. "The average fan didn't start paying attention to Bryan [Berard] until late in his junior year, then he wasn't here for his senior year. Jeff had all that publicity during his junior year; now he's back. A lot of people hate Mount, and they're taking it out on him."

But as much as they sympathized with Jillson's plight, Bill and Dave thought that too often Jillson was using it as a crutch for his own shortcomings. Rather than rising to a challenge, he blamed bad officiating for his erratic play. It's easy to fall into the trap of blaming others for your shortcomings, especially when there's some creditability to the accusations. But Dave and Bill knew the situation wasn't going to get any better and they feared that it could get a lot worse if Jillson didn't start realizing, for the good of the team, that he had to keep his mouth shut and just play hockey.

"The officials are getting tried of him blaming them every time he screws up," said Bill. "I've motivated a lot of players, but I can't seem to motivate him to the next level."

When the players walked into the dressing room for a game with Hendricken the night after the Burrillville victory they were greeted by sign in big, black block letters that read:

Keep Your Mouth Zipped.

Everyone read the sign, but there was no question it was directed mainly at Jillson.

The game was a repeat of the previous night. Mount held a 12–5 shot advantage in the first period, but the score was tied 0–0. It was the same scenario in the second period. Going into the third, the game was still scoreless. Despite the lack of goals, neither Dave nor Bill was upset in the locker room between the second and third periods.

"You're playing good position," Dave complimented them. "Keep doing that and the opportunities will come."

Even Oliver, who had been in Bill's doghouse the previous night after allowing two soft goals in the third period against Burrillville, had earned Bill's praise.

"My goalie is playing a great game," he declared.

Finally, five minutes into the third period Snizek scored on a nice pass from Cardillo. The goal held up and Mount escaped with a 1–0 victory, pushing its league record to 9–1. It was also encouraging that they hadn't incurred any stupid penalties. In the forty-five-minute game, Mount received only one penalty. But Bill knew they were lucky. They had given Stokinger some playing time and although he was never sent to the penalty box, he easily could have been.

"He could have had two penalties," Bill said after the game. "One time he hooked the kid and pulled his helmet right off, but it was away from the puck. It was a good thing the official was looking the other way."

Jillson had played a nice steady game, nothing spectacular, but he also didn't give the officials any lip. That can't be said for his opponents.

"He's taking a lot of verbal abuse," Dave said in Jillson's defense. "When we were shaking hands after the game, I heard some of the Hendricken players say 'NHL, that's a joke.' They wouldn't say it to Jeff's face of course. They waited until after they had passed by him in the line. But I was three or four people behind him so I heard it. I wouldn't be surprised if Jeff heard it, but he didn't say anything."

There was one month remaining in the regular season. They had won five straight games since the loss to Catholic Memorial in the Holiday Tournament title game. They led their league with a 9–1 record and were 12–2 overall against some of the top high school competition in New England. Most high school coaches would have been ecstatic with that record, but the Belisles were worried.

"We're not finishing off. We're not strong. We're not really focused," Dave said

He picked up a copy of the schedule sitting on the training table in the middle of the dressing room. On Tuesday there was a nonleague game with Fairfield Prep, the alma mater of the Buffalo Sabres' Chris Drury. Fairfield is always one of the top teams in Connecticut. The following Friday they had a league game against Toll Gate in Warwick and then another nonleague game against Belmont Hill Prep of Massachusetts in ten days.

"If we don't lose two of those three games it will be a miracle," Dave sighed.

CHAPTER 23

ave had thought he was only kidding Saturday night when he said it would be a miracle if Mount didn't lost two of the next three games. But six days later he was starting to worry that maybe he was right on target. On Tuesday, Mount had beaten Fairfield Prep 5–1, but it didn't take the Belisles long to realize that the current 1997–98 Fairfield Prep team wasn't in the same class as the Chris Drury–led Fairfield teams of the early nineties.

Three nights later, Dave's Saturday night trepidation proved accurate. It was a game against Toll Gate, a team Mount had already beaten twice by at least three goals each time. But this game was at Thayer Arena in Warwick, a rink in which Mount has never played well. Part of the reason for Mount's poor showing at Thayer may be that the rink is often used for figure skating, which means that it's always kept warmer than the frigid temperatures Bill maintains at Adelard. Warm temperatures in a rink can mean soft ice and soft ice can slow down a team.

Right from the beginning the coaches knew it wasn't going to be a good night. Toll Gate jumped out to a 1–0 lead only a minute after the opening face-off when Oliver let an easy shot slip past him. Fede tied the score nine minutes later, but Toll Gate regained the lead again with about two minutes left in the first period. Jillson tied the game again with a rink-long dash shortly after the start of the second period, but that was the last bright spot of the night for the one hundred or so Mount fans who had traveled to Warwick. Toll Gate took a 3–2 lead with two minutes to play in the second period and then added three more goals in the third period. Mount was flat. Nothing was quick. To make matters worse, Oliver didn't have a good night: he wasn't focusing at all. He let two more easy shots past him in the third period and his teammates weren't able to provide enough offense to make up for his lackluster play. When the final buzzer sounded Toll Gate had a 6–2 victory.

The dressing rooms at Thayer are only a few feet from the gate. By the time the Mount players began filing into the aisle between the rink and dressing rooms, it was already jammed with Toll Gate fans eager for their team to come off the ice. Music was blaring from a large boom box and the fans were clapping in the faces of the Mount players.

"Listen to that. They love beating us," said one Mount player as he wove his way through the fans.

Bill and Dave walked into the dressing room behind the last player and immediately slammed the door shut. The sudden closing caught Mount's two managers still standing outside in the mob of Toll Gate fans, but both knew it wouldn't be a wise move to knock just then. So they stood there, wearing their Mount Saint Charles hockey jackets, with music blaring and Toll Gate fans chanting all around them. The managers stood there for fifteen minutes before the door finally reopened.

As soon as the door had closed Bill launched into a speech. Surprisingly, he wasn't yelling. He almost looked bewildered about what he had just seen.

"It's my fault," he said. "I've failed you. We've worked on moving the puck quick and you hold the puck too long. My captain gets a nice goal, but then he gets beat for a goal. He gets mad and he retaliates. You're not in shape. That's my fault. That's the coach's fault."

In an era when it's becoming increasing popular for a coach to respond to his team's loss with the cliché that "they didn't come to play," Bill never passes the buck. If his team loses, it's because he didn't prepare them correctly. Pure and simply. You'll never find him blaming a loss on the players. He may feel that they're not working hard enough, that they're not focusing, that they're not following his or Dave's instructions. But in his mind, it's the coach's fault that his team is playing that way. That's why after a game Bill will sit in his little office in the locker room until one or two o'clock in the morning drawing up new drills that will help his players master the skills needed to win.

"I wish they never put the scoring in the paper," Bill said referring to the weekly statistics provided to the Rhode Island media by the Coaches Association. "That's all you're thinking about."

When Bill finished, Dave immediately picked up the dialogue and he wasn't as mild-mannered as his father.

"You're insulting that man," Dave screeched as he pointed to his father. "He tells you what you need to do, then you go out and do what you want to do. Only one person, this young man, does what his coach tells him," Dave said pointing to senior Chris Lentini. "If the coach told him to shit on the ice, he would take down his pants at center ice and do it. Everybody else, you do what you want to do."

"Am I missing anybody Coach?" Dave asked his father.

"No," Bill said.

Lentini tried not to change the expression on his face. He didn't want to embarrass any of his teammates, but he had to feel good about himself. He was one of those no-name Mount players who's never going to play in the NHL or even see his name in the headlines, but who is essential to the success of Mount hockey.

But Dave wasn't finished and any exuberance Lentini felt for being singled out for his dedication quickly faded. He was part of a team whose character was being questioned. All along the bench were expressionless teenage faces. A few players had quickly taken off their game shirts, shoulder pads, and tee shirts before the coaches started speaking. They had been sitting stripped to the wrist in a somewhat chilly dressing room, but no one attempted to put a tee shirt back on to protect themselves from the chill. They just sat and stared at Dave.

"You allowed that coach over there to out-coach this man," Dave continued, first pointing toward the Toll Gate locker room and then pointing to Bill. "I'm physically exhausted. I had a JV practice at six o'clock this morning. I worked all day, then I come here and see you insult this man. I'm not going to let that happen."

Dave refuses to accept losing. He will deal with it, but he won't accept it and he doesn't want his players to get in the mind-set of accepting it either. They have too much talent for that. It's like the smart kid who accepts the B when, if he put in an extra effort, he would earn an A.

There's nothing wrong with a B, except for a kid who has the talent to get an A.

The fact of the matter is Mount Saint Charles hockey isn't fun.

Some people may think that's terrible. They don't understand that there can be a difference between enjoyment and fun when playing sports beyond Little League. The thrill of victory doesn't always come with a laugh. There aren't many teenagers who have fun studying chemistry or physics. Yet when they get an A on a test because they put in hours of work, there's a great feeling of satisfaction.

Mount Saint Charles hockey is chemistry and physics on ice.

Mount hockey isn't right for every young hockey player. But if a kid is willing to spend hours studying under the watchful eyes of no-laugh tutors, he can achieve an immense feeling of accomplishment.

Bill has reached the point where a loss doesn't seem to affect him as much as it does Dave. Contrary to what people think, every loss doesn't transform him into a raving maniac. What does send him over the edge, however, is individual failures, especially if they continually happen. These days he seems to see his job as developing the individual player as part of the whole Mount package. Winning the game is now Dave's responsibility. He decides how to defend against a specific opponent. Bill's job is to give him the material, ready for production.

It was 11:30 by the time the blue bus pulled back into the Adelard Arena parking lot after the Toll Gate game. The players stowed their equipment in the locker room and quickly exited. Parents waited for the younger players in the parking lot. A few of the seniors, however, made some quick plans to meet elsewhere. Sure they lost a game, but there was still time to salvage something out of the evening. When everybody finally left, Bill and Dave retired to the locker room office. They would be there until 1:30 in the morning, wrestling with the necessary line changes.

"Maybe we've gone too long with some of the seniors," said Dave. "Our defense is what's hurting. We need good games from Oliver. When he's plays well, we do well."

Dave knew it was only going to get tougher keeping Oliver focused on the challenge. Bill's fear that without Pete Capizzo at practice, Oliver wouldn't feel challenged was proving true. The last thing Mount needed was a complacent Brian Oliver.

"If Capizzo was here, I would put him in there and Oliver would never get back in," grumbled Bill.

Capizzo was never going to be able to challenge Oliver, though.

Doc Guay had taken Capizzo for X rays because he feared the young goaltender had pneumonia, but the X rays didn't show any signs of it. Gus and Stephanie Capizzo were relieved, but they still wanted to know why their son was coughing up blood. Until they had a definite answer, Pete wasn't going back on the ice. On the day Mount was losing to Toll Gate, Capizzo was in a Boston hospital undergoing a series of biopsies that the doctors hoped would help pinpoint his problem.

Capizzo hadn't been in school for two weeks, but almost every day he would call either Matt Kasberg or Chris Snizek, his two closest friends on the team. The calls made him feel like he was still part of the team. Snizek and Kasberg would supply updates on what had happened at practice; they would tell him how the coaches had changed the lines around or how Bill had been screaming at Oliver. Capizzo would lie in his bed, holding the phone and letting his mind re-create the practice session that his body wouldn't allow him to attend. Sometimes the calls lifted his spirits, but other times they sent him into a state of depression and self-pity. Why did this have to happen to him now? Why couldn't the doctors just send him home with a prescription that would clear up the problem in a few days? He had been taking a variety of medications for a few weeks. One doctor had said he thought it was just a bad case of the flu, but if that was the case, he should have started feeling better by now. Instead, he actually felt weaker. He had been in the hospital for a few days and still no one seemed to have an answer. He was sick, but the depression was causing him more suffering than the physical ailment. As the days turned into weeks and he hadn't seen any chance of a quick return to the team he wondered if there was something seriously wrong, something that might mean he could never play hockey again.

He had been in one Boston hospital for a few days when his parents told him they weren't happy with the care he was getting. They were hiring an ambulance and having him transferred to another hospital. It was all very confusing to a teenager. Why couldn't the doctors in this hospital help him if it wasn't anything serious like some of the other doctors had said?

The only slight glimmer of hope that came out of the Toll Gate game was that Pelletier was back in the lineup and picked up an assist. He had missed five weeks with a dislocated shoulder suffered in the first Toll Gate game back in mid-December. Dave was happy, with Pelletier back he could make some moves with the lines. But he knew everything was different for Pelletier now. If he hadn't been hurt, he would have been one of the team's top scorers, and college coaches would be taking notice. The honor roll student didn't need hockey to get into a good college, however. He wasn't talented enough to generate a host a Division I scholarship offers, but if he had scored a high number of goals to go along with his impressive 1,200 SAT scores he would have made some coach's recruiting list. Dave knew that although it was too late for Pelletier to prove anything to college coaches, it wasn't too late for him to help Mount win another title. Maybe it wasn't a scholarship offer, but being the hero of a Mount Saint Charles playoff victory can make up for a lot of disappointments.

There was no game scheduled for Saturday, January 31, the night after the Toll Gate game. There were other Rhode Island high school games for that night at Adelard, but that wasn't going to stop the Belisles from holding practice. The situation was turning desperate, and waiting until Monday to start making changes wasn't an option. So Mount players lined up inside the doors of the rink, watching the final period of the second game of a high school doubleheader. It was 10:00 p.m. and there still was ten minutes to play. It would be at least 10:30 before the first Mount players took the ice for warm-ups. Every other high school hockey player in the state had already finished his night's work, but the Mount players had just begun.

Dave hadn't arrived when the players started warming up, but Bill didn't wait to start making changes. He stood on the ice next to the bench and called to players as they skated past. One of the first things he did was order Pelletier to change shirts with Cardillo. He was dropping Cardillo from the white line, the top line.

Cardillo's stomach flip-flopped even as he tried to hide his dismay. It was the same feeling of frustration he had felt back in his sophomore year, back when he was ready to leave Mount because he couldn't understand why the coach didn't appreciate his talent.

From a coaching point of view, the move was a no-brainer. With Cardillo, Ridolf, and Snizek on the same line, they had three guys who seemed to be concentrating on their own agendas more than the team's. A "team of centers," as Dave put it. Cardillo had spent three years playing in the shadows. From the opening day of practice, he was determined to make this season the year the spotlight shone on him. Ridolf had lost half of his senior year; he was left with only a few months to show college coaches he could play at the next level. Snizek may have been only a sophomore but friends and family were constantly telling him that he was one of the best players in the state. "Everything should work around you," they would tell him. Replacing Cardillo with Pelletier meant that at least there was one member of the line who was willing to do some of the dirty work around the cage.

Even Cardillo might have understood it if he had stepped back and taken a logical look at what had been happening the previous few weeks. But when you're seventeen years old and you think somebody is ruining your dream, logic isn't always part of your thought process.

Cardillo wasn't the only one who started the practice depressed. Jackson had been moved onto a line with Chaput and Vincent, a freshman and sophomore. A few weeks earlier he had asked what he was doing wrong and he tried to correct it. Now he was being teamed with two players younger than him, who hadn't seen a lot of playing time in the first half of the season. His first thought was that the coaches had given up on him. Even if that were true, he wasn't going to give up on himself. Both Chaput and Vincent were talented young players so Jackson tried to rationalize that maybe the coach was trying to mix his experience with their raw talent to give the team a new scoring threat. Maybe it's a promotion rather than a demotion, he told himself.

There was no question what it meant to Kurt Stokinger when he was teamed with freshman Dustin Demianiuk. Stokinger might not have seen as much action as he hoped during the first two months of the season, but at least he was occasionally alternating on one of the top two defensive tandems. Now it looked like he was completely out of the regular defensive rotation. Things were going from bad to worse.

Most high school and college hockey teams, following the example of the professional teams, silk-screen players' names across the back of their game shirts. There has never been a name on the back of a Mount Saint Charles hockey jersey, and there never will be as long as Bill is coach. In his mind, a name on a shirt is a sign of individuality. Mount Saint Charles hockey is a team, not a group of individuals.

There are some people who say Bill has another motive for never putting names on the shirts. It's a lot easier to take a shirt away from a player on the varsity who he thinks isn't playing up to his potential and give it to some hard-working kid on the junior varsity if you don't have to change the name on the shirt.

For two decades, the fear of having a junior varsity player move up and take your varsity shirt had been one of Bill's main weapons in his daily demand for excellence from Mount hockey players.

For two hours that night they skated up and down the ice. Breakout drills with a forward and defenseman at each end of the rink on the same side. The forwards start skating toward each other full speed but look back at the defenseman. They don't look at the other forward skating toward them until they take the pass from the defenseman. The ideal situation is for the forward to take the pass at his own blue line and then break across center ice. But if the pass is late, the forward could crash right into the other forward coming at him from the other end of the rink. It's kind of a game of hockey chicken. You keep you attention focused on your defenseman so you'll get the pass. You don't worry about the other guy skating directly at you. The idea of course is to condition players to not worry about getting hit. It's a nice theory, but often one of the forwards will try sneaking a look at the oncoming player so that he can avoid a bone-crushing collision. He knows that he sneaks that look at his own peril because if Bill sees him he's either doing push-ups or, worse, told to "Get out of here."

They worked face-off drills, more breakout drills, and backchecking drills. They worked drills for ten and fifteen minutes, nonstop. At one point, they went about forty minutes without Bill calling for a water break. It was Saturday night, their friends were out partying, probably having a few beers, while they were going forty minutes without a drink of water.

They were tired and thirsty, but no one wanted a break. The only time anyone gets a break is when Bill gets mad at him for doing something wrong and tells him to sit down.

"Go sit down," he screamed at Pelletier during a backchecking drill.

Pelletier spent five minutes sitting on the bench, looking like a little kid who has been told to sit on the side of the pool while his friends are having fun swimming. Sure, he was getting a rest with a water bottle right beside him while his teammates were out on the ice, on the verge of puking. He waited nervously for Bill to order him back out on the ice, back so he too could feel the satisfaction of being on the verge of puking.

Out in the lobby, a few fathers waited for the practice to end. They could hear the sounds on the ice so they didn't dare open the rink doors. Out in the parking lot, a few other parents were waiting in their cars with younger children asleep in backseats. Chris Minor's parents were sitting in a van with the motor running to keep the car warm. It was after midnight and they still had an hour ride back to their home in Tiverton. They would have rather been sitting home watching *Saturday Night Live*, but nobody was going to complain to Bill or anyone in the Mount administration. They knew what their son was getting into when he said he wanted to play hockey at Mount Saint Charles and they knew it was going to mean some long nights for them as well.

"It would have been a lot easier on me if he went to Hendricken or La Salle because they were much closer to our house," said Jack McHugh, father of Sean McHugh, the member of the 1987 team who will never forget the night Bill had the team skating in the dark after a loss.

"The first two years he was on the JV, so he had to be at school for 6:00 a.m. practices. It was a long, long grind for me," McHugh stated about the daily one-hundred-mile round-trip to Mount. "But it was something he wanted to do. The kid has to want to be there. It can't be just something the parents want."

It was almost 1:00 a.m. as Bill went around the Mount dressing room picking up pieces of rolled-up tape that had been dropped on the floor after the practice. Normally Bill would be furious if players had left tape or anything else strewn on the locker room floor. It's their responsibility to keep the dressing room clean. Bill usually doesn't accept any excuse for sloppiness, but that night he was willing to accept the fact that at 12:30 in the morning even Mount Saint Charles players can be excused for a little sloppiness.

"These kids have more than kids used to have," Bill said. "It's good their parents are better off and can give them more, but they're not as hungry as the kids use to be."

He had finally taken a seat in his locker room office. He was almost seventy years old and he hadn't sat down in at least three hours, including two hours on skates. It seemed that every year he was finding it increasingly difficult to pound the middle-class comfortableness out of a bunch of teenager hockey players.

"It's getting tougher. Last year was the toughest to get to them and this year seems even tougher," Bill said. "There's nothing comfortable about hockey. It's a tough, physical game."

"Sometimes I don't understand anymore. Before, the only thing parents and kids thought about was getting to college, maybe a college scholarship. Now they want to be pros. That's more important to them than the team."

He had six weeks left to convince twenty-five teenagers that the team was more important than their personal needs. He knew it wasn't going to be easy.

CHAPTER 24

"Tom Laidlaw called today," Joel Jillson told me as we stood waiting for the start of the Mount–Belmont High game on February 2 at Adelard.

"He said he was calling because some Florida [Panthers] scouts called him asking if he could help them get to talk to Jeff after the game," Joel continued. "They're trying to get an idea whether or not he's going to opt into the draft. We like Tom, but I told him no. We had to put a stop to agents talking to Jeff."

Laidlaw is a former NHL player turned agent. He was Bryan Berard's agent and Berard's parents had been giving Linda and Joel Jillson glowing reports about how he had helped Bryan.

"He's like an older brother as well as an agent. We know he really cares about Bryan," Pam Berard had said.

But by that time in the 1997–98 season, his parents had declared all agents, even the good ones, off limits to Jeff.

"I'm finding it amazing how there's no restrictions on these guys," said Joel. "They can get a kid when he's fifteen years old then they have control."

The stories of guys who were serving a dual role of scout and agent getting attached to young hockey players in Canada are legendary. The best known tale is how Allan Eagleson, at the time a Toronto lawyer, started negotiating deals for Bobby Orr when Orr was only twelve years old. So when Americans started filling the NHL ranks it was only natural that the agents would be spending time around American high schools. The NCAA rules prohibit agents from dealing with college players in any sport, so once an athlete becomes a college student they are shielded, at least in principle, from the onslaught of agents. But there's no protection for high school athletes. Their only protection is parents like Joel and Linda. That was one of the other big reasons Linda wanted Jeff to stay at Mount for his senior year. She had already seen a sampling of how agents operate during Jeff's junior year. As bad as it was with Jeff playing at Mount, she knew the agents would be even more intense if he was playing junior hockey and didn't have his parents there to protect his interests.

"I'm learning something new every day. When this is over, I could be an agent," Joel said with a disgusted laugh.

It was the first week of February and Jeff still hadn't announced whether he would opt into the NHL draft in the spring; therefore three scouts planted themselves in the top row of the bleachers at Adelard to watch the Mount-Belmont game. Belmont is a private school nestled among million-dollar homes in Belmont, Massachusetts, a Boston suburb. Belmont plays in the tough New England Independent Schools League so it's the days when Mount plays teams like St. Sebastian's and Belmont that the scouts come out so that they can see Jeff compete against bigger and older players.

Joel was glad it was an early five o'clock game. That meant Jeff could play a game, get home, and finish his homework and still get to bed at a decent hour. Like Dave, there had been times during the previous few weeks when both Joel and Linda had worried about their son's health. He seemed tired, which immediately triggered fears of a mononucleosis relapse.

"But all his tests are fine," Joel assured me.

"He just slept yesterday. It's the first time he's had a chance to just relax in a long time."

Sunday is supposed to be the day Mount players catch up on everything from sleep to studying for upcoming exams. There's never practice on Sunday, even through Bill could easily arrange for the ice time. But most of the season Jeff couldn't relax, even on Sunday.

Two weeks earlier, University of Michigan coach Red Berenson had flown in on Sunday morning and spent the afternoon in the Jillson's living room. He was trying to convince Jeff that Ann Arbor would be the best place for him for at least the next two or three years.

Berenson is an icon among college hockey coaches. He was an all-American at Michigan during his four-year career in the early sixties, when it was still written in stone that you couldn't make the pros right out of college. Yet the day his Michigan team lost in the semifinals of the 1962 national NCAA tournament, Berenson signed a contract with the Montreal Canadiens and the following night he was in Boston Garden playing for them against the Bruins. He went on to enjoy a seventeen-year NHL career. Shortly after he finished playing he returned to his alma mater as head coach. He had directed the Wolverines to the semifinal round of the NCAA national tournament several times and won the 1996 national crown. In 1998, his team was once again considered one of the best college teams in the country.

Michigan draws the largest crowds of any American college hockey team. The Wolverines usually play their home games before SRO crowds at the 6,300-seat Yost Ice Arena on the Michigan campus. But for the big games they play in Detroit's Joe Louis Arena. It's not surprising that Berenson doesn't have to go chasing after too many recruits. Usually his assistant coaches will do the home visits and the prospect will meet the coach when they visit Michigan's 36,000-student campus. But if there was a chance a player with Jeff's potential might go to college rather than jumping right into the big-money world of pro hockey, Red Berenson was more than willing to spend a Sunday afternoon sitting in a living room in North Smithfield.

There are coaches who might stroll into a top recruit's home wearing a five-hundred-dollar suit and launch into a nonstop sales pitch for their program. Berenson took a different approach.

"He took his shoes off, put his feet up on the hassock, and we watched some Michigan tapes and talked hockey. He was a real regular guy," Joel said about Berenson's visit.

That night Jeff and his father drove Berenson to the airport for a flight back to Michigan. The next morning Jeff was on a plane for the trip to the University of Maine. It had been nonstop for two weeks. Even when Jeff was home, the phone always seemed to be ringing with some coach on the line wanting to know how he was doing. There were times his schedule seemed more hectic than a cooperate CEO's. This Sunday was the first day he had been able to lie back a little, but on Monday afternoon he was right back in the spotlight.

Once the game started, Jeff didn't make the scouts wait long to see something special. Only eleven seconds after the opening face-off, he picked up the puck at center ice, made a nice move around a defender, and fired a blast from just inside the blue line that sailed into the goal.

Joel couldn't help but think that there finally was going to be a night when he could just sit back and enjoy a game without controversy surrounding his son. He should have known better.

Belmont tied the score midway through the first period while Mount was trying to kill an Esposito penalty. Jeff thought the penalty was a bush call. He was frustrated further when Belmont scored, and he let the officials know it. The officials let Jillson know that they don't like a teenager questioning their calls.

It was bad enough that his team had given up a shorthanded goal, but then Bill glanced across the rink and saw his star player heading to the penalty box, and they hadn't even dropped the puck since the goal.

"What did he say?" Bill yelled to the referees.

Neither of the two referees came over to the bench to give him a full explanation. One did skate slowly past the Mount bench, however, and yelled something about Jeff making disparaging remarks about Rhode Island officiating. As soon as the penalty expired and Jeff skated back to the bench, Bill jumped down from his spot at the far end of the back bench and positioned himself directly in front of the gates that open onto the ice. Jeff didn't even have a chance to sit down on the bench before Bill grabbed him and yanked him down the runway toward the Mount locker room. There may have been stranger occurrences at Adelard Arena over the years, but the sight of a six-foot-three, 210-pound kid, who a halfhour earlier had pro scouts literally begging for a few minutes of his time, being pulled along by a five-foot-seven, sixty-eight-year-old man definitely ranked as an Adelard classic. Bill pushed Jillson into the locker room and slammed the door behind him. Every player on the bench had turned his attention toward the locker room door rather than toward what was happening on the ice.

"Pay attention to the game," Dave yelled

Dave tried concentrating on the game himself, but he was more concerned about what was happening in the locker room. He knew his father thought Jeff wasn't living up to his potential. He knew Bill felt Jeff was more concerned about himself than the team. Dave was worried that his father had finally had enough and would tell Jeff to get out. His father *had* mellowed over the years, and it was unlikely that he'd grab Jeff's equipment and throw it out the door as he had to some other Mount stars in the seventies and eighties, but he wasn't entirely sure. Even if his father didn't throw Jeff off the team he was worried Jeff could start feeling persecuted. If that was the case, rather than stepping up his game over the final month of the season, he could just shut down and go through the motions. No matter what happened during the final month of the season, every college coach in the country would welcome him with open arms. Even if he didn't look good in the playoffs, people would just say it was because he was bored playing against high school kids. Jeff didn't need Mount, but Mount needed Jeff and Dave knew it. So Dave tried keeping his attention on what was happening in front of him on the ice, but he was far more concerned about what was happening behind the closed locker room door.

Bill slammed the locker room door shut because he wanted it to be just him and Jeff. But it was impossible for anybody outside the locker room door not to know what was going on inside.

"Keep your mouth shut. Keep your mouth shut," Bill could be heard screaming at Jillson.

There were a few more minutes of inaudible Bill screams punctuated by the occasional sound of something hitting Jeff's shoulder pads. A video cam was necessary to get the picture of Bill putting some emphasis into the discussion with a few whacks at Jeff's shoulder pads. Eventually the door opened and Jeff clomped out followed by Bill. Some kids might have been embarrassed to be singled out for reprimand, but it didn't seem to bother Jeff. He went back to the bench and Dave didn't hesitate sending him back out on the ice. No one was happier than he was to see Jeff and his father walk out of the dressing room together.

In between the first and second period Bill went over to Jeff and told him to apologize to the referees for saying anything about Rhode Island officials.

"I didn't say anything about Rhode Island officials," Jeff offered in defense.

"Apologize anyway," Bill said.

His players aren't the only ones Bill plays head games with.

If Dave thought his problems were over when Jeff and his father walked out of the dressing room together he was badly mistaken. Mount had taken the lead in the second period, but every time Charlie Ridolf went on the ice, Dave became more upset. Ridolf was an increasingly frustrated player. The goals hadn't been coming as easily as they did the previous year. During the 1996–97 season things seemed to flow for Ridolf, but this season they always seemed to be getting clogged up. He hadn't been able to leap right in and pick up his hockey timing after he returned from his suspension. He didn't have that special sense that enables you to get a jump on the other guy, whether it's going into the boards or going after a rebound in front of the cage, so Ridolf began pushing rather than flowing. He worried about scoring goals rather than playing a complete game. Dave's frustration equaled Ridolf's, but for entirely different reasons. Even when Ridolf was on the bench he was pushing, trying to compensate for his lack of productivity on the ice.

"Come on you fucking mutes," he shouted at his teammates. "What's a matter with you guys? Are you fucking mutes?"

Fuck may be the all-purpose word of most American male athletes over the age of fourteen, but it wasn't a word heard often around the Mount hockey team—until Ridolf returned. Neither Bill nor Dave was in any mood for a player using profanity as a way of showing how tough he was.

"Watch your mouth," Bill reprimanded him while still looking straight out at the action on the ice. He didn't need to look at the bench to know who was using the "fuck word."

Ridolf didn't help his case the next time he took the ice.

"Pick up somebody; you're circling around out there," Dave yelled at Ridolf as he circled center ice without paying much attention to the Belmont player near him.

As soon as he came off the ice, Ridolf fired back at Dave.

"Who do you want me to cover? I'm on the wing," Ridolf screamed.

After his father's blowup with Jillson, the last thing Dave needed at that moment was somebody else questioning the coach's instructions. He jumped down off the bench, grabbed Ridolf, and hauled him down the runway and into the locker room. It looked like an instant replay of Bill's episode with Jillson. But unlike Bill, who followed Jillson into the locker room, Dave slammed the door behind Ridolf and went back to the bench. Unlike Jillson, who patiently stood there and listened to Bill's ravings, Ridolf didn't take Dave's criticism quietly. He stomped through the junior varsity room, throwing his stick, gloves, and anything else he could pull off.

"I'm sick of this shit," Ridolf howled to an empty dressing room. "I'm quitting."

He slumped on the bench shedding his equipment, knowing that he really didn't want to quit, but his pride was on the line. By the time the team came back into the dressing room between the second and third periods, his shirt, shoulder pads, and elbow pads were off, and he was sitting on the bench with the suspenders of his hockey pants down off his shoulders. A few players approached him and told him to take it easy. "Everything will be all right," they said.

But to Ridolf, he was being used as a pawn in the coaches' head games.

"He's just acting for the crowd," Ridolf sneered pointing toward Dave, who was walking through the dressing room door.

Dave didn't hear the entire accusation, but he heard enough to know Ridolf was criticizing him. He rushed over and bent his face down within a few inches of Ridolf's.

"You want a piece of me? Go ahead—you and me," Dave screamed into Ridolf's face. "You don't like it here? You can get out. You want to quit? Go ahead. I don't care."

There wasn't a sound in the dressing room. Every eye was fixed on Ridolf and Dave.

"You think I don't get criticized? I've been criticized by that man since I was playing," Dave said, nodding in Bill's direction. "You think I'm doing something wrong. Go ahead tell me what I'm doing wrong. I can take it. But you better be able to take it back or get out of here."

Dave kept talking, but now he was backing away from Ridolf. He had made his point. He met Ridolf's challenge to authority head-on and he could tell by the look in his eyes that he really didn't want to argue anymore. It was time for Dave to lure one of the key members of his flock back into the fold.

"Are you okay?" Dave said as he extended his hand while walking toward Ridolf.

Ridolf reached up and grabbed Dave's hand without saying a word.

"I know you're frustrated," Dave conceded. "Just play your game. It will come."

Ridolf wore the look of a little kid who has just escaped what he knows would have been a justified punishment. His temper had backed him into a corner he really didn't want to be in. He didn't want to quit—hockey was his life. Dave could have made him squirm. He could have made Ridolf swallow his pride if he wanted to stay on the team. But Dave was more concerned about the Mount hockey team than about proving that he can outwit a defiant teenager. The team needed Ridolf, but they needed him playing under control. If a handshake could do that, Dave had no problem extending his hand.

CHAPTER 25

"Garth Snow called from Vancouver today," Bill mentioned one day in early February as we sat in the locker room office before the start of practice.

"What did he want?" I asked

"Just checking to see how things are going. He always calls a couple of times each year."

"What did you tell him?"

"I told him we needed more guys who were willing to work like he was."

Snow had been cut four times from various Mount Saint Charles teams before he finally got a chance to wear a varsity Mountie uniform in his junior year in 1986. Even then it wasn't until his senior year that he finally played in a varsity game. That's not exactly the usual storyline for an NHL goalie's amateur career, but then Snow isn't your routine hockey success story.

He had started playing goalie when he was about five years old because no one else on his mite team raised his hand when the coach asked if anyone wanted to play goal. Little Garth thought it would be fun to wear the big leg pads and catching glove and, besides, he was somewhat of a roly-poly kid who kind of flopped around the ice on his skates. Yet, even as a little kid, even when he wasn't a good skater and was about as far from being a pro prospect as you can get, he was always all business. He always concentrated on what he was supposed to be doing.

"You put some kids in the goal and their minds are always wandering. They're always looking in the stands for their mother or father and eventually somebody scores from sixty feet out because they're not paying attention. But not Garth. From the beginning he was all business. His head was always in the game, and he was a feisty little kid," Snow's former youth hockey coach once said.

Snow's skating gradually improved, but he was never a youth hockey superstar. That didn't stop him from deciding that he wanted to play at Mount Saint Charles, even though the school was twenty miles from his home in Wrentham, Massachusetts.

"If you wanted to be a good hockey player that was the only place to go," Snow said.

So every day, from the time he was in the seventh grade, his parents drove him to Woonsocket. After he was twice cut from the junior high team and twice from the varsity, you would have thought that his parents would try to convince him that if he really wanted to play hockey he might be better off at some other school. But if their son was willing to keep trying, they would keep taking him. Then between his sophomore and junior year at Mount he grew from five feet, eleven inches to six-two. A year later he added two more inches.

"I don't think I've had anybody come back as many times as Garth," Bill said. "There were just better goalies in front of him. But he kept working and never gave up. He became the coolest goalie under pressure I have ever had. You can tell when kids are nervous. They want to go off by themselves, especially goalies. But Garth wasn't that way."

"He just refused to let us cut him from the program," said Dave. "He never quit working. When he was younger, he had a very quick glove, but he wasn't blessed with great balance. He was big and somewhat awkward. He knew he had to learn to control his body, so he worked at it."

Dave still remembers walking into Adelard Arena on many mornings at 6:00 a.m. for a junior varsity practice to find that Snow was already there. He would be on the ice by himself, practicing with the puck machine firing shots at him.

Snow is one of the glowing examples of Bill's devotion to his seniors. If Bill didn't remain committed to him, it's unlikely that Snow would today be playing in the NHL.

All his work had finally earned him a starting berth in his senior year in 1987. But midway through the season he gave up six goals in the first two periods of a game against Hendricken and Bill pulled him in favor of a younger, more promising goalie. On some teams that might have been it for Snow's hockey career. The senior, who never was a superstar to start with, has a bad game and is replaced with a younger player who looks good. Many coaches would said they had given the senior a chance and he didn't do the job, so now it was time to plan for the future. But not Bill: his seniors are like his family, and you don't give up on a family member because of a few bad days.

On the bus ride to the next game four days later, Bill called Snow to his seat in the front of the bus and told him to sit down next to him. This was serious business. No player ever sits in the front seat with The Coach. Snow couldn't help but think Bill was going to tell him he was sorry, but he had to change goalies.

"How are you doing in school?" Bill asked him.

"Okay," Snow replied. "I'm just sorry I let everybody down last week."

"Wait a minute," Bill said. "You're still studying, aren't you? You're still going to class? That's what's important. Now when we get off the bus, get ready, because you're playing tonight. You're still my goalie."

By the quirk of scheduling, Mount was playing Hendricken again that night. This time, Snow turned in a sensational performance in a 4–2 Mount victory.

That was the start of what in 1998 had become fifteen years of Snow delivering when the chips were down. A few months after that second Hendricken game, he led Mount to the legendary 1987 Rhode Island high school championships. Hendricken was a team loaded with offensive talent. Their roster included two future college all-Americans: Dave Emma, who would become the 1992 Hoby Baker award winner at Boston College, and Rob Gaudreau, who would go on to all-American honors at Providence College. Hendricken had won the regular-season title; for the first time in several years Mount Saint Charles was a state tournament underdog.

The two teams split the first two games of the best of three series, generating so much interest that enterprising high school kids scalped the $5 tickets for the third game for as much as $50. After two periods of the third game, Mount held a 3–2 lead, but with Hendricken's firepower no one, myself included, expected a one-goal lead would be enough. But no one had counted on Snow's ability to deliver under pressure.

"I swear in the third period of that game the puck never left our zone," Dave remembered. "We were just trying to hang on."

Dave was right. At one point late in the game, Snow stopped three point-blank shots within ten seconds. When the final buzzer sounded Mount was still leading 3–2 and had another state title.

Six years later, Emma had lost games in the Olympics and the national NCAA tournament, but he would still say that third-game loss "was the most disappointing game of my life. In that third period Garth Snow was the best goalie in the world."

"He should have been allowed to take the trophy home with him," Dave said about Snow.

There's a huge sign that once hung on the wall of Brown's Meehan Auditorium still tucked away in a back room of Snow's parents home:"

Only God Saves More than Garth Snow

Bill gives Snow credit for his determination, once noting that in all his years of coaching, "I never had anyone work harder or practice more to make himself better. He wouldn't take no for an answer."

Despite those sensational performances, Snow didn't receive any scholarship offers in his senior year at Mount. Both Bill and Dave called college coaches trying to convince them that Snow could be an outstanding college goalie, but no one was interested. Snow was hurt, angry, and puzzled, yet he wouldn't quit. After graduating from Mount, he moved to Canada and played a year in the Junior B league. When there were still no scholarship offers he enrolled at the University of Maine and introduced himself to Shawn Walsh. All Walsh gave him was an invitation to try out for the team. Walsh admitted that he thought Snow would make nothing more than a capable practice goalie.

"I figured he would get as much ice time as the Zamboni," Walsh was once quoted in a USA Today story about Snow.

But just as he had at Mount, Snow refused to accept "no" about playing time.

He red-shirted for a year, then rode the bench for two. Then as a junior he got a chance to alternate with Maine's regular goalie, Mike Dunham and did the same thing in his senior year. Maine reached the NCAA Final

Four that year and it was Snow's turn to start in the semifinals against Michigan. He turned in a sensational performance as Maine beat Michigan 3–2 in overtime.

Because it was his turn, Dunham was the starter in the title game against Lake Superior. But after two periods, Maine was down, 4–2. His team needed some kind of spark so Walsh sent Snow into the game.

"We had to change the tempo of the game and I knew Garth could do that for us," Walsh said at the time. "He's very aggressive. He's always going out after the puck."

Snow proved to be the spark that Maine needed. Maine tied the game and then won the national title with an overtime victory. One of the other heroes of that Maine national title was junior Keith Carney, who had been a sophomore on the 1987 Mount team that Snow backboned to the Rhode Island title. The following summer, Snow beat out a dozen of the best young American goaltenders for a spot on the 1994 Olympic team. He began as the team's backup at the Olympic games in Norway, but by the time the competition was over he had become one of the heroes on a young American team that almost won a medal.

After the Olympics, he signed with the Quebec Nordiques, who had drafted him a few years earlier. He played a few games for Quebec in the NHL, but spent most of the 1993–94, and 1994–95 seasons in the American Hockey League. Many observers thought that his grit and determination had taken Snow as far as his talent would allow him to go—a journeyman AHL goalie. That's not bad. A lot of players would love to accomplish that, but it wasn't enough for Snow. He kept working, doing whatever it took to earn a spot on an NHL roster. He donned shoulder pads and a chest protector that were so wide on his six-four body that they virtually covered the entire width of the goal, anything to make it appear tougher for opposing forwards looking for an opening. One sportswriter wrote that he must be taking two-by-fours from his family's home supply store and putting them across his shoulders. He became ever more of a roamer than he was in college, and he wasn't afraid to skate out of his crease to help one of his teammates in fights. NHL fans, who weren't accustomed to seeing goalies out of the cage brawling in a center-ice fight, loved Snow's style. He eventually earned a spot on the Quebec roster before he was traded to Philadelphia to serve as a backup to veteran Ron Hextall. But when Hextall developed problems toward the end of the 1996–97 season, Snow became the starting goalie and his sensational performances helped the Flyers reach the Stanley Cup finals in 1997. Ironically, Philadelphia felt another former Mountie, Brian Boucher, was their goalie of the future. They traded Snow to Vancouver, where he was splitting time as the Canucks starting goaltender in 1998.

With his perseverance, Snow probably would have made it to the NHL even if Bill hadn't given him a second chance back in 1987, but Snow will never forget that Bill had confidence in him when a lot of other people didn't. He still calls Bill a few times each season, not only to find out how things are going at Mount but also just to let Bill know how critical a role he played in making what most people thought was Snow's impossible NHL dream a reality. That year, Snow's call couldn't have come at a better time. It reminded Bill that he has always had faith in his seniors, and that they have always delivered for him. The 1997–98 seniors were testing that faith, but Snow's call reminded Bill just how important it was that he didn't give up on them.

CHAPTER 26

There had only been a few years in its twenty-one-year reign as Rhode Island state champion that Mount Saint Charles didn't have the regular-season title clinched by the time it played its final regular-season home game. But a few days after Garth Snow called Bill, Mount was scheduled to play its final regular season home game of the 1997–98 season against La Salle, and it still hadn't clinched the title. There were three games remaining on the regular season schedule: the home game against La Salle and then road games against Burrillville and Hendricken. All Mount needed was one victory and the title would be theirs. It should have been easy, but then, during that season, nothing was easy.

These days, most high school sports teams use the final home game of the regular season as a night to honor its seniors. A group of parents get together with the coach and plan a pregame ceremony. Usually the players present their mothers with flowers and then have their photographs taken with their parents. The Mount Saint Charles girls and boys basketball teams both have senior nights, the soccer teams have senior days, but the Mount hockey team has never had a senior night—and probably never will as long as Bill is coach. He considers it a distraction at a very critical moment in the season. Furthermore, it would mean parent involvement in the game's preparation—and parents aren't members of the Mount hockey team. Yes, Bill's always telling his players how much they should appreciate what their parents have done for them, but they should show their appreciation every day at home. A few flowers that someone else bought isn't a real thank you, at least in Bill's mind. So on February 6, the parents of the thirteen seniors on the 1997–98 team sat in the stands just as they always did and watched as their sons took the ice for their final regular-season home game.

Chick LaBreche was also sitting in the stands that night. No one outside of the Belisle family worried more about Mount Saint Charles losing than LaBreche. He'd been watching Mount hockey since 1934. He was there when Brother Adelard was coaching, and he was there when they built Adelard Arena. And every time a Bill team won a state championship, he had been there.

A retired machinist, LaBreche was one of the devoted fans whom Bill shut out of Mount practices when he became coach in 1975. LaBreche didn't hold a grudge, however; whenever Mount played, Chick was there to support the team, home or away.

When Woonsocket had a heavy French-Canadian population there were hundreds of guys like Chick who followed Mount hockey because it was part of their heritage. But the ethnic makeup of Woonsocket had changed dramatically and, by the late nineties, the Mount fan base was mainly students, parents, and young hockey players from the Woonsocket area. Mortality had also taken its toll on the old-time Mount fans, but in 1998 a dozen still made the games on a regular basis. The 1997–98 team wasn't kind on their aging hearts.

"You never know what team is going to show up," LaBreche said one night. "When they want to, they can beat anybody. But sometimes they don't seem to care."

LaBreche was trying to stay optimistic about the title string continuing, but on some nights it was hard. The team didn't seem to be able to put games away. They would control the action, but they continually failed to take advantage of scoring opportunities. Even when they won, the outcome was usually in doubt until the final buzzer.

"This could be the least-talented team Bill has ever had," LaBreche said. "They don't know how to score."

Nothing changed against La Salle that night. Only forty seconds into the game, Oliver let a fairly easy shot bounce off his catching glove for a goal. It was purely a case of not concentrating.

It was quickly looking like one of those nights when Mount hadn't "come to play." Only three minutes into the game, Mount was behind 2–0 to a team it had already beaten twice. Hutchins finally cut the deficit to one at 5:44 of the period, and then Jillson tied the score with an unassisted goal with a few minutes to play.

Between the first and second periods, Dave paced the hallway behind the Mount bench trying to figure out how to get everybody focused on the game. They were outshooting La Salle at least two-to-one, but the score was only tied. They weren't taking advantage of their scoring opportunities, and once again Oliver was letting up some soft goals.

"How do we get him up for big games?" Dave asked about Oliver to anyone around him who wanted to offer an answer.

Things didn't get much better in the second period. Mount continued to dominate the action, but couldn't put the puck in the cage. La Salle broke the tie with three minutes to go in the period, before Cardillo once again tied the score only a minute later. When the period ended and the team headed to the dressing room for the ten-minute Zamboni break, Dave knew his father was in the mood for some ranting and raving. But Dave felt the game was winnable, even if there wasn't a radical turnaround in the team's focus. They should be able to score a goal or two in the third period, but they couldn't make any more defensive lapses as they'd done in the first. If his father started screaming, a few of the players might start trying to make things happen offensively and make defensive mistakes.

"Take it easy. We can't have any defensive mistakes," Dave quietly pointed out to his father as they walked into the dressing room.

Ten years earlier, there wouldn't have been any hope of Bill not going on a rampage between periods, but if that was the way Dave wanted it that was the way it would be that night. Bill knows he's lucky: the closest most guys his age come to getting their competitive juices flowing is the weekly church bingo game or the monthly trip to the casino with the senior citizens group. He wouldn't be actually feeling the thrill of victory rather than just watching a game on TV if it wasn't for Dave.

Very low-key between periods, Dave talked about finishing off plays and about looking for the second chance rather than just skating away if they missed their first shot. It was nothing the players hadn't heard before and most of them were surprised that Dave didn't seem all that upset. They knew they hadn't played well and they had expected to hear chewing out from either Dave or Bill, probably both. Most of them, especially the younger players, were pleased that neither coach yelled at them, but not everyone. Charlie Ridolf was sitting on the bench, bent over, eyes on the floor. As usual he seethed frustration. Nothing seemed to be clicking, and in his opinion it was because the coaches had him teamed with the wrong players. He wanted to yell out for everyone to get their fucking asses moving, but he knew he couldn't. If the coaches were keeping it low-key, he couldn't explode. Across the dressing room, near the door, Jillson also was frustrated. Why couldn't the team score more? Why was every game a struggle? Oliver's letting up soft goals increasingly irritated him. A hockey team can't go into a game worried that their goalie was going to give up easy goals. If they're always worrying about having to cover up for him, it's going to hurt their offensive play. None of them said a word out loud, but some of the other seniors were starting to think Oliver just didn't care enough. He was looking for any type of physical problems that would give him an excuse to avoid practice.

Maybe Oliver intercepted his teammates' mental vibes or maybe it was his own determination, but in the third period he played a solid game. It was fortunate that Oliver finally got his head back into the game because once again, despite a huge shot advantage, Mount couldn't score a goal. Oliver's play helped keep the game tied through the third period, and the one sudden-death overtime that's played before the game was declared a tie, which gave Mount the point it needed to clinch at least a tie for the regular-season title. Now all they needed was a tie or victory in one of the final two games to be the outright champion.

Most teams would have been celebrating, but the mood in the Mount dressing room after the game was very subdued. It had been the second game of a doubleheader and it was now eleven o'clock. Within about thirty minutes, the entire team, except Jillson, had showered and left the locker room. Even though it was approaching midnight, and his parents were waiting for him in the lobby, he wasn't in a hurry to leave. He wanted to talk to the coaches alone. He was upset about what was happening and was beginning to worry that he was going to be the captain of the Mount team that lost the title. He was trying to be a leader, but he was learning that leadership doesn't automatically come with talent. So he sat down with Bill and Dave to discuss the team's next move.

"What do we need to do, coach?" he asked.

"Maybe it's time for a good old-fashioned practice," Dave answered with a sly smile.

It wasn't unusual for Adelard Arena to be nearly dark when the players file into the rink after school and head to the locker room to dress for practice. Bill doesn't waste electricity. Most days the rink is empty for the few hours before the end of school, so Bill leaves only the exit lights illuminated. He doesn't switch on the others until just before the start of practice, so when the first few players took the ice to start warming up and there were still only a few lights on at the far end of the rink they assumed that Bill just hadn't had a chance to put on all the lights. But when Bill came charging through the locker room blowing his whistle for the start of practice and the lights *still* weren't on, everyone knew they were in for a long afternoon.

The rink was lit only by the scoreboard lights as it had been in Sean McHugh's days. There was enough light that players could see where they were skating, but you wouldn't want to be a goalie trying to find a slap shot at your head in that kind of lighting. But that wouldn't be a problem, because nobody would be shooting pucks that day. They had heard all the stories about the daily torture tests during Bill's early years as Mount coach. The members of the 1997–98 team were now finding out what an old-fashioned Mount practice was really like.

They skated for two hours without shooting a puck. Bill set up four lanes with traffic cones and had the scoreboard clock set to forty-five minutes, the minutes in a game. The twenty-five or so players were divided into four groups skating up and down the lanes. There was no circling around the back of the cage, no chance to float. Just skating up and down the rink. First it was from one end of the rink and back again. Then it was stopping at the blue line, back to the goal line, up to the red line, and back again. First they skated nonstop for fifteen seconds, then twenty seconds, then twenty-five, and then thirty seconds. Forty-five minutes of nonstop skating. When the clock finally expired, Bill had it reset and then started doing skating drills by lines and defensive units.

Dave arrived about a half hour after the start of practice, but didn't even go out on the ice. He just went up to the press box and starting marking down which lines were skating best.

Suddenly Venice skated over to the bench.

"I don't feel good," he said. "I think I'm going to puke."

On the other side of the rink Bill saw Venice leaning over the boards near the bench. It was a sight he had seen many times through the years.

"If you're going to puke get off the ice," he yelled. "And don't do it in the locker room. Use the toilet."

Venice charged off the ice. Soon he was kneeling at the toilet in the dressing room.

"I think I have a cold," he said when he finished and sat down on the bench.

A few minutes later, Pelletier limped into the dressing room complaining that he had pulled "an ass muscle." Within five minutes, a few other players also came in complaining to Doc Guay about muscle pulls.

"Doc, you have to come out and tell coach we can't practice because we have pulled muscles," Pelletier pleaded.

But Pelletier didn't have to worry about an alibi. Out on the ice, Bill was finally calling an end to the practice. One by one the players stumbled into the locker room. Most of them just wanted to take a warm shower and head home. A few were already in the shower when Bill strolled into the locker room.

"Out of the showers! Everybody in here," he yelled as he herded the few players who were still coming off the ice into the locker room. He slammed the door and ordered everyone to sit down. Four or five players sat with just towels around their waists, still dripping wet from being pulled out of the shower.

"This is just the start," Bill informed them. "Today you had an old-fashioned Mount practice, and there's going to be more of them. We have a lot of work to do, so you better be ready."

He went on for nearly ten minutes, going from player to player telling them what they had to work on. When Bill finally finished and walked into his office, just about everybody started scrambling for the showers. But Joe Peters headed out of the locker room doorway toward the weight room across the hall. The previous week Peters had come into the office once again to ask Dave what he had to do to see more playing time.

"What do I say to him?" Dave had remarked after Peters left the office. "He's a weak skater. His strides are short and he gets tired easy because he only started skating at midyear."

What Peters possessed, however, was willingness to work and physical strength. So Dave told him that the team needed to get physically stronger. He told Peters that they were getting pushed away from scoring opportunities in front of the cage because they were weak. Peters got the message. Not only was he going to the weight room after practice, he was now coaxing other players to go with him. The last place Mark Esposito felt like going after spending two hours of skating drills was the weight room, but Peters had laid down the challenge. Rather than head for a warm shower, Esposito followed Peters.

CHAPTER 27

Paul Fede was sitting in the snack bar at the Sportsplex in Manchester, New Hampshire, and he wasn't happy. It was 4:30 on the afternoon of February 12 and Mount Saint Charles's exhibition game with Bishop Guertin High of Nashua wasn't scheduled to start until 6:30.

"Why are we here so early?" Paul fumed. "We should have left an hour later. I had a lot of things I could have done with that hour."

Paul's high school career was a classic case of teenage achievement addiction. His goal was to be the all-American boy—a star athlete, a brilliant musician, and an outstanding student. But he wasn't a math whiz who could scan a calculus problem and instantaneously compute the answer. He needed to put in the extra time with homework. He was a capable musician, but only because he practiced regularly. His hockey game didn't flow instinctively; it improved step by step with practice. In order to achieve his goals, he needed every minute he could find to balance all of his activities. seemed he was always rushing, always trying to fit an hour's worth of work into fifty-five minutes. At times, his life was a whirlwind that he didn't know how to escape.

After practice the previous night, the entire team—except for Paul— had gone to Jeff Jillson's house for a spaghetti and meatball dinner. Paul had to rush right from hockey practice in Woonsocket to a practice session for the all-state band in East Providence about twenty miles away. He then headed home to study for advance-placement history and English tests. He, Jillson, and Cardillo were best friends, and although all three were dealing with that sense of uncertainty every high school senior feels, Paul's was far more complex than his friends'.

Jillson was debating between turning pro and attending college. Agents called his home every day, urging him to turn pro. But if he decided he wanted to go to college first, it was just a matter of whether he would go to Harvard, Michigan, or Maine. Everybody wanted him.

Cardillo planned to combine his love of hockey and music in a college career; it was just a matter of where. Holy Cross, one of the most selective colleges in the country, was high on his list. Even though he was registering good numbers and coaches were noticing him, Cardillo would probably need a little help with the admissions office. Nonetheless, things looked like they were falling into place.

Paul, however, still had no clue where he would be the following fall. Holy Cross was a possibility for him, too, but he wasn't sure if the Holy Cross coach would use his influence with the admission office for a hockey player who wasn't certain he wanted to go to the school. His brother Frank suggested West Point. It was late to start thinking about the Academy but as a hockey player he could probably still could get an appointment with admissions. Frank was sure that Paul had the talent to play Division I hockey, even if there were no Division I coaches calling him. Frank kept telling him it was the same situation he had been in five years earlier.

Paul's game was also starting to improve. He had gotten over the trauma of being separated from Jillson and was starting to recognize that maybe the coaches were right. He was much more valuable as the top man on the second defensive unit. He wasn't trying to match Jillson, but he also knew that when he was out on the ice he needed to be focused at all times. He was playing most often with Esposito, whose game had steadily improved since the start of the season, but who could still make mistakes and wasn't much of an offensive threat. Paul was the key to the defense when the two were on the ice. Even though Bill seemed to find fault with his moves at nearly every practice, he was feeling good about his play.

Yet as much as he enjoyed playing hockey, as much as he thought he had Division I talent, he was beginning to realize that he wasn't as obsessed with proving he could play at the Division I level as his brother had been. He lacked the hockey passion that he would need to justify the rigors of a West Point plebe year. Furthermore, if he was really serious about a medical career, the program at the University of Pittsburgh was his best option. But it would mean no more hockey.

But his own future wasn't the only thing concerning Paul that February afternoon. He was also worried about the Mount tradition. He was a more integral part of the Mount tradition than anyone else on the team. His mother sat in the stands with her rosary beads tightly wrapped around her hands, praying that her son would play well, and she also was praying for Mount. His brother was one of the great Mount success stories: the guy who never would have become a West Point graduate if he hadn't played hockey at Mount Saint Charles. Paul felt an obligation to protect the Mount image, not just for the school but also for his family.

So on that day, he sat in the snack bar worrying about a Mount win, about attracting the notice of college coaches, about acing his upcoming calculus test, and about wasting time.

In his opinion, Bill's obsession with detail had cost him precious time. When estimating how long the Woonsocket to New Hampshire trip would take, Bill had factored in the possibility of encountering Boston metro traffic. But there hadn't been any traffic; the bus could easily have left Woonsocket an hour later. But Bill is never going to take a chance that his team will be late for a game because he hadn't thought about a detail such as a traffic jam.

Most of the players were content to hang around the rink's snack bar playing video games, but Paul was sure that their early arrival was just one more case of Belisle head games.

Bishop Guertin came into the game with a 12–1 record against other New Hampshire high schools, but there was a big difference between the top level of New Hampshire high school hockey and the top Rhode Island and Massachusetts teams. In three games at the Mount tournament that December, Guertin had lost twice. They were also scheduled to play Catholic Memorial that year, but CM had canceled out because it had scheduled too many games and Bill Hanson felt Guertin was the weakest team on its schedule.

So a home game against Mount Saint Charles was one of the highlights of Bishop Guertin's season. For Guertin players, this would be one of the few times all season that college coaches would watch them play.

They knew it was the Mount Saint Charles players who brought the coaches to the game, but it was still their chance to get noticed.

For two periods, Guertin played one of its best games of the season, holding Mount Saint Charles scoreless despite being severely out shot. On the Mount side, Joe Peters was playing his ass off—he's obviously taken Dave's message about the team needing to be more physical to heart. It wasn't in Peters's nature to be mean, even on the ice, but if pushing a few people around was the way he could help Mount, he would go against his natural feelings. A few times he had muscled his way into an advantageous scoring position in front of the cage, but just couldn't convert on passes, although he was providing the team with the physical presence in front of the cage that had been so sorely missing. He was setting up screens in front of the goalie for the shots from the point and he was getting some rebounds. If only if he didn't have hands of stone.

It was starting to turn into another typical Mount game in which they dominated the action, but couldn't score goals. After two periods, it was still scoreless, but finally, early in the third period, Snizek tipped home a pass across the front of the crease. Five minutes later, he made it 2–0 with another tip-in. That was the way it ended giving Mount its sixteenth victory of the season. Dave was a bit frustrated that they didn't convert some good scoring opportunities, especially on the power play, but the defense was steady and Oliver seemed to stay focused for the entire game.

As soon as the players started filing into the locker room, Fede initiated his campaign to hurry everyone onto the bus and quickly head back home. The victory was nice, but he still had studying to do when he got home. Thanks to Jillson, however, there was no chance of a quick departure.

As he was skated off the ice after the game, Jillson had noticed one of the Notre Dame assistant coaches in the stands. In the locker room, he knew the coach was waiting for him outside, but he didn't want to see him. Although he liked Notre Dame coach Dave Poulin, and the fact that Poulin was a former NHL star, the Notre Dame program was still in the building stages. As much as he enjoyed the atmosphere of a Notre Dame football game, South Bend wasn't the most exciting place in the winter. The Fighting Irish had made his Final Four, but now he had narrowed it down to three other schools: Harvard, Michigan, and Maine. He just didn't want to tell anybody yet. So he undressed even more slowly than usual in hopes that the Notre Dame assistant would become discouraged waiting and simply settle for a conversation with his parents, who were in the lobby.

All the other players had left the locker room and most of them were already on the bus by the time Jillson finally left of the locker room. The Notre Dame coach was still there waiting for him. He cornered Jillson against a wall and launched into his spiel about the enthusiasm that Poulin has instilled in the Irish program. Like a salesman who knows his customer, he emphatically stressed the importance for a young player like Jillson, whose dream was to play in the NHL, to have a former NHL player as his college coach. Many high school superstars in Jillson's position would have just given the coach a quick brush-off if they knew they no longer were interested in the coach's school, and that's exactly what Jillson would love to have done, but his parents have taught him manners. He didn't want to hear the coach's pitch, but he stood against the wall, listening politely. It was a one-way conversation. Jillson didn't have any questions, but the coach had plenty to say and he had Jillson all to himself.

Out in the bus Fede sat fuming. He and the other players had waited for at least fifteen minutes and there was still no sign of Jillson. Back in the rink, Dave had stopped to chat with a few acquaintances from Bishop Guertin, but eventually everyone except Jillson and the Notre Dame coach had left the locker room area. Although Dave didn't know that Jillson had wiped Notre Dame off his list, he could sense that Jillson had had enough. He went to Jillson's rescue, telling the coach they had to get going. Jillson, with the look of a kid who was just let out of detention early, rushed out of the rink—probably the only time all season his teammates saw him in a hurry to get on the bus.

"Why do people hate us?" Bill asked.

He was sitting in his usual spot next to the window in the seat behind the driver as the Mount bus rolled south down Route 495 back to Woonsocket from New Hampshire.

Most people who reach Bill's status in their chosen profession are accustomed to doing the talking. They don't ask many questions; others ask them the questions. Cable news networks, talk radio, twenty-four-hour sports channels—they all need people willing to talk. But when Bill's not on the ice, he's a listener. When he's with people who are not members of his family or part of the Mount inner circle, he's the one always asking questions. He seems to know that despite his reputation as one of the best high school sports coaches in the country he lives in a limited world, the world of Adelard Arena and Manville. He loves to have his former players come back and share their experiences. They open new worlds to him.

Bill's habit of always asking the questions became a formidable roadblock for me as I tried to discover what made this man tick. I was the one who was supposed to be asking the questions, but more often than not Bill turned them right back on me. It was not his way of just making idle conversation or deflecting an invasion of his privacy; he asks questions because he wants to know the answers, to better understand people who live outside his world. He looks straight into your eyes as you answer, no sly glances, no conversations in which you know he's really thinking about something else. When you talk to Bill you're sure that he's focused on what you're saying.

Usually the only person who sits with Bill in the front seat is Dave. But that night Dave had driven his own car to Manchester because he had had a sales call in Massachusetts during the day. So for one of the few times in the ten or so bus trips I took that season, I had a chance to sit with Bill. A chance to have nearly ninety minutes of uninterrupted casual talk. I discovered that these were the times when I could learn the most about Bill, when it wasn't formal interview setting, when he felt like he was just relaxing at his kitchen table. But Bill never lets the conversations go too long before he takes the role of inquisitor rather than informant. We had been idly chatting about hockey in general and how players have changed over the years when he suddenly threw out the "Why do people hate us?" question.

The question caught me off guard, but I didn't have to think very long about the answer.

"Because you win all the time," I told him.

"But isn't that what you're suppose to do?"

It's inconceivable to him that anyone would dislike a team because they win all the time. He's a Yankees fan and a Montreal Canadiens fan because when he was growing up they were the best teams. If the objective when the puck is dropped is to win the game, as long as you play fair and respect your opponent, what's wrong with winning?

He can understand why the fans of the rival teams dislike his team. Like old-time Red Sox fans hate the Yankees simply because the Yankees always beat the Red Sox, two decades of La Salle and Hendricken fans have been frustrated because their teams never beat Mount in the big game. But Bill can't understand why many Rhode Islanders who have no attachment to other teams dislike his. Rhode Islanders should take pride in what Mount Saint Charles has done for the state's sports image. In 1998, there were only five athletes who had played at a Rhode Island high school who were playing at the highest level of their professional sport and four of them, Berard, Carney, Schneider, and Snow played at Mount Saint Charles. In other states, sports fans would consider a high school team like Mount a state treasure, but Rhode Islanders seemed to disdain the Mount success. For years certain Rhode Island sportswriters who have never even met Bill and who don't cover high school sports on a regular basis have taken potshots at Mount hockey. They claim that what Mount has achieved isn't all that special. They insist that Mount has all the advantages because they are a private school playing against public schools. Of course they completely ignore the fact that Mount's main competition are Rhode Island's other private schools. Their criticism began about a decade ago. At first, Bill took it personally, but now he just shrugs if off.

If his team had a reputation as bullies or poor sports, he might understand the animosity. But every year Mount is one of the least-penalized teams among the RIIL's hockey teams. During Bill's tenure they have won the Rhode Island Hockey Officials Association's sportsmanship award more than any other team in the state.

"I thought maybe people hate Mount because they don't like me," he mused. "I know people get upset because I don't talk a lot. But you really think it's because we win?"

Having somebody dislike you just because you win is inconceivable to Bill Belisle.

"I'm putting my job on the line. I'm putting my family's well-being at stake and you don't even care enough to work until the end of practice," Dave screamed.

It was Friday afternoon, the day after the Bishop Guertin game, and Dave was on a rampage. He was in the Mount dressing room following what was the only practice session between the Guertin game and against Catholic Memorial at Boston University on Saturday afternoon. This was one practice Dave wanted to be at from start to the finish. Although they'd won the Guertin game, there were a lot of things that still needed work, especially the power play.

In terms of economic reality, there's no question where Dave's priorities lay between his day job and his coaching job. For all the hours he puts in, hours that include 6:00 a.m. junior varsity practices four days a week, he's only paid a few thousand dollars—not enough money to support a family of four. Dave knows he needs to keep his sales numbers high, which was why he was out bright and early at seven Friday morning although he hadn't made it home from New Hampshire until nearly eleven Thursday. A long list of sales calls awaited him and he wanted to complete them in time to make the 3:00 p.m. start of practice. But every call was taking longer than he had expected, and by noontime it was obvious that he wasn't going to finish. He had to make a choice. Which of his obligations would take priority: his primary source of income or the Mount power play?

It wasn't an easy choice, but he rationalized that he could put in extra time on Monday making up the missing sales calls, but if he didn't get the power play straightened out that afternoon, Mount had no chance against Catholic Memorial the following day.

His father and the players were already on the ice as he rushed through the dressing room to change his skates in the office. No time to change into sweat pants, today his practice attire would be skates, dress pants, and a Mount jacket over his white button-down shirt. It didn't take long for his mood to turn sour. As he sat in a chair at his father's desk tying on his skates, he saw a note on the desk from Pelletier; he wouldn't be at practice. He had mono.

"Boy that's going to hurt us," sighed Dave. "But I feel for the kid more than for us. This was going to be his year. He had worked really hard for this year and he would have been one of the top scorers. He was just starting to get back into shape after returning from the injury, now this. He's finished, and you can't make up your senior year. There's only senior year at Mount."

At least Dave managed a laugh when he headed out of the dressing and spotted the big handwritten sign his father had posted on the back of the dressing room door.

No Exceptions was neatly printed in large letters across the top of the sign. In slightly smaller letters were the following commands:

Unpack Your Own Bag.
Hang Shirts and Socks on the Pipes.
Don't Leave it for the Managers. Managers Aren't Your Mothers,
They're Your Helpers.

Then there was one final warning:

Don't Let Coach Belisle Unpack Your Bag. It Will Take You Two Days to Find Your Gear.

"He wants to make sure they're not getting lazy late in the season," Dave chuckles as he headed onto the ice in his white shirt and dress pants.

Despite Dave's concern about losing Pelletier, practice went well for the first hour or so. Through the drills and the early parts of a controlled scrimmage everything had run smoothly. But when Dave started working on the power play everything seemed to go wrong. Once again, it seemed to be a case of players being more concerned about themselves than about the team. One of the key components of a successful power play is for the forwards on the team with the advantage to keep the opposing players from getting out to the defenseman once the puck goes back to the point. There's a fine line between interference that will get you a penalty and legally bottling up a player for a few seconds so the pointman has a chance to get off a good shot on cage. It's especially important for a team with a defenseman like Jillson. Giving Jillson a few extra seconds to get off his shot could mean the difference between a goal and a wasted power play. The work of the forwards doesn't show up in the stat sheets or get them headlines, yet it's the kind of work that makes a team successful. Nonetheless, for fifteen or twenty minutes no one seemed too concerned about doing the job. Time after time the defensive forwards just skated out and harassed Jillson. Every time it happened further irritated Dave. To make matters worse, no one focused on making the right passes. Either they held the puck too long or they got rid of it too quickly. They had been working for nearly two hours and it was obvious they were thinking more about getting home and enjoying a Friday night with their friends than perfecting their power play. There was still about fifteen minutes left in the normal practice time, but Dave had seen enough.

"Everybody into the dressing room," he screamed.

Once the entire team was assembled in the dressing room, Dave started talking, surprisingly in very even tones.

He spoke for only a few minutes, then he suddenly brought the conversation to a close.

"If you don't care, I don't care," he said with disgust. "Go home. The bus leaves for Catholic Memorial at eleven o'clock tomorrow morning."

He then turned, stomped into the little office where his father was already sitting, and slammed the door behind them.

The players sat dumbfounded, shocked looks on their face. No one spoke or moved for several minutes.

Dave Belisle not caring about Mount hockey? He didn't really mean that, did he?

CHAPTER 28

Bill was walking around the dressing room at Boston University's Walter Brown Arena, shaking hands and telling his players "that's the way to play Mount hockey." If you had just strolled in from outside you would have thought he was congratulating his players on a big victory. But it was only the break between the second and third period of the Mount Saint Charles–Catholic Memorial game and Mount was losing 3–2. It may have been the only time in his twenty-three years of coaching that Bill had congratulated his players when they were losing. But in 1998, any team could be playing a great game and still be losing to Catholic Memorial. CM had won nine of the previous ten Massachusetts state championships. CM coach Bill Hanson had coached some great teams over the previous decade, but he had never coached a team through a perfect season. But with only two weeks left in the season, the 1997–98 CM team had a perfect record. They were 22–0–0 coming into the nonleague game that day with Mount. Hockey insiders were saying it was the best CM team Hanson had ever coached, one with both superstars and lots of depth. A few weeks earlier, in a *Boston Herald* story, Hanson had been quoted as saying his two star defensemen, Jim Fahey and Mike Matta, were playing so well "they could be playing college hockey already."

Fahey had already committed to Northeastern and Ryan Cordeiro, a powerful, high scoring forward had signed with the University of New Hampshire. By the end of the season, three other players would sign with Division I schools. A New England high school hockey team with five players headed to Division I is special.

In December, CM dominated Mount in the title game of the Mount tournament. Bill and Dave will never tell their team another team is better than it, but that year they knew CM was a much better team. To beat CM that year, Mount would have had to play better than it had played in any previous game, and for two periods that's what they had done. CM had opened the scoring late in the first period and then made it 2–0 early in the second. But midway through the period Chris Snizek cut the deficit to 2–1 when he tipped in Joe Cardillo's pass near the right post. A few minutes later, Cardillo's goal tied the score. With only a few minutes to play in the second period, Mount was even with CM. Everyone was working hard. They were moving the puck and except for the goal in the first period when the defense got caught looking for the perfect breakout pass rather than just clearing the puck from in front of the cage, everybody was playing good position hockey.

Dave was psyched. He was seeing more emotion from the Mount players than he had seen in any game all season. A victory over CM was just what this team needed to give them that sense of self-confidence that would be so important in the playoffs. CM dampened his excitement a bit when it scored just before the end of the period, but he still was happy as hell when the team headed to the dressing room between the periods. Mount was trailing 3–2, but it was still anybody's game.

Up in the far corner of the rink a group of about ten guys, some in their late twenties and others closer to middle age, laid down their notebooks as the Zamboni began circling the ice. Some were scouts for professional teams and the others were assistant college coaches—same game, different objectives. The pro scouts were there to watch Jillson, Fahey, Cordeiro, and Matta, another six-foot, two-hundred-pound plus CM defenseman who was trying to decide between a few Division I offers. Although Jillson hadn't made an official announcement, it was becoming obvious that he wasn't going to opt into that year's NHL draft. Playing high school hockey had dropped him off the 1998 draft radar screen. Whether he played college or juniors the following year, the only wise move was to wait until

1999 to enter the draft. The pro scouts were already starting to put together information for the 1999 draft prospects, and Jillson, Fahey, and Matta were prospects. The college coaches were there to see if there was a player besides those known prospects who they might have missed. Someone who might be worth a last-minute offer if they didn't secure all their top choices.

That's why Charlie Ridolf was so psyched for the game. His chances of getting a Division I scholarship had dwindled severely, if not evaporated completely. This game might be his last real opportunity to show the college coaches he had the talent to excite a team. For most players, reaching an emotional high improves their play, but that wasn't always the case with Ridolf. Sometimes for Charlie it was a detriment. Sometimes that enthusiasm sent him right over the edge.

"The refs have their heads up their asses," he yelled right in the middle of Dave's strategy talk between the second and third periods.

The outburst caught Dave by surprise. He was trying to maintain the controlled enthusiasm that was essential if Mount was to have any hope of beating Catholic Memorial and here was Ridolf yelling uncontrollably. He suppressed his urge just to order Ridolf to shut up; he didn't want to upset everyone else's focus. He tried answering Ridolf's outburst without letting it distract the rest of the team from the task at hand.

"Yes, they do. But you can't say anything," Dave said, then quickly turned the subject to coverage in front of the cage. He kept talking but he was constantly worried that at any second Ridolf was going to break out with another diatribe. Finally, he walked over to the small blackboard hanging on the wall. Everyone expected that he was going to diagram some defensive assignments, but instead he scribbled "Mount Pride" in large letters.

"You're learning what it means," Dave said.

Joel Jillson was up in the stands standing at the far end of the rink, talking to Bill Cass Sr. Cass is the ultimate hockey parent. He and Joel had spent a lot of time together during the previous years sitting in the stands of hockey rinks throughout the Northeast watching their sons, who were the same age, play hockey. Although Cass lived in Massachusetts, his willingness to promote his son's hockey career had no mileage limitations. Since Bill Jr. was about ten years old, Cass had driven him to clinics, camps, and leagues throughout the Northeast, nearly twelve months a year. He was a divorced long-haul truck driver, which meant he didn't have a large disposable income or a lot of free time, yet he always found time for his son's hockey career. In a sense, he was always battling to make sure Bill Jr. didn't get lost in the Boston youth hockey circus where money often dictates how far a kid will go. If he had to make an extra run to earn the cash for a clinic or a special summer camp, then that's what he did. It was all part of his master plan to give his son an opportunity to play pro. Bill Jr. wasn't anywhere as talented as Jeff, and also didn't have Jeff's size, but he had been skilled enough to make several of the regional age-group all-star teams over the previous four or five years. So Cass and Joel had shared many hours of conversation over cups of lukewarm coffee. But that day Cass was looking for Joel's help—without really asking for it.

When it came time for Bill Jr. to pick a high school, Catholic Memorial was his first choice because it fielded the best team in Massachusetts. But his father wasn't taking any chances. He had heard the rumors that Hanson played favorites, that there were politics in CM hockey just as there is in the USA Hockey youth programs. He had heard that the kids whose parents are involved with the school, fund-raising and other services, have an advantage when it comes to making the hockey team. He discussed these rumors with Hanson before enrolling Bill Jr. Hanson guaranteed him that he plays the best twenty-five players—no matter who they are—so Bill Jr. enrolled at CM. He played there three years and every year Cass was in the stands with the other fathers. In both his sophomore and junior years, Bill Jr. saw action but wasn't one of the team stars. He wasn't going to be one of the stars of the 1997–98 team, either. Cass was afraid that in a team of so many outstanding players Bill Jr. might get overlooked by college coaches. Bill Jr. therefore left CM before the start of the 1997–98 season to play for the USA Hockey development team in Michigan, one of the teams Jeff had considered when he thought about leaving Mount, but never gave serious consideration. For three months, Cass drove long-haul truck trips during the week and then each weekend hopped in his car and drove to Michigan to watch Bill Jr. play. He had bought a new car in October and by February the odometer already read 35,000 miles.

But the master plan hadn't gone the way either father or son had envisioned. There hadn't been any serious interest by Division I coaches. To make matters worse, a few weeks earlier Bill Jr. suffered a leg injury that kept him sidelined for about a month. There were no scholarship offers, his son was two thousand miles away in what should be the best year of his high school career, and he wasn't even playing. Instead of driving to Michigan, Cass was spending his weekends attending CM games. He knew Jeff was getting a lot of college attention, receiving everything Cass had imagined for his son. College coaches were calling the Jillson household on a regular basis. He didn't say it directly, but he was asking Joel for a favor. If in his discussion with the college coaches, one happened to ask Joel who he thought were the best players Jeff had played against maybe he could mention Bill Jr.'s name.

It didn't take long for Bill and Dave's euphoria to disappear once the third period started. CM came out flying. It was obvious that Hanson had drilled home the fact that the game was still anybody's to be had. He probably played on their pride emphasizing that their chance to be one of the all-time great Massachusetts high school hockey teams would be lost if they let this game slip away. Even if they went on to win the Massachusetts championship Mount could say it was the best team in New England because it beat CM on its home rink. They could finish the season with 27–1 record, but if that loss was to Mount Saint Charles they would never be able to say they were the best CM team ever. Whether it was a prep talk or simply CM's superior talent finally taking control, the tide started turning against Mount only a few minutes into the third period. To make matters worse, CM even had luck on its side. A few minutes into the period, Jillson made a nice diving stop of a shot from the left point. But rather than staying near Jillson's body, the puck took a weird bounce across the ice to a CM player standing alone on the right side of the cage. Normally the player wouldn't have been anywhere near the action, but the lucky bounce put him in the right place at the right time with nobody around him. Oliver, who was standing on the far side of the cage, didn't have a chance to get across the cage in time to stop the rebound shot.

The goal seemed to open the floodgates of Ridolf's frustration. Down 4–2 he knew Mount's chance to win and his chance to show he could play with the best players were quickly fading. He apparently decided if he couldn't make an impression with his goal scoring, he was going to show the scouts and coaches that he was the kind of player who could spark a team with his no-holds-barred style. He started making runs at CM players, with predictable results, especially with out-of-state referees. He picked up a penalty and CM didn't waste time scoring on the power play. The score was 5–2 and for all intents and purposes the game was over.

It would have been much better for Mount if the game *had* ended at that point. When Ridolf returned to the bench from the penalty box, he started screaming.

"That fucking referee is an asshole," he yelled.

"Keep quiet!" Dave yelled back.

But Ridolf wasn't about to suppress his anger. Every time he went on the ice, it was obvious that he was more concerned with making a statement than scoring a goal. Of course the CM players weren't going to back down. They weren't about to be intimidated by a five-nine forward, even if he did seem to be a little crazy. The quality of the game quickly deteriorated. Players on both teams were making runs at each other. Up in the stands, Joel Jillson was incensed. Losing was one thing; he could accept that. After all, CM was a great team. But Mount Saint Charles teams are *never* supposed to lose their cool. That's one of the great things about Bill's teams: he teaches his players how to handle themselves under pressure, how to channel their emotions to their benefit. But this Mount Saint Charles team was going off the deep end. Their emotions were working against them.

Joel knew that his son was getting increasingly frustrated as the game progressed. This was going to be one of the games in which he could demonstrate that he was one of the best players in the country. Unlike at the beginning of the season, when he was still thinking about the 1998 NHL draft, he no longer was worrying about dropping in the draft rankings. Now that his draft was more than a year away, there would still be a lot of time the following season to show the scouts he was NHL material. This game was about personal pride. It was his chance to feel good about himself, and it had started so well. His play in the first two periods was the major reason Mount had stayed with a far superior team. But now everything was falling apart. He was aware that a few of the CM players were trying to prove their potential by showing that they could stop him. They had been taken runs at him all afternoon, many of which easily could have been called penalties. But he knew the Massachusetts referees were going to give the CM kids the benefit of the doubt. He had taken the hits without retaliation in the beginning for the good of the team, but now the game was out of Mount's reach. Now for his own self-esteem, maybe a little for the scouts' sakes, he was going to show that nobody could hit him and get away with it. If other players were making runs, he was going to show that he could hit harder than anybody else could.

Up in the stands, Joel didn't say it out loud, but there was no question that he was blaming what was happening on the ice on Ridolf. It was his runs at the CM players that had turned the game into a festival of chippiness. The game should have just played out without incident. Mount gave it a good try, but CM was destined to win. But instead of just losing a game, Mount had also lost its cool. And when things get out of control, players get hurt. It was at times like this one that one of the CM players might take a cheap shot at Jeff, just so they could brag about having "gotten Jillson."

"He's becoming more of a distraction than a benefit," Joel grumbled about Ridolf.

Joel wasn't the only one starting to question Ridolf's value to the team.

Dave was standing in the hallway outside the Mount locker room after the game finally ended with an angry look on his face. The final score had been 7–2, but that wasn't what had Dave upset. He knew his father was embarrassed by what had happened in the final period. Down the hallway in front of the CM locker room, Bill Hanson was talking to a couple of sportswriters about how this Mount Saint Charles team was out of control. Hanson will never pass up an opportunity to expound on the virtues of his team over Mount, and that day he had a lot of fodder for his campaign. Dave couldn't hear Hanson, but he had an idea what he was saying. They had been several exchanges between the benches during the third period. The CM coaches were calling Jillson and Ridolf "goons."

Losing a game was one thing; Dave could take that. But people labeling a Bill Belisle team "out of control" was a different story. Dave had been one of Ridolf's staunchest supporters; he knew how much hockey meant to him. For months, Dave had also thought that the team couldn't win the state title without Ridolf because he was one of the only players who knew how to score. But after that game's performance Dave was starting to think the team might be better off without him. He wasn't scoring goals the way he had done the previous year, and more important, he was a negative influence.

"I can't figure it. This team is worse with Ridolf," Dave told Chris Murphy.

"I know Hutch and Fede were visibly upset about what was happening on the bench," Murphy replied. "Everything with Charlie is 'fucking this' and 'fucking that.' It's a different atmosphere with him here."

It wasn't an atmosphere that the Belisles wanted around Adelard Arena.

CHAPTER 29

Three copies of the *Sports Illustrated* swimsuit edition were being passed around the Mount dressing room as Bill walked through on the way to his office before the start of practice.

"What are those books doing here?" he bellowed.

"We're just looking at Jeff's picture," one of the players said with a laugh.

Even Bill had to laugh, too.

There have been photos of Mount Saint Charles hockey players in the *New York Times*, the *Hockey News*, and even a few regular editions of *Sports Illustrated*. But until the winter of 1998, Bill had never seen one of his players sharing magazine space with a bunch of bikini-clad beauties.

But when the 1998 *SI* swimsuit edition hit the newsstands there was a page-length photo of Jillson in his Mount uniform right beside the "Girls around the Equator." Jillson was as surprised as anybody that his Old Spice Athlete of the Month feature ran in the swimsuit edition. He was trying to pretend that it was no big deal, but what high school boy wouldn't love to have his picture in the famous swimsuit edition? Along with the photo there was also was a page-length story about Jillson and the Mount Saint Charles hockey program, including several quotes from Bill.

It's a bit ironic that as often as the Mount Saint Charles hockey story had been told on the sports pages of newspapers across the country more people learned about Mount hockey because of a desire to ogle girls in bathing suits rather than any love of the game.

The *Sports Illustrated* edition was a welcome distraction from what had been a tough and often frustrating week of practice. It was winter break in Rhode Island, which meant that the players would be available for double sessions, or at least that practice could start an hour earlier than normal. But as much as Bill would have loved longer practices, Dave's job left him unavailable.

There were two games scheduled for the upcoming weekend, both on the road: Friday night against Burrillville and Saturday against Hendricken. They would be the final two games of the regular season. Mount still needed one point to clinch the regular-season title. They couldn't take anything for granted. After all, Burrillville had already beaten them once that year. But despite the uncertainty of the regular season campaign, both Bill and Dave were already thinking about the playoffs, set to begin in two weeks.

Whatever happened that weekend, Mount would get a bye through the first round of the playoffs because the top two teams both received first-round byes. Dave had mulled over meeting with Charlie Ridolf before Monday's practice. Should he scream at him and tell him this was his last chance? Or should he try approaching it in a more businesslike manner? He could quietly sit with Ridolf and point out that if he seriously wanted to play college hockey he had to get his act together quickly and systemically show him how it would be a risky business decision for a college coach to make a commitment to a kid playing like he was. But eventually Dave decided to keep his mouth shut. If Ridolf didn't understand what Mount Saint Charles hockey is all about by the time he was entering the final few weeks of his senior season, there was nothing more Dave or Bill could do. Ridolf's hockey bill was finally coming due. All the second chances he'd been given over the past few years, all the times they had stretched their tolerance because they understood how much hockey meant to him had finally reached the limit. If he didn't realize that his drive for personal achievement was hurting the team more than it was helping, Dave had to move somebody else into his spot. It would be a gamble because there was nobody else with Ridolf's talent. But unless things changed over the next week to ten days, Ridolf would be watching most of the playoffs from the bench.

* * *

I was standing near the gate that opens onto the rink when the Mount players came out of the dressing room and headed toward the ice for their game with Burrillville.

"Chris, you've got to score. You're only four points ahead," said the young woman standing a few feet away from me.

The challenge was directed at Chris Snizek.

The Rhode Island Hockey Coaches Association keeps a summary of the individual statistics of every player in the league and publishes the leaders in each category on its Web site. Each year there are more than 30,000 hits to the site. There's no award for the highest individual scorers; neither the RIHCA nor the RIIL officially honors the champion. But that doesn't stop the players, and probably even more so the parents and friends, from keeping a close eye on the individual scoring race.

Going into the final weekend of the season, Snizek was leading by four points. His team needed a victory or at least a tie to add another chapter to its storied history, but to a few of Snizek's relatives and friends the primary concern was winning individual honors.

If there ever was an illustration of what Bill, and most likely every high school coach has to deal with these days, it was that moment. Bill and Dave had just spent ten minutes passionately touting the virtues of thinking like a team and the first words Snizek heard when he left the locker room was a cheer for individual honors. If Bill, a man who has become a national high school coaching legend because of his ability to get teenage athletes to suppress their individual wills for the good of the team, is constantly struggling with the "me first" attitude of today's young athletes, what chance does a coach of an average high school team have?

Most of the one thousand or so seats at the Burrillville rink were filled, and the fans were standing two and three deep at both ends of the rink by the time Burrillville and Mount took the ice for their 9:00 p.m. game. It had been two months since Burrillville pulled off that 2–1 upset over Mount back in December. Many Burrillville fans had missed that game: Why bother going to see Mount beat their team again? But they weren't going to miss another chance to witness a Mount defeat. Even the 5–4 overtime loss in the second meeting of the season at Mount in January had given the Burrillville fans encouragement. If they could beat Mount at home and only lose by a goal at Mount, they figured anything could happen now that they were playing at Burrillville again.

But it wasn't long before the reality of talent ended their upset dreams.

Hutchins scored only twenty seconds after the opening face-off and Fede made it 2–0 less than a minute later. Then Ridolf scored twice in the second period and Turcotte added another goal for a 5–0 lead after two periods. Neither team scored in the third period, so Mount walked out of the rink with the 5–0 victory and another regular-season title.

Long before he walked into Thayer Arena in Warwick after the Burrillville victory, Dave had a feeling it wasn't going to be a great night.

Dave was afraid there might be a letdown after having clinched the title the previous evening, and it was Saturday night—not a good night for this team to play a game.

"We have a lot of seniors and when you have a lot of seniors, Saturday can be a bad night because they party Friday night," Dave said. "When they're freshmen and sophomores and maybe even juniors, they don't have cars so they come to the games with their parents. But by the time they're seniors they all drive and they can stay out later."

It wasn't a new phenomenon. Dave still remembers how after games in his senior year at Mount he and some of the other Mount players would drink a few beers down near the old-age home in Manville. It's just a reality that a senior team may have experienced players, but it also can have experienced partyers. Yet, Bill has never impressed about curfews on his players. He never considers himself their guardian; they're their parents' responsibilities. He's their hockey coach, and as their coach he expects them to come to a game ready to play. They know that means they should get plenty of rest the night before a big game. For several years after he became his father's assistant, Dave called the players the night before a game to make sure that they were home by a decent hour; but he no longer makes those calls. He has adopted his father's philosophy that the players know what is expected of them. It's up to them to conduct their social lives to fit their roles as Mounties.

To make matters worse, that Saturday night the first thing the Mount players saw when they stepped on the ice in Warwick was a large group of Hendricken fans who had gone to elaborate lengths to ridicule Jillson. The Hendricken fans had cut out the *Sports Illustrated* photo of Jillson and pasted his face on the body of a few of the issue's bathing beauties. They then enlarged the eight-and-a-half-by-eleven-inch composites and glued them onto placards with handles.

They'd also come up with their version of a Dave Letterman's Top Ten List and "Ten Reasons Why I'm Not an NHL Player" was scrawled below the photos.

None of the lines made much sense, of course, especially Number 4.

"I don't pay anything to go to Mount."

"Boy, do I wish that was true," said Joel Jillson as he stood near the Mount bench looking up at the posters. "What I owe because of tuition payments for Jeff and his sister, and we still have to pay for [Jeff's younger brother] Nick."

As soon as Jillson stepped on the ice the Hendricken fans started waving the posters and yelling a variety of teenage insults. Jillson couldn't miss the posters or the verbal assaults, but he pretended not to notice. Even when the Hendricken fans booed him during the announcement of the starting lineups he didn't even glance upwards. Had an incident such as this one occurred at the start of the season, he might have reacted differently, losing his cool and gesturing toward the stands. But over the past three months he seemed to have learned you can't let other people distract you from your goal. He was learning how to keep his focus. If there was one aspect of his game that had received a better test by his staying at Mount it was how to react to boorish comments by jealous fans. If he was playing in juniors, he wouldn't have been the center of attention like he was in Rhode Island. He wouldn't have been the target of the fans' wrath. The maturity needed to not let those remarks affect his play wouldn't have been tested like it was in almost every game with Mount. There had been many occasions over the first few months of the season when he reacted like an immature teenager, not thinking about the consequences to himself, and even more important, to the team. But he now seemed to better understand the basis of Bill's coaching philosophy that you don't let anyone or anything distract you from focusing on your goal. That's not always easy for a seventeen-year-old, but Jillson was learning.

Bill Belisle ignored the posters. Later he would say he didn't even see them, but Dave Belisle did and they annoyed him. Some people would say it was all in good fun, but he failed to see the humor. Sure Jillson was getting a lot of publicity, so one could argue that it was the price a star pays for being in the spotlight. But Jillson was still just seventeen years old and seventeen-year-olds shouldn't be the fodder for sick humor, no matter how hard they can shoot a hockey puck. Dave would have liked to have said something to the game officials, but he knew better. No one was going to feel sorry for Mount Saint Charles. And even if the officials reprimanded the Hendricken fans it would only aggravate the situation. So Dave let it go, especially when he saw that Jillson wasn't concerned.

After the first ten minutes of the game Dave started thinking that maybe he'd been wrong to be worry about the Saturday-night blurs. Rather than mouthing off at the fans with the posters, Jillson was getting his revenge by scoring goals. Six minutes after the start of the game he blasted a shot past the Hendricken goalie from the blue line. Two minutes later, he increased the lead to 2–0 by literally going through the entire Hendricken team on a solo trip from the defensive zone to about twenty-five feet from the Hendricken cage where he fired home the goal.

But it wasn't long before Dave's fears of a bad night became reality. Oliver let a long, soft shot from the right point bounce off his catching glove and roll into the cage for a goal. A few minutes later, while Hendricken was on a power play, a pass from the left boards deflected off Jillson's skate and rolled over to the other side of the Mount zone. Instead of quickly reacting to the puck's sudden change of direction, Oliver froze in the middle of the cage. That meant the Hendricken player standing by himself on the far right side of the cage wasn't even challenged as he slipped the puck into the wide open right side of the cage. Standing on the back bench looking over the chain-link fencing that encircles the players' benches, Bill looked like he wanted to jump on the ice and pull Oliver out of the cage. To him, the goal was another example of Oliver's lack of focus. There are occasions when nothing can be done about deflections that suddenly change the direction of the puck. It's a bang-bang play and there isn't time for the defensive player to react to the change of direction. But this wasn't bang-bang. It took a few seconds for the puck to roll across the ice to the Hendricken player on the other side. If Oliver had been focused on what was happening and acted instinctively he would have been over on the right side. But instead of moving across the cage, he stood as if his skates were encased in cement.

Back in the eighties, when Tony Ciresi was an assistant coach, Ciresi would work on techniques with the Mount goalies. But these days Mount goalies receive very little technical instruction. Bill leaves that to the goalie experts at the summer clinics and hockey schools. His work with his goaltenders almost exclusively involves getting them to stay focused on the play in front of them. It's not just shooting drills; it's everything from the minute they step on the ice until the minute they leave. The result has been a string of solid Mount goaltenders, especially by the time they're seniors. But here was Oliver in the final week of the regular season of his senior year, and his mind always seemed to be taking a break from the action. For Bill there's nothing more frustrating than a lack of focus by a senior, especially his senior goalie.

Oliver wasn't the only Mount player who was having focus problems. In the second period, a lack of back-checking by the Mount forwards gave Hendricken a three-on-one break. Instead of coming out and challenging the Hendricken skaters, Oliver backed into the cage as the action moved closer to his crease. That left him little chance of stopping a shot from about five feet out.

By the end of the second period, Mount trailed 5–2.

Between the second and third periods, Chris Murphy tried whipping up some emotion with a pep talk laced with four-letter words. Dave and Bill also did some screaming, minus the four-letter words. At the start of the third period, it looked like the coaches' tirades had had some effect. Sophomore Josh Lanni cut the deficit to 5–3 only thirty-four seconds after the third period face-off, but that was the last bright spot for the Mount fans. Mount failed to convert several good scoring opportunities over the next ten minutes and then Oliver let a rolling puck slip under his pads with nobody around him. It was still 6–3 when the final buzzer sounded.

By the time Bill made his way through a crowd of jubilant Hendricken fans into the Mount dressing room, all the players were sitting on benches wearing the look of little kids waiting for their parents to administer punishment for some misdeed. This loss, probably more than any of the others all season, was playing havoc with their psyches. Friday night they had rolled to victory over Burrillville. They couldn't help but think that the typical end of the year Mount domination had started. It was as if all they had to do was turn on a switch and the goals would start flying into the cage. But now that feeling of invincibility had evaporated, and it had only taken twenty-four hours. They had suffered one of their worst losses of the season to a team they had already beaten twice. They all expected Bill to start screaming once the dressing room door was shut to the outside world.

Bill was the first person to speak once the door was shut, but there was no sign of panic in his voice, no screaming.

"This is the end of the regular season. You gave me a championship. Thank you," he said in even tones.

The lack of any outbursts caught the players off guard. They had expected to take a verbal beating; instead they were being congratulated.

But Bill didn't give them much time to savor his praise.

"Monday starts a new season," he continued, still in even tones. "Now we start working toward winning the state championship. Get your studying done before you get to school. No more staying after school for extra help. No more college visits."

The message was clear. For the next three weeks, they all belonged to Bill Belisle.

Dave had let the team sit in silence for a few minutes before he took his turn. It was his way of putting emphasis on his father's declaration of dedication.

Finally, he spoke, his tone far more amplified than his father's had been.

"You think just because you're wearing that shirt that everybody's going to sit down. You think just because they hadn't scored much in the other games that they were going to think they couldn't. Well they didn't quit and neither will anybody else. If you play like this, you're in for a tough series.

"You're afraid of losing. You haven't heard us talk about losing. We talk about Mount Pride. When they score, you get scared. You can't play scared."

Later Dave was standing outside the dressing room watching the players file out and head to the bus.

"I knew it on the bus," he said. "I didn't say anything to my father, but I knew it. In past years that bus would have been rocking. We had won the regular-season title Friday night and we dominated. Other years, the kids would have been talking about how they were going to do the same thing to Hendricken. But these guys just go along quietly. This team doesn't know how to dominate. We have to teach them—and we're running out of time."

CHAPTER 30

Brian Lawton and Bryan Berard were both the first player selected in their respective NHL drafts. Keith Carney and Mathieu Schneider have enjoyed long and successful NHL careers and Paul Guay played for the U.S. Olympic team. But some observers who have seen every player who has worn a Mountie uniform during the Bill Belisle era insist that one of the most naturally talented players Bill ever coached was Jim Colucci.

Colucci was a Mount sophomore when Bill became coach at the start of the 1975–76 season. He was a defenseman who skated faster than most of the forwards on the team. He had a great shot, he liked to hit people, and he was a great passer. But he knew he was talented and he was extremely strong-willed. He wasn't the kind of kid who enjoyed having other people tell him how to play. It's therefore not surprising that there are a few classic stories about Colucci and Bill.

"Bill would get infuriated with Jim. Everybody else was buying into Bill's philosophy, but Jimmy was stubborn. He wasn't going to change his game," Tony Ciresi related.

Ciresi still remembers the day Bill got so mad at Colucci that after a practice he grabbed Colucci's equipment bag, went to the locker room door and threw the bag out into the hallway. He then told his best player to get out and don't come back.

"Jimmy's father, Tony, was a hockey maniac," said Ciresi. "He was very involved with Jim's career, so we figured he would go crazy when Jim told him Bill had thrown him off the team. We knew he was out in the lobby waiting for Jimmy that day. About ten minutes after Bill threw Jimmy out there was a knock at the locker room door. We knew it had to be Tony. When Bill opened the door Tony was standing there with Jimmy's bag. I figured he was going to start screaming at Bill, but instead he threw the bag back into the locker room and said, 'Coach, if you don't want him, I don't want him either.'"

Tony Colucci then asked Bill to please take his son back on the team and assured him that there wouldn't be any further challenges to Bill's coaching techniques. From that point on, there was never a question about who was boss. Colucci was one of the main reasons Mount won its first state title in 1978. But even though he followed Bill's instructions throughout his high school career, to this day, Bill insists that Colucci was one of the few players he has ever coached that he couldn't totally convince to play Mount hockey.

Colucci went on to a solid college career playing for Lou Lamoriello at Providence College. He never made it to the NHL as some of the other great Mount players did, but twenty years after he graduated from Mount, he was still playing in age group leagues around New England. He may not have always agreed with Bill, but he always had a deep respect for his coach. So every year, when Dave calls in early March to ask Colucci if he'll come up and help Mount get ready for the playoffs, Colucci's there.

No coach wants his team to have a terrible performance in the last game before the start of the playoffs. He doesn't want his players coming into the do-or-die postseason play with lingering doubts about their ability to get the job done. After their terrible performance again Hendricken in the last game of the regular season, Dave and Bill would have preferred to have had their team get right back into the action the following weekend so that they could quickly regain their confidence. But, along with a lot of other things that season, even the schedule was making the Belisles' lives more difficult than usual. Although Mount finished its regular season against Hendricken on February 23, there still was another week of regular season games on the RIIL schedule before the start of the playoffs. A two-week layoff before the start of the playoffs was bad enough, but because there were only six teams in the RIIL's Championship Division, the top-two regular-season finishers earned first-round playoff byes. That meant Mount wasn't scheduled to play a game for nineteen days after the Hendricken debacle.

Although the three-week layoff was unique, the Belisles were accustomed to dealing with two gameless weeks between the end of the regular season and the playoffs. There haven't been enough teams in the Championship Division to have four opening-round series for more than a decade. No coach wants to go two weeks without playing a game at this time of the year, but the only teams still playing are the playoff qualifiers—and no other high school team wants to scrimmage Mount Saint Charles a few days before a playoff game.

So each year Dave made calls to former Mount players who live in the Rhode Island area and set up alumni-varsity scrimmages for the weekend before the start of the Mount's first playoff series. Bryan Berard, Keith Carney, Mathieu Schneider, and Garth Snow may have been busy playing NHL games, but with a few calls Dave put together a team of former college players, including former U.S. Olympian Paul Guay.

The alumni knew what their job was. They were there to give the Mount players both competition and help. Paul Guay may have been in his late thirties in 1998 and it may haven been 14 years since he played in the Olympics, but he still was faster than most sixteen- and seventeen-year-olds and had a lot more hockey savvy. Peter Belisle came down from coaching at the University of Connecticut to help out, Chris Murphy switched from the Mount bench to the other side of the rink, and at least ten other guys who had played college hockey were there.

They scrimmaged for almost two hours: no breaks, no cleaning the ice. Rather than standing on the Mount bench, Bill sat up in the press box, taking down notes. Every so often he would scream down at some varsity player for not backchecking or for coasting rather than slingshotting toward the cage when Jillson fired a shot from the point.

"Shit, it's bad enough when he's on the ice; at least he misses some stuff from there. He doesn't miss anything up from there," one player groaned after being administrated a verbal beating from on high.

The two teams played on even terms until just before the end when Murphy and Pete obviously decided that they needed to show the young kids that they still had a lot to learn and scored three goals in about five minutes.

Long after everybody else had left the ice, Jim Colucci stood at center ice talking with Jillson. Some of the Mount old-timers said that despite all the great defensemen that had played for Bill, Jillson was the only one who had a shot that rivaled Colucci's. Colucci was impressed with what he saw from Jillson in the scrimmage, but he thought Jillson might not be as intimidating as he should be with his shot. He told Jillson he needed to scare people at the start of the game.

"Don't worry about scoring on one of your first few shots," he told Jillson. "Let it rip high and hard at the goalie's head. It will make him think every time he sees you shooting. It also will make some forwards a little hesitant about rushing out to the point to block a shot."

Bill was sitting on the bench in one of the little dressing rooms on the opposite side of Adelard Arena from the Mount dressing room. All around him, the former Mount Saint Charles players who had just played in the scrimmage were sitting with cans of beer in their hands. Everybody was drinking, except Bill.

"If I don't go to heaven for this, I never will," he said with a laugh as he looked at his former players enjoying their postgame brews while he sat empty-handed.

If it had been any other time of the year, Bill would have matched gulp for gulp with his former players. There's nothing he likes more than drinking a beer while talking about hockey, especially with his former players. But it was Lent, and he never drinks beer during Lent. The Roman Catholic tradition is that during the forty days of Lent you show your devotion to God by abstaining from something that means a lot to you. There aren't many Catholics these days who make a greater Lenten sacrifice than Bill's giving up beer for forty days.

"It's kind of ironic that he has never been able to celebrate any of his state championships with a beer after the game because the playoffs are always in Lent," said Peter. "But that's him. A lot of people would probably say it's okay to have just one beer to celebrate, but not my father. If he makes a commitment, he doesn't look for ways to get out of it, even at his age."

But just because he couldn't sip a beer didn't mean that Bill wasn't going to show his former players how much he appreciated that they were willing to take time away from their own families on a weekend night to help him round the current Mount team into shape for the playoffs. After the scrimmage, he filled up a twenty-gallon tub with ice and two cases of beer and had the student managers carry it into the alumni dressing room. He then sat and listened as the players, most of them now in their late twenties or early thirties, regale each other with their Mount experiences. They had reached an age when they can finally tell Bill their treasured stories about how they occasionally outwitted him.

"I remember the time your dog got loose from the chain in the back of the rink," said Bill Dean, a Mount player in the late eighties and now a lawyer. "We were all ready to go on the ice, but you came into the locker room and told us all to go out around the streets looking for the dog rather than go on the ice. We find him the next street over, but we didn't bring him right back because we knew we would have to start practice right away. So we put the dog in the car and took him with us to the Burger King."

Everyone, including Bill broke into laugher, but then without losing a beat Bill's face turned stone solemn and he yelled "Give me twenty" at Dean.

Dean's first reaction was to drop to the floor and try reeling off twenty push-ups—once you've played for Bill you never completely escape the gut reaction to jump at one of his commands. But Bill's face quickly changed back into a smile so Dean knew it was safe to do arm curls with his beer can rather than push-ups on the floor. It went on that way for almost an hour after the scrimmage. Slowly the benches emptied as the players showered, got dressed, and headed home to their families. But Bill lingered until the last few players finally declared that they had to get going. The coach sat there looking as if he hated to see it end. When they played for him, he did all the talking. Now he generally enjoys sitting and listening to them talk about their lives. It's as if their lives are part of his. He never intended it to be that way. Some men go into high school coaching with the hope that they can both win games and help develop lifelong traits of character in young men. Bill didn't get into coaching because he felt he could help mold the future lives of teenagers. He got into it because he felt he knew how to win hockey games, and he certainly has. But somewhere along the line, probably without him even realizing it was happening, he moved into another realm. Into the realm of developing life skills as well as hockey skills. It all came about because of his passion to win hockey games but now the state championship banners hanging on the Adelard Arena wall are only part of the benefit.

So he loves to sit and listen to his "boys." The only thing that would have made it better was if he was drinking a beer.

•   •   •

After two weeks of what too often had been chaotic practices, both the coaches and the players needed the diversion that the alumni game presented. On most high school teams what had happened over the previous two weeks probably would have been considered run-of-the-mill teenager confusion. But in the Bill's world of orderly perfection it was disorder. Both Dave and Bill had assumed that the Hendricken game would be a wake-up call to the team that it was time to forget about all of the personal goals and all of the outside distractions and focus on the objective of doing whatever was necessary to win the state championship. Dave hoped that the Monday practice after the Hendricken game would be the start of three weeks of focused, old-fashioned Mount Saint Charles practices.

It didn't take long for that illusion to evaporate.

Any hopes Bill had for spending a practice working on basic skills that he and Dave felt had been lacking during the final few weeks of the regular season disappeared early Monday afternoon. As soon as he arrived at the rink following his daily ritual of noontime mass at the nearby Catholic church, Bill discovered one of the two compressors used for ice-making had broken down. The ice would stay frozen with only one compressor working, but if anything happened to that compressor the rink would have to close down. Bill may be known nationally for his coaching accomplishments, but to the good brothers at Mount Saint Charles his talents as a mechanic are equally important. Every year he saves the school thousands of dollar with his ability to repair machinery in the rink rather than call for outside help. At a school run by an order of fiscally conservative—some people would say "cheap"—Roman Catholic brothers anyone who saves money is in line for sainthood. Therefore, rather than being on the ice for practice that Monday afternoon, Bill was in the back of the rink fixing the compressor.

That meant Chris Murphy ran the practice alone until Dave arrived from work.

"They think some of those practices last week were tough, wait until they see today," Chris said.

For almost forty-five minutes Chris directed the team through nothing but skating drills. There was no shooting, no pucks on the ice, just skating. It was his way of telling the players that he felt they were lazy, that they weren't working as hard as he thought they could. He had told them as much when Dave gave him a chance to talk between periods of a few games during the previous weeks, but that day he had a chance to put his words into action. It was his chance to show the players that, despite what they thought, they didn't have the staying power that was the key to past Mount success. When other teams got tired, that's when Mount shifted into high gear. Murphy was afraid that this team still didn't have what it would take to make the shift.

Dave grinned as he headed onto the ice. He knew Chris had become extremely frustrated with what he felt was a lack of a work ethic in a few of the players. It crossed his mind to just let Chris run a whole practice of skating drills, but he needed to do some work with the lines. He couldn't believe that this far into the season he was still changing lines.

"We've never gone this late into the season without having the lines set," Dave said. "Usually by this time you're fine-tuning, but I'm still looking for people who can work together."

"Get showered fast, but don't leave. We're going to have a meeting," Dave yelled to the players as they head off the ice after practice.

Most people outside the Mount family probably think that with all the media attention about Mount Saint Charles tradition, Bill and Dave are constantly showing films of former great Mount Saint Charles games to inspire current players. But even Bill knows a steady diet of forced nostalgia isn't going to inspire many of today's teenagers. This was a group of kids who were growing up with the History Channel and ESPN Classic. For them there's nothing unique about watching great moments in history, even Mount Saint Charles hockey history, but Dave had decided that the 1997–98 team needed something special. He dug out the tape of the 1988 title series, the series in which Keith Carney strapped himself in a harness because there was no way he was going to miss the last game. Dave figured if a Mount hockey player wasn't inspired by watching the final game of that series, there wasn't much more he could do.

Dave was sitting in the coach's office after the meeting and film presentation, watching the last few players leave the locker room. When everybody was gone, he turned to Chris Murphy.

"I've been thinking about my speech in case we lose in the playoffs," Dave said.

"Yeah, you should tell them I hope you all remember this the rest of your lives. How you lost this because you weren't willing to work," Chris said with disgust.

"I would never do that to a kid," Dave said.

"You should," Murphy said as he rose from his chair and headed toward the locker room door.

Dave waited a minute until Chris was out of earshot.

"He's the true Mount spirit. He will do anything that's necessary to win," Dave offered about him. "That's why he's so important to have around here. He wouldn't really say that to the kids, but he just doesn't understand why some of these kids aren't as dedicated as he was. It isn't a generation gap. He's not that much older than the seniors."

Dave hadn't thought he could be any more discouraged with the way things were going than he was after the Hendricken loss. But when he skated onto the ice for practice the Monday afternoon following the Hendricken game and didn't see Joe Cardillo he sunk into a new level of depression.

Cardillo had missed the Hendricken game because he had been seriously dehydrated by the flu. After the game, Dave had talked about how his absence played a big role in the team's poor performance.

"In some ways he might be more important to us than Jeff because of his work ethic," Dave noted.

Cardillo may not have been quite as talented as Chris Murphy when it came to scoring goals, but Dave always felt Cardillo was the one player on the team with the same "willingness to do anything for the team" attitude that made Murphy such an outstanding high school player. Most teenage athletes can talk about teamwork, but few really understand what it is. For most of them it's simply something they have been hearing about from coaches since they started playing sports around the time they also started kindergarten. Yet in reality, a sport is an individual human activity, even in the so-called team sports. Every athlete must make an individual effort to train and perform. Athletes are naturally ego-centered individuals. It isn't until an athlete reaches a certain level of maturity that he or she can understand the true concept of meshing your talent with that of others to achieve a common goal, even if that means sometimes changing the way you like to do things. There aren't too many sixteen- or seventeen-year-olds who have achieved that level of maturity.

On many high school teams kids become team players because they don't have the talent to be anything else. That of course isn't the situation on the Mount Saint Charles hockey team. Every player who makes the Mount team thinks he has the talent to be an individual star—and most do.

The secret to the Mount success is that the Belisles have been able to convince a lot of teenagers who thought they should be in the spotlight to accept the shadows for the good of the team.

Most former Mount players will admit that they didn't really understand what teamwork was all about until their senior year. Before that they were just doing what Bill told them to do because they wanted to play. Cardillo seemed to understand the concept almost from the time he made the varsity as a sophomore. It may have been because he had been forced early in his high school career to question just how much playing for Mount meant to him. It may also have had to do with his background in music where it's necessary for talented people to combine their efforts to create harmony. Musicians learn to practice both their individual skills and their ability to work in concert with others. Cardillo knew that only when talented people are willing to put the needs of their team ahead of their personal needs would they produce beautiful music—and championships. There was no one on the team who worked harder than he did to help the team be successful, which was why Dave was so upset when he wasn't at Monday's practice.

The night after the Hendricken game had been the night of the state high school coaches association annual senior all-star game. The top senior players from every team in the state played a game for the benefit of a coaches scholarship program. Cardillo was one of six Mount players who had been selected to participate. After the way Cardillo had felt Saturday night Dave didn't expect he would play Sunday, but when he walked into the all-state game, Cardillo was there. Dave understood that this game was more than just another game between the top players in the state. In addition to raising money for scholarships, it is one more chance for the seniors to showcase their talents. The high school coaches make a big push to get the college coaches to attend the game. The game always attracts a large number of them from the lower Division I schools in the Northeast as well as the coaches of New England Division II and III teams. So while the game didn't mean much to sought-after players such as Jeff Jillson, it could have meant a lot to Paul Fede, Mark Esposito, Jerry Turcotte, Charlie Ridolf, and Joe Cardillo.

Cardillo had decided that if he was accepted he would go to Holy Cross, but there was still a question of whether he would be accepted. Although he was a member of the National Honor Society and had college boards scores in the high 1,100s, he didn't quite have the academic resumé of the average Holy Cross student, which in 1998 included scores higher than 1,300. Cardillo's likelihood of acceptance would be furthered, however, if a Holy Cross coach flagged his application as a student the coaching staff wanted. Cardillo had informed the Holy Cross coach that the Cross was his top choice; he just wanted to make sure that he was one of the Cross's top choices. He assumed that the Holy Cross coach, or at least one of his assistants, would be at the all-star game because there were a few other kids playing in the game who had applied to there. He still needed another day to completely recover from the effects of the flu, but he felt that this was an opportunity to strengthen his standing. He couldn't pass it up, after all this was his future.

Yet the next day he again felt sick so he didn't go to school or practice.

"He felt well enough to play Sunday night, but he can't make school or practice on Monday," groused an irritated Dave as soon as he noticed Cardillo wasn't on the ice. "That's because he's thinking about college and not about this team. I expect that from some kids, but not from Joe."

Cardillo was back at practice on Tuesday. Dave didn't make a big deal of it in front of the other players, but he quietly let Cardillo know he was disappointed to have seen him play Sunday but then miss practice on Monday. If it was somebody else, Dave probably would have vented his displeasure in the locker room in front of the whole team but he figured Cardillo would get the message without having to be reprimanded in front of his teammates.

So what if his team had only won one of its last five games? So what if the playoffs were only a few weeks away and there seemed to be missing parts in the Mount offensive machinery? Bill wasn't going to change his practice style.

For all the stories about the puke buckets and players skating in the dark, the real key to Bill's coaching success has been his ability to develop individual hockey skills. That wasn't going to change, even if things weren't going well in the win-loss category.

That late in the season, most coaches use practice sessions to develop plays or playing styles that will provide a victory in the next game. Most coaches feel it's too late to work on individual skills. The time for that is early in the season or at the summer clinics. But a few weeks before the start of the playoffs, Bill was still looking to improve the basic skills of the members of the 1997–98 team. He would stop a practice and keep twenty-four other players waiting while he pointed out to a player a small fault.

"Use your power stride," Bill said as he stopped a drill to show freshman Chris Chaput how to improve his skating technique. That Chaput might not see much ice time during the playoffs didn't make any difference when Bill saw a fault that needed to be corrected. A few of the seniors standing along the boards near the Mount bench looked irritated with him for taking time out of practice to work with a freshman who wasn't going to play much. They knew that every minute Bill used for working on basic skills meant another minute of practice. It wasn't like during the regular season when other teams rent the ice after the Mount practice so that practice ends at a specific time. All of the other high school teams had finished their seasons and there was no one waiting to get on the ice. The practice would go on as long as the coaches thought necessary.

"Why is he wasting time working with that kid? He isn't even going to play," one of the seniors mumbled.

No one bothered to answer his question. They all knew the answer already. That's the way it's always been. It's the way it was when they were freshmen and for a long time before. In the father-son coaching partnership that now is Mount Charles hockey, working on the power play or penalty-killing are Dave's responsibility. Bill works on basics and Mount Saint Charles hockey is basic hockey. So Bill had Chaput perform the drill again while the rest of the team stood around watching.

"No," Bill screamed. "That's still not it. Do it again."

Once again Chaput went back into the zone and skated out under the watchful eyes of Bill and his teammates. It was a simple drill, one he had been doing for years in youth hockey. But no one had ever told him before that he wasn't skating correctly.

"You're not paying attention, get out of here," Bill yelled, pointing to the locker room.

Chaput didn't say a word. And just skated toward the Mount bench. All eyes were on him, but no one said a word. When he reached the boards in front of the bench, he finally let out his frustration by flinging his stick into the alleyway behind the Mount bench. As he stomped toward the locker room you could see his eyes behind the bars of his face mask. He was ready to burst into tears, frustrated with himself for not being able to do the drill the way Bill wanted him to and mad that the coach threw him out of practice. Other players had done things just as stupid and they weren't thrown out. What he didn't realize was that he might have been just another victim of the mind games Paul Fede claimed are such a big part of Mount Saint Charles hockey.

Was he being singled out because he didn't perform the drill? Or was it because Bill needed to send a message that everyone needed to focus harder and nothing gets that message across more vividly than someone being thrown out of practice. Many Mounties through the years have suffered the misfortune of being Bill's messenger.

Chaput stomped into the dressing room, slamming the door behind him. The slam echoed out on the ice, but no one looked away from center ice where Bill was working with another player on the same drill. Slowly, without saying a word to anyone, Dave skated over to the bench and headed to the dressing room. He spent about ten minutes talking to Chaput. Finally the freshman came out of the room, still fully dressed in his practice gear, and retrieved his stick. Dave hadn't given him a pardon to get back on the ice, but he had obviously convinced him that he was still part of the team. Chaput returned to the locker room, killing time by taping his stick, taking ten minutes to tape a stick that he could do in thirty seconds if he had someplace to go. Some players would quickly undress and get out of the locker room before the coach returned after practice, but Chaput was still in his skates and pads when practice finally ended. He knew by staying around he could be leaving himself open to further ridicule. Out of sight, out of mind is one sure way of avoiding any additional Bill reprimands. But his dream was to be in that locker room. He wasn't going to be scared out of it, even if he had been on the verge of tears.

Like an enraged bull, Bill charged into the Mount dressing room on Monday afternoon, March 2. After five days of long, often torturous practices following the Hendricken loss, Bill had given the team Saturday off. Coupled with their usual Sunday off it meant that they had the first two-day break in more than a month. He'd also made another concession. Despite his declaration following the Hendricken game that everybody better get their work done so they didn't need to spend time after school getting extra academic help, he heard some of the kids in the locker room grumbling about not being able to see a teacher because they had to get right to the rink for practice. So rather than practice right after school as they had the previous week, that week he had pushed the start of practice back to 4:30, which would give everyone more than enough time to meet with their teachers or finish other schoolwork. Of course, it also gave Dave more time to complete his sales calls so that he could be there for the entire practice.

Normally Bill parks his pickup truck at the back door of the rink and never goes out into the front parking lot. Unfortunately for the players, that day he altered his regular route, walking from the back of the building into the front parking lot about forty minutes before the scheduled start of practice. Just as he turned the corner of the rink and headed for the front door he noticed several players piling out of cars that were parked in the far end of the lot. He may have been sixty-eight and his eyesight may not have been as good as it once was, but he didn't have any problem seeing that there also were several girls in the cars. When the players finally strolled into the rink to get ready for practice, he walked over to the cars and found an empty can of Copenhagen chewing tobacco. That in itself might have been enough to set him off, but then he walked into the dressing room and was greeted with the news that Stokinger wouldn't be at practice because he had an appointment to get his car windshield fixed.

Stokinger had made the windshield appointment based on the assumption that practice would be at 2:30 and he could go afterwards. When Bill announced on Monday that he was changing the practice to 4:30, Stokinger had to make a choice: drive with a cracked windshield or make practice. He chose the windshield.

For Bill that was the last straw. He could understand college visits and doctor's appointments, even a family photo session at Christmas, but a windshield? He banged the locker-room door shut and yelled to the managers to clear out of the room. Knowing that the locker room wasn't going to be a fun place to be just then, they didn't hesitate taking advantage of the command to disappear.

"Shut off that music," Bill screamed.

No one really wanted to leave the security of their spot on the bench for fear they might become the target of Bill's wrath, but slowly one of them crept over and flicked the CD player's power button.

As soon as the music stopped, Bill started.

"I changed practice to help you, and what do you do?" he said as he reached into his pocket and pulled out the Copenhagen can. He held the can in the air so everybody could see it. "I found this outside one of your cars." He then flung the can across the room. The toss was high enough that it wasn't going to hit any of the players sitting on the bench against the wall on the far side of the dressing room, but no one was taking any chances. Four or five players ducked and covered their heads with their arms to avoid any rebound off the wall.

Dave, Doc Guay, and I had been sitting in the coach's office when Bill burst into the room. From where he was sitting, Dave could see his father. When he saw the Copenhagen can, he cringed.

"Oh no," he said just above a whisper so he wouldn't be heard outside the little office. "I saw some of them with that stuff a few weeks ago. I knew some of them were using it and I told them they better not let my father see. But they don't listen."

"You're not in the cafeteria studying; you're in cars with your coochies," Bill continued screaming. "School gets out at 2:30. What are those girls still doing here at 3:30?

"That's it. No more late practices," Bill snarled as he turned and headed out of the locker room. Rather than putting on his skates as he usually did, he just stood outside the locker room watching as the players rushed out of the dressing room onto the ice. No one needed to be told that they had better be on the ice ready to go at 4:30.

At exactly 4:30, Bill stood barking orders while standing behind the bench.

Still sitting in the office, Dave could hear the *swhoosh* of the skates on the ice. "He's got them flying," he said with a laugh. "The girls in the car and the Copenhagen upset him, but I think the windshield thing is what set him off. I better get out there before he kills them."

CHAPTER 31

No one has to tell Dr. Mark Guay what it's like to be on the receiving end of Bill's wrath at practice. The fact that he was Dr. Jean Guay's son and Bill had known him since he was an infant didn't save Dr. Mark from being the target for Bill's ferocity.

Although he never obtained the fame of his older brother Paul, Mark was an outstanding goalie for the Mounties back in the early eighties. He went to Notre Dame after Mount and played for the Irish hockey team before going on to medical school. He's now an ear, nose, and throat specialist in the Cleveland area.

He never will be considered one of Mount's all-time great players, but he does hold a special place in Mount hockey history. He was in the goal the night Burrillville ended an eighty-five-game Mount victory string back in 1982.

"I'll always be remembered as the guy who gave up those goals," Mark said one day in 1998, finally able to laugh about that fateful evening.

He is now also able to laugh about the physical pain he suffered because of Bill's intensity.

"Bill used to shut off most of the lights, then he would take the puck machine out just beyond the blue line. He would turn it up to eighty miles an hour and start firing at me in near darkness. He would be out there moving the machine around so I never knew where the puck was coming from until the last few seconds. The pucks were whacking off my shoulder and hitting me right in the spot between the pad and arm. My father bought that machine and Bill was nearly killing me with it, but I loved it."

He was in Rhode Island for a few days in late February 1998 visiting his parents. But even though he didn't say it, he also was on a mission for his alma mater.

When Mark had visited Notre Dame during his senior year, one of the players who showed him around campus was Dave Forbes, then the Notre Dame hockey captain. Forbes did a convincing job selling Mark on Notre Dame although Forbes graduated by the time Mark arrived and went on to play in the National Hockey League. Yet he and Guay maintained a friendship. In 1998, Forbes was the Notre Dame coach and he wanted Jeff Jillson. He knew Mark could get into places at Adelard Arena that neither he nor any of his assistant coaches could, so he asked him to do some recruiting for Notre Dame. A few days before the alumni scrimmage, Mark was in the Mount dressing room after practice. His father had asked him to check on a couple of players who were having bronchial problems. Doc Guay suspected that it might be some type of viral infection. Coincidentally one of the players was Jillson. Jillson still hadn't told anyone that Notre Dame no longer was in the running so long after he's checked out all the players, but long after all the other players had left the dressing room, Mark and Jillson sat on the bench, discussing medications and Notre Dame.

The last spaghetti dinner of the season was at Brian Oliver's house on Wednesday, two nights before the first playoff game. In addition to death and taxes it's virtually a certainty in Rhode Island that when a group of people from various parts of the state get together there's going to be at least one good Italian cook. In terms of per capita population concentration, Rhode Island is the most Italian state in the country. And although Mount Saint Charles hockey may be more associated with French-Canadians, a look at the rosters of Bill's teams over the past two decades tells you that players of Italian ancestry had played big roles in the twenty state titles prior to 1998. The dinners are usually laid-back get-togethers where the players load their plates with pasta and then retreat to another room to play video games or watch a game on TV. The parents, meanwhile, sit at a kitchen or dining room table chatting about everything from hockey to the stock market. Bill and Dave rarely attend the dinners. They are social events, and there's nothing social about coaching Mount Saint Charles hockey.

The dinner at Oliver's, however, took a slightly different turn than all of the others when, after every one had finished eating, Richard Oliver called all the players into the family room in the basement. The look on the faces of some of the players, especially Jillson and Fede, made it clear that they weren't excited about having some sort of team meeting with a parent. But they were in Oliver's home—there wasn't much they could do but oblige.

Oliver had been involved with amateur hockey programs for almost twenty years, coaching several teams to regional youth hockey championships. For years after the high school season and during the summer he had coordinated some of the most popular invitational tournaments in New England for high school–age players. With all of his experience, he was convinced that he knew as much about hockey as anybody, probably more than most. He wasn't afraid to stand at Mount games and second-guess Bill and Dave's coaching decisions, but he also was the first to admit that, "You can't argue with success." It was why his two sons played at Mount, even if it meant he had no direct involvement with the team. Yet on that night he saw a chance to bestow his coaching wisdom on a team that needed help. Here were all the players with Bill nowhere in sight. For a hockey fanatic, it was just too much to pass up. This may have been the only time in the history of Bill's coaching career that a parent had been bold enough to give his team a pregame pep talk.

Oliver began with a few familiar pointers.

"You have to skate both ways. You have to give second efforts," he said.

The players had heard it all before since they first put on a pair of skates back in elementary school.

But then he said something the players had never heard in the Mount dressing room.

"You hear all the talk about playing for Mount. You're not playing for Mount. You're playing for yourself. You're playing for personal pride. You have to have pride in yourself to be successful in anything you do."

Probably without realizing it, Oliver had just exemplified why from day one of his coaching career, Bill has kept parents, and everyone else, outside the closed doors. What Oliver was preaching was the exact opposite of Bill's Mount Pride.

To most people Oliver's words would sound logical. Of course you need personal pride, but the way in which you obtain it while playing for Mount is what separates Mount Saint Charles hockey from so many other teams on all levels of sports. Today, for most athletes, the personal pride comes first and then they can help the team. To Bill, making the team a winner is your primary responsibility, and when you do that you automatically develop a sense of personal pride that few people enjoy.

Most of the players sitting around the room had tuned out Oliver from the second they sat down. *Just let him talk so we can get out of here* was the message conveyed from the expressions on most faces around the room. So no one jumped up and informed Oliver that what he was saying wasn't the Mount way. No one cried "heresy." Besides, all season long there had been a question of whether this year's Mount team even thought that Oliver's philosophy was wrong.

"Do you think you guys are as scared of Coach Belisle as the players used to be?" I asked Jeff Jillson one day as he sat in a near empty dressing room after practice.

He didn't need to think very long about the answer.

"We may not be as scared, but I think we respect him more than they did," he said.

The reply caught me off guard. All season long I had been hearing from people who had been around Mount hockey for a long time that the 1997–98 team didn't seem to understand what Mount Pride was all about. That its players seemed to follow their own agendas. A "team of centers" as Dave had dubbed it. But here was Jillson saying that he thought he and his teammates respected Bill more than some legendary Mount Saint Charles players of the past.

"From what I hear some of the guys in the past did things the coach said because they were afraid of what he might do if they didn't do it." Jillson said. "We do it because we know how much it means to him. You watch him at practice every day and you know how much it means to him. That's why it means so much to us."

CHAPTER 32

"We're in trouble," Dave said.

It was Friday, March 13, and Dave feared that the Mount Saint Charles luck had at last run out.

He was sitting with his father in the coach's office. It was almost midnight. About two hours earlier, father, son, and about a thousand Mount fans watched in shock as a fluke goal gave La Salle a 3–2 sudden-death overtime victory in the first game of their best-of-three playoff semifinal series at Adelard. It meant Mount was on the verge of elimination from the state tournament in the semifinal round. No one could remember the last time that a Mount team lost a game in the semifinal round. To keep the hope for another state title alive, they would need a victory the following night in the second game of the series at Thayer Arena in Warwick.

That's why Dave was so worried.

"We lost a game and now we have to play at Thayer. We *never* play well at Thayer. We're definitely in trouble," he said with a rueful laugh, the way a guy facing a root canal tries bringing humor to the situation.

Dave had learned not to be surprised about anything the 1997–98 team did. But he had to admit, he didn't expect to lose the first game of the playoffs, especially since it was at Adelard. After a couple of weeks of up and down practice sessions the last three or four practices had been excellent. Everyone focused. To Dave, it looked as if the seniors were finally realizing what being a Mount senior was all about. That the abstract known as Mount Pride was finally surfacing. The only downside had been that Oliver had missed three of the final four practices. He'd attended practice on Tuesday, but then on Wednesday there had been a note on Bill's desk explaining that his hamstring was bothering him again. What bothered Dave the most about Oliver was that he didn't seem to care enough about the team to be at practice, even if he couldn't skate. Other guys had been hurt and couldn't practice at various times during the season, but unless they had treatment scheduled for the same time as practice they would be in the dressing room. For six months, the hockey team is their family and the family home is the locker room. But to Oliver, if he wasn't going to play, there were more productive things to do than sit around a dressing room or stand in a rink watching other guys practice.

"You would think that he would want to be here to show his support for his teammates, especially at this time of the year," Dave sighed when he first saw the note.

All season Dave had questioned just how much playing at Mount meant to Oliver. Sure he enjoyed the honor of wearing the Mount hockey jacket and the excitement of the games, but at times he seemed to be burned out. He lacked the same passion that fired the other players. He had been playing hockey virtually his entire life, but how many of those hours at rinks throughout New England had been spent because of his love of the game and how much was because of his father's hockey passion and the fact that his big brother was a hockey player? Would he ever even play at Mount if his brother hadn't done so first?

He had also never paid the dues to earn a starting berth as most of the other players had. He moved up as a varsity regular in his sophomore year simply because there were only three experienced goalies. In his senior year, he won the starting berth as much by default as by spectacular play. If Pete Capizzo hadn't gotten sick, Dave had no doubt that by midseason either Oliver would have had to work harder or Capizzo would have been the starting goalie. But with Capizzo out of the picture, Oliver knew the job was his no matter what he did, or didn't do. No one wanted to play for Mount more than Jason Catalano, the other senior goaltender, but "Cat" just didn't have the talent to be the starting goalie. Even though there were nights Dave and Bill would have loved to put Cat in the game just to shake up Oliver, they were realistic enough to know that the move wouldn't have been fair to the rest of the team, or to Catalano himself. So Oliver was the goalie, even if he had only been at three of the last sixteen practices before the first playoff game. It all came down, as usual, to getting him to stay focused for any length of time. His father said it was the same way with his schoolwork. When he paid attention and completed all of his assignments he was a good student, but there were times he struggled in the classroom because of his inability to maintain his focus. Some people would say he might have attention deficient disorder; others would say that's typical behavior for a lot of teenage boys. His problem was that he still hadn't realized that when you're wearing a Mountie uniform you're not a typical teenager.

Dave knew there could be difficulties in the goal, but if the Mount forwards and defensemen had dominated as they were capable of doing it shouldn't have mattered. And that's how it went at the start of the game. Mount dominated. They took three shots for every one of La Salle's. By the end of the first period, Mount had tallied twenty-four shots and La Salle had only six, but there was still no score. Then in the second period, a La Salle player fired a soft shot toward the top right-hand corner of the cage. Unfortunately, Oliver misjudged the speed of the shot and it floated past him for a goal. Later in the period, Oliver made a save, but lazily tried to cover up the rebound. One of the La Salle forwards was anything but lazy. He slammed the puck into the cage before Oliver could grab it. Less than five minutes into the second period, Mount was trailing 2–0.

"We're playing well, but you can't recover from plays like that. Bantam goalies make those saves," Jillson said disgustedly when he returned to the bench after the La Salle goal.

Mount did take the action right back into the La Salle zone following the second goal and kept it there for most of the final ten minutes of the period, but they still couldn't score. At the end of two periods, Mount was trailing, 2–0.

"You don't want to listen to me," Bill screamed in the locker room between the second and third periods. "You think you know everything. You think those guys are just going to step aside because you're Mount Saint Charles. Well this is what happens when you think that way."

That was all he had to say. He turned and stalked from the middle of the dressing room, out the door into the junior varsity room, and plopped down onto the bench in the empty JV room, out of the sight of the players in the varsity room.

268

The players froze. They had expected Bill to scream for most of the break. But he only talked for a few minutes and then walked out on them. But he wanted them to sit and stew over what he had said. The players looked toward Dave, expecting he would immediately step in and pick up where Bill left off. But Dave just leaned in the doorway of the coach's office. He knew what his father was trying to do and he wasn't going to let the players off easy. After a few minutes of awkward silence, he finally spoke up about defensive assignments and the importance of getting position in front of the cage. He then walked out and joined his father in the junior varsity room. The players sat in silence for a few more minutes until they finally heard the Zamboni driving off the ice.

"Let's go," Jillson barked as he led them out of the dressing room past their two coaches who were sitting by themselves in the empty JV room.

Jillson didn't waste any time directing Mount to the comeback trail. Only three minutes after the start of the third period, he scored an unassisted goal. Seven minutes later, Hutchins tied the score. Mount continued dominating, but once again they missed a host of scoring opportunities. It went the same way through the first sudden-death overtime period: Mount dominated, but La Salle held the fort. Then shortly after the start of the second overtime, a La Salle player fired a shot toward the Mount goal from out near the blue line. He really was just trying to get the puck on the cage in hopes that one of his teammates might be able to pick up a loose puck in front of the cage. But Oliver wasn't ready for the shot. He dropped down to his knees thinking the shot was low. Then, when he realized the shot was high, instead of just reaching up and grabbing it with his catching glove, he instead tried bringing his big blocking glove and stick all the way across the front of his chest. Every Little League baseball player knows how tough it is to backhand a glove across the top of your body with any type of quickness. It's twice as tough to do with a heavy goalie blocking glove and stick. By the time Oliver brought his glove over, the puck was past him into the cage. It was a fluke goal, but goals don't come with quality points. It was a goal—and it meant that Mount had lost.

Jillson was one of the first players back in the dressing room after the game. He sat in his seat next to the locker-room door watching the other players file in. No one said a word—they didn't need to say anything; their faces told the story. If a picture is worth a thousand words, the faces in the

Mount dressing room read like a novel. They were expressions of anger and disbelief. This wasn't supposed to happen to them. They were Mount Saint Charles, and Mount Saint Charles always wins this type of game. The Mounties always find a way to win the important playoff games. But not that night; that night they lost. What made matters more confusing to them was that they felt that they had outplayed the other team.

No one's face showed more pain than Jillson's. Some of the other's had looks of disbelief, but Jillson had an expression of anger. He was angry about the fluke goal, but probably angrier with himself. It was the first time all season that he was accepting blame for the team losing a game. Ironically, he had played one of his best games all season. On an individual basis, even Bill would have given him at least 2.5 out of a possible 3 for his performance. But the team had lost and it seemed Jillson was suddenly realizing he had a special responsibility. Whatever he did individually, unless the team won, his season was a failure. Finally, the anger and frustration built to a point where he no longer could stay seated. He jumped off the bench and strode into the junior varsity room. The managers, rushing to pile all of the equipment into the dressing room before the coaches came in and slammed the door shut, had stacked all of the extra sticks on the training table in the middle of the JV room. For Jillson, the sticks were the perfect targets upon which to take out his frustrations.

"Shit, shit, shit," Jillson yelled as he picked up the sticks one by one and flung them against the JV room wall. Dave and Bill stepped into the room just as Jillson began the stick-flinging, but neither said a word. They hardly even glanced at their captain as they walked past him into the varsity room. Under normal circumstances Bill would have been livid seeing one of his players abuse valuable equipment. But this time, he let it go. It was the most emotion he had seen out of Jillson all season. It would cost him a few broken sticks, but he finally knew that Jillson really did care about the team. All season long, it had appeared as if the team had been secondary in Jillson's hockey priorities. Until that game, what little emotion Jillson had expressed was over an individual situation; either it was an argument with Bill or Dave or he was upset because the officials were letting the opponents cheap-shot him. Now he was finally showing frustration and anger because of what happened to the team. Veteran coaches say you should learn from every loss. Maybe Jillson had learned an invaluable lesson, but had he learned it too late to save the season?

• • •

Dave and Bill stood in the middle of the varsity room without saying a word, patiently waiting for Jillson to finish his tirade in the adjacent JV room. Eventually Jillson returned and slumped into his spot on the bench next to the door.

Bill let Dave do the talking.

"You didn't lose from lack of effort. You played your hearts out, especially in the third period," Dave said in a very composed tone. "Now you need to come back tomorrow night. If you win tomorrow, you will win the state championship. If you lose, you lose it. You have to come out firing. You have to shoot low."

He talked for a few minutes longer, preaching out the usual basics such as working harder around the cage. He then asked if anyone wanted to say anything.

Charlie Ridolf was the first to speak up.

"We need to keep it under control. We can do it," he shouted out.

Ridolf's declaration surprised everyone. Here was probably the only player in the history of Mount Saint Charles hockey to jump into the stands to celebrate a regular-season goal, pronouncing that the key to victory was keeping everything under control.

If Ridolf could keep his game under control, anything was possible.

But the most potent declaration came a few minutes later when Jillson spoke.

"We're not going to lose," Jillson matter-of-factly shouted. "Mount teams have been down like this before. This is what Mount hockey is all about. We're not going to lose."

So what if they had only won one of their last six games? So what if they lose games despite outshooting the other team by a two-to-one ratio? So what if they needed to win at Thayer Arena, a rink where they always seem to have trouble? So what if their only goalie had made only three of the last sixteen practices? If Jillson said they weren't going to lose, if he finally seemed to understand what Mount hockey was all about and was willing to put all his energies and talents into making the team a winner, there was hope.

Most of the players had showered, changed, and left the dressing room when Oliver came into the coach's office after the La Salle game.

"I want to apologize for that goal. I saw it," he said.

"You don't have to apologize," Dave assured him. "That's what can happen when you let a game get into overtime. There have been years we got goals and we didn't know how the puck went in. Tonight that happened to us. Now you're going to come back tomorrow night and stone them. Don't worry about it."

Dave probably would have like to have said, "You dumb bastard. How did you let an easy shot like that get past you?" But you can't do that when you're a high school coach, even a Mount Saint Charles hockey coach.

Bill ordered the door to the Mount dressing room at Thayer Arena closed. Outside the door, a packed house was awaiting the start of the second game of the semifinal series between La Salle and Mount. The only reason a lot of the fans were there was to see Mount get beat. They hoped that years from that night they would be able to say they were there when Mount Saint Charles finally lost the state championship, just as for decades probably a million New England sports fans have claimed they were at Fenway Park that September day back in 1960 when Ted Williams hit a home run in his final trip to the plate.

Of course not everyone was there to see Mount lose. Somewhere in the crowd Jo-Anne Fede frantically fingered the rosary beads in her coat pocket, silently reciting a Hail Mary for every bead she touched.

The Mount–La Salle game was the second game of a playoff doubleheader and because the first game had gone into sudden-death overtime the players were forced to sit in the dressing room without any idea of when they would finally get a chance to take the ice. Surprisingly, the forty-five-minute bus ride from Woonsocket to Warwick hadn't seemed much different then the ride to an early regular-season game. If the Mount players were nervous about their upcoming face-off with destiny they didn't show it. It was the usual sounds of teenage chatter coming from the back of the bus mixed with music from the bus radio. There were no panicked faces.

Dave had planned the departure time from Woonsocket so that the players wouldn't have to spend a lot of time sitting around the rink with nothing to do but think about their upcoming game. But the overtime in the first game had disrupted the schedule, forcing the players to sit around and wait. The longer they waited, the more the magnitude of what they were about to undertake took a toll on their nerves. Most of them had been playing hockey games since they were five or six years old. Even though they were only fifteen, sixteen, and seventeen, most of them had already played several hundred games during their hockey careers, yet they've never dressed for a game like this. In one corner of the room Paul Fede sat looking up at the ceiling.

He tried keeping them hidden from teammates, but you couldn't miss the rosary beads that he was holding in his lap. Maybe tradition and all the other stuff wasn't that important to some of the other players, but it was to him. It had been part of his family for almost a decade. Now the streak could end in his senior year. Maybe he'd worried about too many other things all season long but at that moment the band practices and the college trips didn't mean anything compared to winning the championship.

"Please, God, give us a great game," he seemed to be saying as he gazed toward the ceiling.

Finally, one of the managers came rushing through the dressing room door with the news that someone finally scored in the second sudden overtime of the first game.

"Get ready. We're on as soon as they clean the ice," Dave instructed the team.

A few minutes later Bill came in and ordered the door closed.

Once the door was shut, he waited a few minutes without saying a word before jumping onto the bench at the far end of the dressing room so that everyone could see his five-eight frame.

"Stand up. Everybody up," he yelled.

Almost in unison, twenty-five teenagers stood up on their skates.

"That's the way you play tonight. You stand tall," he told them.

"I love you guys like I love God. You're my boys. I love you because you're dedicated. You're willing to put up with my yelling at you."

There was minute or so of complete silence after Bill finished, and then Dave began: "You are the defending champions. You have the experience. Play with confidence," he challenged them.

Then he raised his voice.

"You're playing for him," he said, pointing toward his father, who by now was jammed between the sink and a toilet in the tiny bathroom of the dressing room.

"Picture that maniac on the ice," he said as he continued pointing toward his father. "Do you think anybody would want to try taking the puck away from you if you play like he would if he was out there? Grab his energy. That's what I do. I'm him. You think I'm this way all the time? You know I'm not. He gives me energy. Grab *his* energy."

Whatever the source, the Mounties didn't waste any time getting energized once the game started. Oliver came up with a couple of big saves in the first five minutes that kept the game scoreless. Had his apology the previous night meant he finally was ready to focus on his job? Did he finally realize that nothing comes automatically in the game, not even for a Mount Saint Charles goalie? Only a few minutes later, Snizek carried the puck into the zone and fired a shot at the La Salle cage. The La Salle goalie made the save, but the rebound bounced a few feet out in front of the cage. A La Salle defenseman got a stick on the puck, but Joe Peters came charging in. He muscled the puck away from the La Salle player and slipped it over to Turcotte on the right post. Turcotte had no problem banging it home for the game's first goal. Just over a minute later, Turcotte struck again when he banged home a Snizek rebound.

It was what Turcotte had dreamed about during all those years he was growing up in Woonsocket and going to Mount games as a little kid. The dream that some night he would be the star of a Mount Saint Charles playoff victory. It was why he was willing to wash dishes to play for Mount.

Joe Peters was also rewarding Dave's faith in him. A few weeks earlier, Dave had moved Peters up to the top line with Snizek and Turcotte. He knew Peters wasn't a scorer like the other two, but he was willing to work around the front of the cage collecting the garbage. He was the kid who had come into the coaches' office a few days after Dave had joked about shitting on the ice and said: "If it will help the team just tell me where to shit, Coach." It hadn't come to that, but Peters *was* taking a lot of shit from opposing players while working around the front of the cage. When he stripped off his tee shirt after games you could see the welts all over his upper body. He was constantly getting jabbed with the butt end of the defensemen's sticks as he tried establishing position in front of the cage while one of his linemates was digging the puck out of the corner. The defensemen were wrapping their sticks around his arms and chest as they tried pushing him away from the cage, not to mention the times he was getting cross-checked when the defensemen knew the officials were busy watching the action away from the cage. He could feel every hit, but he kept coming back, time after time. For weeks, his work hadn't produced many dividends. There were more missed opportunities than goals scored because Peters didn't have the hands to make him a scorer. But now his hard work had produced, and Dave couldn't be happier for any player. He felt that Joe Peters was one of the few members of the 1997–98 team who could have survived on *any* Mount team.

With three minutes remaining in the first period that determination paid off for Peters. Stationed in front of the cage, he won a battle with two La Salle defensemen for a loose puck and banged it home to give Mount a 3–0 lead. There was still two periods to play, but this wasn't going to be one of those nights when anybody wearing a Mount uniform let up. The best La Salle could do was cut the deficit to 3–1 early in the third period, but Mount came right back with goals by Cardillo and Josh Lanni. Mount was still holding the 5–1 lead when the final buzzer sounded. The best-of-three series was tied at a game apiece. They would be back at Adelard on Monday for a winner-take-all third game.

Dave perched on the dressing room bench after the game as the players packed their equipment and made their way out to the bus. He was glancing at the game stat sheet one of the league officials had just handed him. After each game, the coaches select three stars. Snizek was the first star, Turcotte was the second, and Oliver was the third. For the first time all season, Oliver was a legitimate star.

"Oliver had a good game," Dave noted. "Maybe he's finally coming around."

By the time the blue school bus pulled out of the Thayer parking lot it was after midnight.

"He's tired," Dave said as he looked over at his father, who was sprawled in the seat across the aisle with his eyes closed and his head resting against the bus window.

"How many guys his age could do what he did tonight?" Dave asked. "I'm tired, too. I'm not sure how much longer we're going to be doing this. You know it's only fair that somebody beats us before we give it up. But I'm going to do my best not to let that happen."

Two nights later, Mount earned its twenty-second consecutive berth in the Rhode Island state title series with a 3–0 victory over La Salle at Adelard in the deciding game of their best-of-three series.

"Give me a hundred percent effort and I won't let you lose," Dave had said before the game.

Twenty-five teenagers gave him what he asked.

It looked like the game would be scoreless after the first period until Jillson blasted home a shot from the point with only a second to play in the period. Then Jillson and Fede set up Ridolf for a second-period goal. Peters took any remaining suspense out of the game with a goal midway through the third period. Three goals by three seniors with Oliver playing another strong game in the goal. After giving up three goals in the first game of the series, Oliver gave up only one goal in the next two games. The seniors, including Oliver, finally were rewarding Bill's confidence in them.

For his pregame captain's speech, Jillson had read an excerpt from the poem, "The Man in the Glass."

> When you get what you want in your struggle for self,
> And the world makes you king for a day,
> Just go to a mirror and look at yourself
> And see what the man has to say
> For it isn't your father or mother or wife
> Whom judgment on you must pass
> The fellow whose verdict counts most in your life
> Is the one staring back from the glass.

Pat Hutchins sat on the bench in the locker room after the game savoring the moment. The state title series would be played at Providence College so this would be Hutchins last night sitting in the Mount dressing room after a game. He wasn't in any rush to shower.

"Jeff's poem was corny, but he was right," said Hutchins. "We all needed to look at ourselves in the mirror."

CHAPTER 33

Pete Capizzo only had one question for his parents when he was released from the New England Medical Center in early March of 1998.

"If we make the finals, can I sit on the bench in my uniform and pads?" he asked.

At the time, Stephanie and Gus Capizzo didn't give Pete's request much thought. Their main concern was getting their son home and restoring some sense of normalcy to his life. Rather than having been on the ice at Adelard Arena, Pete had spent the better part of the previous month in a hospital bed. The X rays that Doc Guay had ordered hadn't shown any signs of pneumonia, but when Pete still had a runny nose and sore throat after a week of treatments for flu and possible pneumonia, Stephanie and Gus decided it was time for hospital tests.

But even a few days in one hospital didn't ease the Capizzo's anxiety. The doctors couldn't agree on what was causing the problem. They kept saying the bleeding was just an irritation, caused by the flu symptoms. But each day his parents visited him in the hospital they felt their son was growing weaker. Finally, the Capizzos decided they had to make a move. They informed the doctors that they were taking Pete to the New England Medical Center for further tests.

"Some of the doctors at the hospital that he was in weren't happy about it, but it was something we had to do," said Stephanie.

They tried staying optimistic as Pete underwent scores of blood tests and biopsies, but at times they couldn't help but be certain that their son had serious a health problem. Although they never said it to Peter, they often thought he might never play hockey again. But if the loss of hockey was the only price to pay for their son's health, it would be a bargain.

Unfortunately, giving up hockey wasn't going to cure Wegener's granulomatosis.

WG is a chronic, uncommon, autoimmune vasculitis disease that causes inflammation of the blood vessels. It can seriously endanger the sinuses, lungs, and kidneys. It's a very rare disease. Only two in every million Americans are diagnosed with WG each year. That's only five hundred new cases in the United States each year. The odds of somebody under the age of twenty contracting the disease are even slimmer. Approximately 85 percent of the patients are above the age of nineteen.

Sixteen-year-old Pete Capizzo had become the one-in-a-million American teenager with Wegener's granulomatosis. But in a sense, Pete Capizzo was lucky. Because laboratory tests are not specific for WG, on the average it takes from five to fifteen months to diagnosis once the symptoms appear. It had only been about a month from the time Doc Guay sent Pete to the hospital for X rays to the time diagnosis was made. Unfortunately, a relatively quick diagnosis didn't mean Capizzo was cured. There's no quick cure for WG. The hope is that the disease can be forced into remission with drug treatments and chemotherapy. So while his Mount teammates were battling through the final weeks of the regular season and gearing up for the playoffs with some old fashioned Mount-style practices, Pete was in a Boston hospital undergoing treatments that sapped his strength and at times made him downright sick. Because of his talks with Chris Snizek and Matt Kasberg, he at least knew he wasn't the only Mount player puking during those weeks before the start of the playoffs.

The doctors didn't pull any punches when they talked to Gus and Stephanie. Their son was a sick young man. His lungs and kidneys might already have been affected, and if that was the case, his hockey career was over. That's why his parents kept hedging whenever Pete brought up the subject of playing again. They didn't want to tell him the doctors' fears because they were afraid it would deflate his spirits during the treatments. Even though he had been released from the hospital in late February, they knew he was going to need another series of chemotherapy treatments in April. He needed to keep his spirits up because the next series of treatments would be tougher than what he had already endured. But when Mount won the third game of the semifinal series a few weeks after Pete was released from the hospital, Stephanie asked his doctors if he could dress for the playoff series and skate in the pregame warm-ups.

The answer delighted Pete and shocked his mother.

"If you can carry your gear, then go for it," one of the doctors told Pete.

Later, they told Stephanie and Gus that fortunately there didn't seem to have been any organ damage. The disease had been caught in time. If Doc Guay hadn't noticed the blood on the towel, if Pete had gone a few more months struggling with what he thought was just a stubborn cold, he might have incurred liver or kidney damage. In most instances, the doctors probably would have prescribed a longer rest for someone who had gone through what Pete had during his hospital stay. But Pete's love of hockey was no secret to the people who had been treating him at New England Medical. Every doctor who entered his room quickly became an expert on Mount Saint Charles hockey. The doctors were still trying to find the right combination of drugs to fight the physical effects of the disease, but they knew the perfect medication for this teenager's damaged psyche was getting him back into a hockey uniform.

So on Friday, March 20, Pete skated onto the ice at Providence College's Schneider Arena for the warm-up of the opening game of the title series against Hendricken.

Technically, he had been back at school for two weeks, but he was far from a normal student. He was so weak he couldn't manage more than a few classes a day. Just carrying his equipment the fifty feet or so from the Mount dressing room to the bus parked outside Adelard Arena for the ride to Providence College made him sweat profusely. Not wanting his teammates to realize what a chore it was for him to simply carry his equipment, he waited until they had all taken their bags off the bus and headed for the dressing room at Schneider before he took it inside. He had sat on the dressing room bench, putting on his uniform, trying to make his slow, methodical dressing look as if he was in deep thought about the game. But in reality, he couldn't put on more than a couple of pieces of equipment without taking a rest.

He hadn't let Dave or Bill know just how weak he really was. He hadn't been at practice for two months so the Belisles knew he couldn't play in a game, but he had the doctor's okay. As far as the coaches knew, Pete was healthy again.

But Stephanie and Gus knew better. They sat in the stands, watching anxiously as Pete stepped onto the ice and slowly started skating around the rink before the start of the game. His teammates were flying at high speed to the sounds of the Mount band's rendition of "When the Saints Come Marching In," but Pete seemed to be measuring every step. After more than a decade of taking skating for granted, he now needed to watch his feet every time he took a stride. For years, Stephanie and Gus had watched Pete play hockey, cheering every time he made a good save. But none of the fifty-save performances he delivered during his youth hockey days brought the Capizzos the same thrill that watching him simply skate around the rink did that night.

Sometimes life's treasures come in small strides.

Veteran coaches like to think that they can get a feeling for what's going to happen in an upcoming game by the way practice had gone for a period of days before the game. Dave had a good feeling going into the 1997–98 title series against Hendricken. With the third game of the semifinal series having been played on Monday night there would only be three days of practice before the start of the title series on Friday, March 20. That wasn't a lot of time. It would have been only natural if the team had come to practice on Tuesday afternoon still on a high from Monday night's victory. They would still be thinking more about Monday's accomplishments than Friday's challenge. But to Dave's surprise, and delight, it wasn't that way. There wasn't much talk about the La Salle victory in the locker room on Tuesday. Some of the younger kids still seemed excited, but the older players seemed more concerned about making sure that they were on the ice, ready to go, when Bill blew the whistle for practice.

Oliver, who came up with a big game on Monday, was one of the older players there ready to go, when Bill blew the whistle. Dave had wondered how Oliver was going to respond to Monday's victory. Dave knew the hamstring pull was still bothering him a little, he could see it in the way Oliver was moving Monday night. But he'd fought through the discomfort, not letting it disrupt his focus. He had stayed alert, keeping his head in the game for the entire forty-five minutes. But Tuesday could be a different story. Dave wouldn't have been surprised if there had been a note on his father's desk from Oliver saying that he was going for treatment rather than coming to practice. The kid had the perfect excuse to take the easy way out.

But Oliver was there.

Like Hutchins, Dave had thought Jillson's "The Man in the Glass" poem before Monday night's game had been a little corny. He loved that Jillson was taking on a leadership role, and he had obviously given serious thought to what he felt the team needed to do. But as Dave stood watching a six-foot-three, 220-pound kid standing in the middle of the locker room reciting poetry he wondered how seriously a bunch of teenagers were going to think about what Jillson was trying to say. But it just showed that you never know what teenagers are going to buy, especially when the person doing the selling is one of their own. It's a good bet that if Dave, or even Bill, had brought out the poem as a motivational tool many of the players would have passed it off as more coaching clichés. But when Jillson recited the poem it became a peer challenge.

Cardillo didn't need Jillson telling him to look in the mirror, he'd already been doing some serious soul-searching for a few weeks. Was it the all-star game episode that had started him thinking? He hadn't really thought of his participation in it as an insult to the team until Dave mentioned it. Dave had debated whether or not to bring it up, but he felt he had to say something. He just made a quick off-handed remark to Cardillo that he was surprised to have seen him playing in the all-star game after he hadn't been able to play in the Hendricken game the previous night.

He knew Cardillo would get the message.

Bill and Dave knew any trepidation Hendricken players had about not being able to beat Mount Saint Charles because they had lost the first two games of the season had been wiped out by the resounding Hendricken victory in the final game of the regular season. The Hendricken coaches no longer had to fire out a bunch of clichés to convince their team that it could beat Mount; all they needed to say was: "Remember the last time you played them."

Mount was no longer invincible.

Hendricken also had won its best-of-three semifinal series against Toll Gate in two straight games. Hendricken would have a full week's rest before the start of the title series while Mount would be playing with only a three-day rest. In a physical game such as hockey, where injuries pile up at the end of the season, a few extra days to rest battered and bruised bodies can make a significant difference to a high school team. Hendricken also had a capable goalie, so Bill and Dave knew Mount wasn't going to get any gifts in this title series.

The Belisles hadn't expected any gifts, but after the first two periods of the opening game of the title series they were starting to think fate was actually cheating their team of its just due. Hot goalies win playoff games. It's as true in high school hockey as it is in the Stanley Cup playoffs. Over a three- or four-month regular season, the team with the greater overall talent usually emerges as the champion. But in a two or three game playoff series, or even a best of seven series as in the NHL, a hot goalie can make a less talented team a winner. A few times during its twenty-year reign as state champion, especially with Garth Snow in 1987, Mount Saint Charles had won the title, not because of its overall superior talent, but because of its hot goalie.

Now it was starting to look as if Mount's title string might end because of a hot goaltender—and a little bad luck.

In two periods, Mount fired forty shots at the Hendricken goalie while Hendricken had only taken fifteen at Oliver. But despite the one-sided play, neither team had scored.

But it hadn't been like so many other nights during the season when the lack of scoring was a direct result of a lack of focus. The forwards were winning the battles in the corners. They were getting the puck back out in front of the cage and their teammates were getting shots on the cage. But the Hendricken goalie, Kyle McNulty, kept coming up with phenomenal stops. He would kick out a shot with his pads and then reach up and snag the rebound shot that looked like it was headed into the top of the cage.

It wasn't just McNulty who was keeping the game scoreless, however. There's an old hockey saying that goal posts are a goalie's best friend. For two periods McNulty and the posts had acted more like beloved family members than just friends. At least four times, shots off the sticks of Mount players hit the post. The shot could have deflected into the net or bounced back to a Mount forward for another try. But each time the shot either deflected off to the side of the cage or dropped in front of McNulty who quickly smothered it.

Dave and Bill paused outside the dressing room door, talking for a few minutes before going in to speak to the team during the break between the second and third period. They knew that for once the lack of scoring wasn't a result of a lack of focus or hustle, but they couldn't allow a sense of frustration to set in because all of their effort in the first two periods hadn't produced any goals. It's easy for young athletes to start feeling sorry for themselves when what they think is their best effort doesn't produce results. They can start thinking that this just isn't their day, that no matter what they do, fate is against them. Why keep fighting the inevitable? But the frustration can also be a perfect testing round for an athlete's sense of pride. Is he going to let someone else determine his fate or is he going to put in that extra effort that will make him a winner? Bill and Dave knew that they needed to turn two periods of frustration into the catalyst for a demonstration of Mount Pride.

They also needed to make the point clear that this might be one night when the other players couldn't expect Jillson to bail them out with some big offensive play. It had become obvious that despite all the criticism heaped on Jillson by the Hendricken fans and players, the Hendricken coaching staff felt the only way to beat Mount was not to give Jillson a chance to show his offensive talents. All night, even when they were in the Mount zone, a Hendricken player was shadowing Jillson. The Hendricken coaches wanted to make sure the second Jillson touched the puck there was somebody harassing him and they quickly had a second player joining in the forechecking effort against the Mount star. They didn't want Jillson to have a few seconds to think about getting the Mount offense in gear with a good breakout pass or a rink-length solo dash. The strategy would cut down on the Hendricken scoring potential and also open up the rink to the other Mount players, a gamble the Hendricken coaching staff was willing to take. Even though they would never say it, they knew Jillson had awesome offensive talents. They knew if they gave him just a little opening he would burn them. But they weren't sure if any other Mount player would, or could, step up even if they had an opening because of the extra attention being given Jillson.

Apparently they decided to gamble that this was a Mount Saint Charles team of one superstar and a lot of ordinary players who didn't know how to deliver when the pressure was on.

For two periods the gamble had paid off.

CHAPTER 34

"We didn't come out the way we should have," Dave said in a loud but controlled tone of voice as he stood in the dressing room during the break between the game's second and third periods. "We need to be aggressive. Don't let them in the zone. We need to work."

As he paused to take a breath, Bill suddenly jumped into the middle of the conversation from his spot nearer the dressing room door.

"Come on boys, you got to work," he barked. It was like the "Alleluia!" punctuating a revival preacher's sermon.

That's all Bill said. Every player had taken his eyes off Dave in the middle of the room to look at Bill near the door, but now Bill was looking straight back at Dave.

Dave immediately went back to shouting out specific instructions.

"As soon as you see your linemate with the puck yell to him," he bellowed. "Don't wait. Do it the split second he gets the puck. If you don't yell, if you wait two or three seconds, they may be on you. When you hear the voice, pass the puck. Don't wait."

Suddenly Bill's voice erupted again.

"Don't wait! Don't wait!" he yelled, pumping his fist in the air.

Once again, that's all he said.

It went on that way for three or four minutes. Dave shouting out his laundry list of specific assignments and Bill punctuating the message every thirty seconds or so with his version of hockey alleluia.

"Mount Pride, boys. Mount Pride!" Bill shouted one final time as the team charged out the door for the third period,

Just under a minute after the start of the third period, Mount Saint Charles's luck went from bad to worse.

Hendricken had fired the puck into the Mount zone shortly after the third period face-off. One of the Mount defensemen had been the first player to the puck and he immediately looked to feed one of the Mount forwards who had started breaking out of the zone. Unfortunately, the pass was a few inches off the mark. Rather than smoothly slide onto the stick of the Mount forward as he broke out of the zone, the puck hit the back of the skate of a Hendricken forward, who a second earlier had been behind the play. Suddenly, rather than having to chase the action, the action had come to him. He didn't waste any time taking advantage of his golden opportunity. He saw a teammate still near the Mount cage and quickly fed him a pass. It all happened so fast that neither the Mount defense nor the Mount forwards, who had been breaking out of the zone, had time to recover. Nor did Oliver have much of a chance when the Hendricken player let loose with an unmolested shot from out about five feet away.

The goal naturally sent the Hendricken fans into an uproar. For two periods they had watched their team being dominated. They couldn't help but think it was just a matter of time until Mount began scoring goals. But suddenly Hendricken had scored the game's first goal. It wasn't pretty, but the scoreboard still read 1–0 and there were only fourteen minutes to play.

Dave stood at the back of the Mount bench watching the Hendricken players celebrating on the ice. He knew Mount had to get that goal back fast. He knew the longer Mount went without scoring the more frustrated his players would become—and frustrated players can become stupid players. He also knew that the longer Hendricken held onto the lead the more confident their players would become that they could pull off a victory despite being outshot almost three-to-one. Mount needed a goal and needed it fast.

"If you want me to shit on the ice just tell me where," Joe Peters had said to Bill and Dave that day he had come into Bill's little locker-room office.

Bill didn't say anything about shitting on the ice, but he did slap Peters and his linemates on the back and issued a command as they took the ice following the Hendricken goal.

"Work hard," Bill shouted.

Peters had his order and nothing was going to stop him from carrying it out.

Snizek and Turcotte, who were now Peters's linemates, worked the puck into the zone following the face-off. Snizek had taken a Turcotte pass just inside the blue line and was working his way toward the Hendricken goal. Peters knew his job. He needed to get in close to the goal, maybe for a rebound, maybe for a pass, or maybe just to create havoc in front of the cage so that Snizek would have a better chance of scoring.

"Just tell me where," he had said to Dave and Bill that day, so for weeks Dave had been telling him where.

"Use your strength to create shit in front of the cage," Dave had told him although not quite in those words.

Peters was trying to establish a spot in front when Snizek fired a shot. McNulty made the save, but the rebound bounced out a few feet away from the Hendricken netminder. Peters didn't hesitate reacting. He simply outmuscled a Hendricken defender to the puck and banged it home for the tying goal. It had only taken twenty-six seconds for Mount to respond with the tying goal. They had needed a goal quickly and Joe Peters, the kid who had dreamed about some day being the hero in a Mount playoff game, but didn't think it would ever happen, had delivered.

But Peters didn't have time to reflect on the fulfillment of his childhood dreams just then. Mount may have tied the game, but McNulty and his Hendricken teammates weren't about to concede defeat. It was still a tie game and for the final thirteen minutes of regulation play, McNulty made sure it stayed that way with several great saves.

"This is our game," Jillson shouted to his teammates as they stood in the front of the Mount bench waiting for the start of the sudden-death overtime period.

It only took a few minutes for Jillson's declaration to prove true.

Just under four minutes after the start of the overtime Charlie Ridolf beat a Hendricken player to a loose puck along the boards in front of the penalty boxes at center ice. It looked like an innocent enough play, nothing that was going to lead to a goal. But Ridolf made a deft move that left a Hendricken forward standing helpless as Ridolf broke toward the Hendricken zone. Then, somehow, he squeezed between the boards and a Hendricken defenseman. That sent him and Hutchins, who was now skating down the other side on a two-on-one break. Maybe because they knew Ridolf was a player who always wanted to do it all himself, or maybe it was just a natural reaction to move toward the player with the puck, but both McNulty and the Hendricken defenseman directed their attention toward Ridolf. Yet rather than trying to do it himself, Ridolf kept everything under control. When the Hendricken players moved toward him he slid a perfect pass across to Hutchins who was now all alone on the left side. He quickly fired a shot high into the left corner for the game-winning goal.

At the far end of the bench, Bill pumped his arm in celebration. Once again his boys had come through under pressure, and once again it was seniors who had delivered the big plays.

On the other end of the bench, Dave had more of a look of relief than jubilation. He knew Mount had escaped a scare. They had outshot Hendricken 57–23 yet they needed to go into overtime to win. The bottom line, however, was that they *had* won. There were a lot of reasons why. But two of the biggest were because Joe Peters was stronger than the other players going for that rebound and when he had a chance to try doing it all himself, Charlie Ridolf thought more about the team than himself.

In 1998, Mike Campagna was the producer of a popular sports talk radio show in Providence. He had been a student at Hendricken during the great Mount Saint Charles–Hendricken title series in the late eighties so he knew all about the Hendricken-Mount hockey rivalry.

"I've been there before," Campagna said a few days before the first game of the title series. "The first game will be close, but Mount will win. The second game will be a runaway."

Campagna knew what he was talking about.

Dave had seemed more relaxed on the bus trip to the second game of the title series on Saturday night than he had been on any other road trip all season. A one-game lead in a best-of-three series gives any coach a small sense of security, but Dave's sense of tranquillity was prompted more from what he thought was going to happen than what had already occurred. He had been sensing for a few weeks that the seniors finally understood what being a Mount senior meant. It hadn't automatically turned every game into a rout; this team just wasn't that talented. But they had faced close calls, they had been on the verge of losing, but they didn't quit. The previous Saturday night, in a do-or-die second game of the semifinal series with La Salle, Monday night in the third game of the semifinal series, and then again in the first game of the title series. They had all been close calls, but each night they delivered, especially the seniors.

Dave sensed that the seniors had taken control. As much as he tried, he had never quite been able to put as much faith in his seniors as his father had through the years. But now he was starting to feel that faith. It might have been a tougher job turning these twenty-five players into a team than any other one in his father's coaching career, but it had been accomplished. So he sat with his father in the front seat behind the drive enjoying the moment. They had been taking these bus rides for playoff games together for nearly twenty years now. He never thought he and his father could have this kind of relationship, and it wouldn't have happened without hockey. He wanted to enjoy the ride. After all, how many more could there be?

Jeff Jillson didn't waste any time taking control of the second game of the series.

Just about a minute after the start of the game, he picked up a loose puck near the Mount blue line. First he strong-armed his way around a defender at mid-ice and then, before the Hendricken defense could catch him, he blasted a shot from about forty feet away from the Hendricken cage. McNulty didn't even have a chance to react before the puck was in the upper-right corner. Only a minute and five seconds after the opening face-off, Mount had a 1–0 lead. The quick goal forced Hendricken to change its strategy. It could no longer play defensive hockey and hope to win by getting one good break. Now Hendricken had to play catch-up, but there wasn't going to be any catching Mount that night. By the end of the first period, Mount was ahead 3–0 as Snizek scored about nine minutes into the first period and Hutchins added his second goal in two nights eight seconds before the end of the period.

That was more than Mount actually needed, but midway through the second period Joe Peters once again won the battle for a rebound and drove the puck home for another goal. It was the fourth-straight game Peters had scored a goal. In his first seven games back after rejoining the team at midseason, he didn't score once. But in the playoffs, in the four most important games of the season, he was a star. He had become what he always dreamed of being, the kid who comes out of the shadows and becomes a Mount Saint Charles playoff hero.

Jillson dominated throughout the game. When he wasn't scoring or setting the Mount offense in motion with great breakout passes, he was playing solid defense. By the start of the third period, Mount was ahead 4–0 and there was no question that Jillson would be the tournament's MVP. But just for a little flourish, Jillson blasted home another goal, forty-seven seconds after the start of the final period of his high school career.

When the final buzzer sounded, Mount had a 5–0 lead and its twenty-first consecutive state title.

Joe Cardillo sat with his back resting against the wall of the dressing room watching his teammates celebrating the title. He had seen a similar celebration the two previous years, but this one was special. This was his senior year. This was his team. It was his and Jeff's and Paul's and Hutch's and all the other seniors. There were times when some people thought that their team would be the team that finally lost the title. But they had delivered, just like other Mount seniors had done for two decades.

"We started turning it around once we put all the other stuff aside the past three weeks. Once we started playing as a team and stopped thinking about impressing college coaches and building our stats," Cardillo said. "We needed to stop worrying about ourselves and start thinking about the team."

There are people who feel that something as abstract as pride in a tradition is lost on today's teenagers.

They say that kids of today, especially youth athletes who have grown up in a world that's changing faster than New England weather aren't worried about their place in history. Most of the time they're right. Too many of today's young athletes are motivated by the material rewards that sports provide, rather than the spirit of the game. It starts with the trophies in Little League and continues with dreams of college scholarships and big-money professional salaries. They're part of the "Me Generation" of sports. Take care of yourself first—and worry about the team later. But every year for almost three decades, at some point in the season, a bunch of teenagers wearing Mount Saint Charles uniforms realized they were the guardians of a tradition—and they accepted the responsibility.

"We needed to stop worrying about ourselves and think about the team," said Cardillo.

It's what American team sports are supposed to be all about. Unfortunately it just doesn't happen that much anymore, except behind the closed doors at Adelard Arena.

They call it Mount Pride.

EPILOGUE

About a month after the final game of the 1997–98 season Jeff Jillson called to tell me that he was enrolling at the University of Michigan. Red Berenson had won the recruiting battle. Of course it didn't hurt Berenson's recruiting effort that a few weeks after Mount Saint Charles won its twenty-first consecutive Rhode Island title that winter Michigan won its ninth NCAA national title with a 3–2 victory over Boston College in the title game of the national tournament at the Fleet Center in Boston. Jillson was at the game.

Jillson enjoyed an outstanding freshman season at Michigan in 1998–99, and in June of 1999 was the first-round selection of the San Jose Sharks in the NHL draft. The fourteenth player selected overall, he was the first American collegiate player selected. Despite an attractive offer from San Jose, he decided to remain at Michigan. In his sophomore year, he earned first-team all-American honors, the first Rhode Island native to earn that honor since Keith Carney and David Emma in 1991. He had hoped to lead Michigan to the Final Four of the NCAA national tournament, especially since the tournament was played in Providence, but Michigan lost in the quarterfinal round. That summer he told me he was going back to Michigan for his junior year because he felt, despite having an all-American season, he didn't do all he could to help Michigan win a national title. Although he didn't earn another all-American honor he had a great 2000–01 season, and so did Michigan, its best season since the 1998 national championship season. He was named the Outstanding Defenseman in the Central Collegiate Hockey League and the Wolverines reached the national Final Four where they lost to Boston College, the eventual national champion.

Jillson also was close to accomplishing another of his goals by the spring of 2001. By taking extra courses during the regular academic years and staying at Michigan for summer courses, by the time he finished his junior year he was only a few credits short of his bachelor's degree. He could finish his degree requirements with a few summer or extension classes. Although his parents insisted that it was his decision to turn pro or go to college, he knew how much they valued education. While most athletes who play in big time college sports program need a few extra years to complete their degree requirements after their four years of athletic eligibility runs out, Jillson only needed three full years and he had proved all he could in college hockey. A few weeks after the 2001 national tournament, he told Red Berenson he wouldn't be back for his senior year. Although he hated losing one of the best defenseman in Michigan history, Berenson knew Jillson was ready. That Sunday afternoon in 1998, while sitting in the Jillson's living room, he had promised then that when he felt that Jillson was ready for NHL he would give him his blessing to move on. In the spring of 2001, he gave Jillson that blessing. A few weeks later, Jillson signed a pro contract with the San Jose Sharks worth several million dollars. He chose Brian Lawton, the former Mount star whom he had met for the first time that December night in 1997 when Mount Saint Charles played St. Raphael in Pawtucket, to be his agent.

In November 2001, while playing for the Sharks in a game against the Dallas Stars, the official handed Jillson an unsportsmanlike conduct penalty because he was giving them too much lip.

"I didn't really say that much, but that's no excuse. Being a first-year guy I've got to gain the respect of the officials," Jillson said after the game. "I guess I've got to keep my mouth shut."

Back in Woonsocket, Bill was happy to hear that Jillson had finally gotten the message that he had posted on the dressing room wall that night in 1998:

"Keep your mouth zipped."

On a Friday night in May of 2002, Jillson was in uniform for the Stanley Cup playoff game between San Jose and Colorado in San Jose. Immediately after the game, he rushed to the San Jose airport and caught a red-eye flight to Michigan. The following day he was in a cap and gown taking part in the University of Michigan commencement. In only four years after graduation from Mount Saint Charles, he had become a NHL hockey player and a college graduate.

In 2003, the Sharks traded Jillson to the Boston Bruins, who then traded him to the Buffalo Sabres in 2004. He spent the 2004–05 NHL lockout season playing for the Rochester Americans, Buffalo's AHL affiliate.

Joe Cardillo graduated from Holy Cross College in the spring of 2002. He had played for the Holy Cross hockey team in each of his first three seasons, but injuries limited his playing time in each of them. Finally, at the start of his senior year, he decided that music and a band that he had formed had become more important to him than hockey.

He returned to Rhode Island after graduation and joined his family's trucking business. Although he was making a good living, in the spring of 2005, he decided that the business world was not for him and launched a career as a professional musician. He still remains a very good friend of Jeff Jillson and Paul Fede.

Joe Peters never played another organized hockey game after the final game of the 1998 state tournament. He enrolled at Norwich University in Vermont in the fall of 1998, never planning to try out for the school's hockey team. "I knew my hockey talents and nothing would ever match playing for Mount Saint Charles," said Peters. "Being part of that championship team in 1998 was a dream come true for me. I knew it would never get any better for me hockey-wise so it was time to get on with other aspects of my life." After one semester at Norwich, he transferred to Rhode Island College, where he chose to pursue a major in education. The move also brought him closer to home, where he could be closer to his mother during her battle with Parkinson's disease.

After the 1997–98 season Chris Snizek left Mount to attend the Choate School, where his scholarship stipulated that he would repeat his sophomore year. He played three years at Choate and was one of the team's leading scorers each year. He was recruited by a few Division I schools and in the fall of 2001, he enrolled at Dartmouth College and played four years of varsity hockey for the Big Green. Chris's younger brother, Steve, entered

Mount Saint Charles as a freshman the year after Chris left. Steve played his entire high school career at Mount. During the 2001–2002 season he was one of the top defensemen in Rhode Island and played a major role in Mount winning its twenty-fifth consecutive state championship.

PAUL FEDE, the kid for whom hockey had been a major part of his life since kindergarten, also never played another organized hockey game after that championship game of 1998. When the hockey season ended that year, he still wasn't sure whether he wanted to go to Holy Cross where he could play hockey or the University of Pittsburgh where there was no hockey team, but a great premed program. The Holy Cross admissions office made his decision easier when a few weeks after the hockey season ended it informed Fede that he had been placed on the waiting list for admission to the Class of 2002. His wavering about where he wanted to go to school may have meant the Holy Cross coaching staff didn't make him one of their A-list recruits. As Fede made plans to attend Pittsburgh, in early April he finally got around to opening a pile of mail that had been sitting unread for days. One of the letters contained a full academic scholarship offer from Canisius College in Buffalo, New York, a school to which he'd applied, but wasn't seriously considering. The scholarship offer, however, was too good to pass up. He enrolled at Canisius in the fall of 1998 and graduated as a member of the class of 2002. After graduation, he returned to Rhode Island to work in his family's retail liquor business. He now lives in Newport and owns a sailboat.

CHARLIE RIDOLF never received the Division I hockey scholarship that his father had dreamed about. But he did play Division I hockey—at least sort of. Peter Belisle recruited Ridolf to play at the University of Connecticut. UConn doesn't award hockey scholarships, but in 1998–99 it began playing in a new Division I Metro Northeastern Hockey League. Ridolf didn't play much his freshman year in 1999, but in 2000 he started seeing regular action. Although he never was a star, he was a solid contributor to the Connecticut team that won the 2001 Metro championship. At last sighting he still didn't own a Harley.

BRIAN OLIVER enrolled at American International College in the fall of 1998 and played for the hockey team. He left AIC after only one semester, however, and later attended the Community College of Rhode Island, where he didn't play hockey.

Jerry Turcotte went to college at the University of Massachusetts, Dartmouth while still working at Wright's Family Restaurant to help pay his college tuition, just like he did to help pay his Mount tuition.

As the only senior letterman on the 1998–99 Mount Saint Charles team there was never any question that Sean Jackson would be captain. Unlike all the other years, Jackson had no one to share the responsibility of being a Mount senior. After having lost thirteen seniors from the 1998 team, including one of the best players in Mount history, many observers assumed that 1998–99 would be the year Mount finally lost the state championship. Even though they won the regular-season title, nobody was really surprised when Hendricken posted a 6–2 victory in the first game of the state title series. On Saturday, March 16, 1999, it was a sold-out crowd at Providence College's Schneider Arena—everyone wanted to be there when Mount finally lost. Yet Mount won the second game and then came back two days later and won its twenty-second consecutive title with a victory in the third game. He wasn't the leading scorer or even an all-stater, but Sean Jackson earned a special spot in the Mount Saint Charles hockey annals as the only captain of a Mount Saint Charles team that had only one senior starter. He went on to play varsity hockey at Assumption College in Worcester, Massachusetts.

Dave didn't recognize Peter Capizzo when he saw him in May 1998 at the awards banquet for the 1997–98 team. A few weeks after the state title series, Peter began a series of chemotherapy treatments in an effort to stem the effects of the WG. The treatments caused Capizzo's entire body to swell up and distort. "I honestly didn't know who he was until he came over and said 'Hello coach,'" Dave recalled. Dave also remembers thinking that night that Capizzo would never again play Mount hockey. But when practice started the following fall for the 1998–99 season, Capizzo was on the ice and looked better than ever. The WG had gone into remission. The chemo treatments had ended in late May, which meant he was able to spend most of the summer on Nantucket. He also received the okay from the doctors to resume playing hockey in late August. For the first time in his coaching career, Bill allowed a player to determine whether or not he would come to practice, relying on Capizzo to tell him whether or not he needed a rest. Because he was afraid Capizzo might not tell him when he wasn't feeling well, he also asked Doc Guay to keep an eye on him. The one thing Bill told Capizzo before the start of the season was that if Doc Guay said he shouldn't practice, he didn't get on the ice. Yet Capizzo made nearly every practice that season and was feeling so well that his doctors cut back just about all of his medications.

On the ice, Capizzo became one of the inspirational stories of the year in Rhode Island. He was the starting goalie for virtually every game. Although at times the young Mount team struggled, Capizzo was solid in the goal. Unlike most Mount teams that always dominated the other Rhode Island teams, there were nights when Capizzo had to make more saves than the opposing goaltender. In the final two games of the state titles series, he made a host of impressive saves—one of the key reasons Mount won the state title. For his performance throughout the season, he was named the goalie on the *Providence Journal* all-state team. Later than spring, he was named the Rhode Island recipient of the U.S. Olympic Courage Award. He received the award at a national ceremony in Disney World.

But unfortunately, medical reality intruded on the story. In the summer of 1999, Capizzo came out of remission. His senior season in 1999–2000 was a year of ups and downs. Unlike his junior year, he constantly missed practices because he was weak from medication and renewed chemo treatments. There were periods during the season when he felt fine, but also times when it was even difficult for him to attempt playing hockey. Fortunately for Mount, young Tony Ciresi, by then a junior, had developed into a steady goaltender. He and Capizzo alternated throughout most of the season. Even though Capizzo was a returning first-team all-stater, many observers dubbed Ciresi Mount's top goalie.

With almost the entire team back from the 1998–99 season, everyone expected Mount to roll to the 1999–2000 title, but it didn't happen that way. To everyone's surprise they had to settle for a regular-season co-championship with La Salle because they lost the last two of their three regular season games with La Salle. They even lost the first game of their semifinal series against Toll Gate. But once again they came back and won the next two games.

Although it only went two games, the title series against La Salle was one of the closest series in twenty-five years. There was only one minute in the ninety minutes of play in the two games when the teams were separated by more than one goal. Mount won the first game, 4–2, but it was 3–2 until an open net goal in the final minute. Only a great goaltending performance by the La Salle goalie had kept the game close as Mount outshot La Salle better than two-to-one.

Ciresi had been in the goal the first game, and some people thought Bill and Dave might come back with him for the second game, especially because Capizzo had missed a lot of practice time because of illness. But Capizzo had given four years to Mount hockey, four years of enduring trials no other Mount player had ever endured. Bill and Dave weren't going to deprive him of his chance to end his career on the ice. For only the second time all year, the other team outshot Mount Saint Charles that night. But Pete Capizzo made some spectacular saves. When the game was over, Mount had a victory and its twenty-third straight state title.

Despite his up and down senior year, Capizzo still had hopes of playing Division I college hockey. He spent a post-graduate year at Berkshire School in Massachusetts. He was the team's top goalie in the 2000–01 season. But he also spent the year on and off medication, fighting the effects of WG. In the fall of 2001, he enrolled at Providence College and although he didn't dress for any games during the 2001–02 season he was a member of the Providence varsity hockey team.

He gave up hockey the following season, however, partly because it was obvious that the PC coaching staff didn't think he would ever be the team's regular goalie. He was also still fighting his on-off battle with WG. Because he spent so much time in and out of the hospital over the next two years he was forced to withdraw from a few of his courses. He hopes to graduate after either the 2006 spring or 2006 fall semester.

MARK ESPOSITO enrolled at American International College in the fall of 1998. He played four years of hockey for AIC and was one of the team co-captains for the 2001–02 season. He came back to work in Rhode Island after graduation and also served as a Mount Saint Charles assistant hockey coach for the 2003–04 season. He was forced to give up his coaching position, however, when he became a Jamestown, Rhode Island, police officer in 2005.

MATT KASBERG, the sophomore defenseman who was given the job of covering up for Jillson when he made his offensive rushes in 1998, eventually became a high school star in his own right. In his senior year in 2000, he led the league in assists and was named one of the Providence Journal's two first-team all-state defensemen.

CHRIS CHAPUT quickly became a high school star after playing in the shadows of Jeff Jillson, Chris Snizek, and Joe Cardillo during his freshman year in 1997–98. In his sophomore year, he was named MVP of the state tournament. He won the honor again in the 2000 state tournament. He accepted a scholarship offer from Providence College before the start of his senior year. Word was that one of the conditions of the scholarship was that he would leave Mount for his senior year and play junior hockey. He left Mount and moved in with a family in the Springfield, Massachusetts area. During the 2000–01 season, he was the top scorer for the Springfield team in the Eastern Junior League. He enrolled at Providence College and was a starter for the varsity hockey team for four straight years. During the 2004–05 season, he was one of the Friars top scorers. He graduated from Providence in the spring of 2005.

Chris Chaput had been JUSTIN LAVERDIERE's closest friend since their freshman year at Mount in 1997–98. After their junior years in 2000, both Chaput and Laverdiere went to Iowa to investigate the possibility of playing junior hockey there instead of playing at Mount as seniors. Iowa wasn't the place where either wanted to spend his senior year of high school. Chaput decided to play junior hockey in Springfield, Massachusetts, and Laverdiere decided to stay at Mount even though some hockey insiders had warned that staying at Mount could hurt his chances with college recruiters. "I wanted to spend my last year of high school with my friends," Laverdiere said. His play helped Mount defeat Catholic Memorial in the title game of the 2000 Mount Holiday Face-off, the first time Mount had beaten Catholic Memorial in six years. But he suffered a rib injury the following week and missed almost three weeks of the season. Although some Division I schools had been talking to him, he didn't have any college offers by early March, which made him wonder if he had done the right thing staying at Mount. But with the Mounties on the verge of losing the state championship in sudden-death overtime of the second game of the state title series, Laverdiere took the puck near center ice, skated past two La Salle defenders, and fired about a forty-foot shot for the game-winning goal. Two days later, Mount won another third game of a state title series.

"This is what it's all about. This is why I stayed," Laverdiere said after the second game. "No matter what happens about next year, it was all worth it."

Laverdiere never received a Division I scholarship offer so he spent the 2001–02 season playing junior hockey in Iowa before turning professional in 2003.

In 1999, the New York Islanders traded BRYAN BERARD to the Toronto Maple Leafs. The trade thrilled Berard. The Islanders had decided that Berard should become more of a defensive-minded defenseman. Toronto, on the other hand, wanted him for his offensive skills. He helped Toronto reach the semifinal round of the 1999 Stanley Cup playoffs and was one of the top scorers on a Toronto team that had one of the best records in the NHL during the first half of the 1999–2000 season. But on the evening of March 11, 2000, while playing against the Ottawa Senators in Ottawa, Berard was struck in the right eye by the Senators Marian Hossa's stick. The instant he was struck, Berard knew that the injury was serious. "It was like my eye had exploded," he would later say.

Back in Woonsocket, Pam and Wally Berard sat in their living room watching satellite TV. Their son lay on the ice in a deep crimson pool of his own blood. Although the TV audio didn't pick it up, Wally could see his son mouthing the words, "I can't see."

The force of the stick had cut the cornea in Berard's eye, detached the retina, and fractured the orbital bone. As he was being helped from the ice, a wave of nausea overcame him—not just from the injury but from what he saw out of his left eye. As he was being helped from the ice, holding a towel over his right eye, his teammates gawked at him with expressions of near panic. These were rough-tough hockey players who were very accustomed to seeing blood, but they had never seen anything like this.

The next day, Berard underwent a four-and-a-half-hour operation to reattach the retina. He knew it was going to be a long battle, but he declared he would return to the NHL. Several more operations followed over the next few months, but he never really regained sight in his right eye. He could see light and make out some images, but his vision wasn't close to the NHL 40/400 requirement.

In March 2001, he announced that he felt it was time to get on with his life and that he was accepting an insurance settlement for a career-ending injury that would give him approximately six million dollars. He was only twenty-three years old at the time and he had already played in the NHL for five years.

Tom Laidlaw, who Berard claimed acted more like a brother than an agent, helped him overcome the turmoil of the injury, offering Berard a position with his firm. Instead, Berard chose coaching. He publicly announced that his hockey career was finished, but in the back of his mind he held out a glimmer of hope that someday he might play again. That spring he was fitted with a new corrective lens, which helped his sight somewhat. In the summer of 2001, he played in an adult men's league at Adelard with a few area college players. He performed well and in August accepted an invitation to skate with the players who would make up the USA team in the 2002 Winter Olympics. The more he skated the more the idea of giving playing another try intrigued him. The more people saw him skate the more interest there was in signing him. Because Toronto had not signed him to a contract after his original expired in 2000, he was a free agent. Six teams showed serious interest in signing him during the fall of 2001.

Finally, a week before the start of the 2001–02 season he signed a contract with the New York Rangers and began what is one of the most amazing comebacks pro sports has ever seen. He played the 2001–02 season for the Rangers, the 2002–03 season for Boston Bruins, and the 2003–04 season for the Chicago Blackhawks. Despite being a defenseman, he was the Blackhawks' second-leading scorer with forty-eight points. He also led the team in assists with thirty-four in fifty-eight games.

In 1999, BRIAN BOUCHER's performances helped the Philadelphia Flyers reach the semifinal round of the Stanley Cup playoffs. In January 2004, while playing for the Phoenix Coyotes, he broke a fifty-five year NHL goaltending record when he posted five shutouts in five straight games. The 2003–04 season was Boucher's forth as a regular NHL goalie. He was signed to a new contract with the Coyotes after that season. During the 2004–05 lock-out, he played hockey in Sweden, but will be back with the Coyotes for the 2005–06 season.

The Chicago Blackhawks traded KEITH CARNEY to the Phoenix Coyotes midway through the 1998–99 season. He was a steady influence on the Phoenix defense. Phoenix felt he was such an important part of their team that the Coyotes signed him to a five-year contract during the 2000–2001 season. After the season, however, he was one of the main players in a multiplayer trade between the Coyotes and the Anaheim Mighty Ducks. The Ducks felt he could be the steady influence that was needed on their defensive unit. In 2003, he played a major role in the Mighty Duck reaching the title round of the Stanley Cup playoffs. After the 2003–04 season, he signed a two-year extension to his contract with the Ducks. He sat out the 2004–05 lock-out. At the start of the 2005–06 season, he has played 798 career NHL games.

Both GARTH SNOW and MATHIEU SCHNEIDER didn't play organized hockey during the 2004–05 NHL lock-out season after spending the 2003–04 season playing for the Detroit Red Wings and the New York Islanders, respectively. At the start of the 2005–06 season, Schneider has played 992 career NHL games, and Snow has been the goaltender in 348 NHL games.

In July 2001, *People* magazine ran a cover story about the "Loves of Julia Roberts." Included were pictures of Roberts at various times over the previous decade with Kiefer Sutherland, Jason Patric, Lyle Lovett, Matthew Perry, and PAT MANOCCHIA. Although his personal training business continues to flourish in New York, Manocchia suffered a tragic personal loss in the summer of 2000 when his friend John Kennedy Jr. died in a plane crash off Martha's Vineyard.

In September 2001, University of Maine hockey coach SHAWN WALSH, the only college coach Bill allowed into his practices, died of cancer. He was only forty-six years old.

Over the years, the Belisle family had developed a tradition of holding their postgame state championship celebration in the kitchen of Bill and Yvette's home. On the evening of March 20, 1998, I sat at the Belisle's kitchen table, sharing a celebratory beer with three of Bill's sons, Dave, Peter, and Bill Jr. Bill was there, too, but it was Lent so he sat watching us drink beer while he sipped a cup of coffee. Shortly before everybody headed home that night, Dave Belisle announced that he had something to tell everybody. For a few seconds I feared that he was going to announce that he and his father were retiring as Mount coaches. Instead, he announced that he and his wife, Nancy, were expecting a baby. Their third son was born during the summer of 1998. At another family gathering in the summer of 2001, Dave and Nancy announced that they were expecting their fourth child in January. John Belisle was born in January on the same night Mount Saint Charles was playing a hockey game. With his wife's blessing, Dave had attended the game, but he told his father he would probably have to leave before the game even started. By the time Nancy called her husband's cell phone to tell him it was time for her to go to the hospital, it was the second period and Mount already had a five-goal lead. Somebody suggested that once again Bill had perfectly planned the night's events so his son could both help coach Mount to a victory *and* be at the hospital for his son's birth.

Bill quickly retorted that God is the only coach that can do that.

On January 5, 2002, Mount Saint Charles defeated Toll Gate in an RIIL game. It was Bill's 696th victory as the Mount Saint Charles coach. It made him the winningest high school hockey coach in America. Two months later, on March 16, 2002, Mount completed a two-game sweep of La Salle in the title series of the Rhode Island state tournament. It gave Mount its twenty-fifth consecutive state championship, a quarter of a century of consecutive titles.

After twenty-six years, the Mount Saint Charles reign as Rhode Island state high school hockey champion finally ended on March 21, 2004, when Toll Gate completed a two-game sweep of the Mounties in the state title series. Two of the stars of the Toll Gate team were David and John Cavanagh, the son and nephew, respectively, of former Harvard all-American, Joe Cavanagh.

"We were beaten by a better team," Bill said after the final game.

As always, Bill was brutally honest.

Many Rhode Island sports fans expected Bill to retire from coaching when Mount Saint Charles eventually lost the title. But in 2004–05 both Bill and Dave were back coaching the Mounties. The 2004–05 Mount team won the regular-season title, but were defeated in the playoffs by Toll Gate, again led by the Cavanagh cousins.

Once again, Rhode Island hockey fans predicted that Bill would retire, but both Bill and Dave plan to be back for the 2005–06 season.

"I'm surprised people would think we would stop coaching just because we finally lost the championship. It's always been about more than winning the championship," Dave said.

Mount Pride Is More Than a Game.